A bee in your bonnet?

By the Same Author

A bee in your bonnet?

An astonishing compendium from the
master of origins, customs and beliefs

R. BRASCH

Angus&Robertson
An imprint of HarperCollins*Publishers*

Angus&Robertson
An imprint of HarperCollins*Publishers*, Australia

First published in Australia in 2001
by HarperCollins*Publishers* Pty Ltd
ABN 36 009 913 517
A member of the HarperCollins*Publishers* (Australia) Pty Limited Group
http://www.harpercollins.com.au

HarperCollins*Publishers*
25 Ryde Road, Pymble, Sydney, NSW 2073, Australia
31 View Road, Glenfield, Auckland 10, New Zealand
77–85 Fulham Palace Road, London, W6 8JB, United Kingdom
Hazelton Lanes, 55 Avenue Road, Suite 2900, Toronto, Ontario M5R 3L2
and 1995 Markham Road, Scarborough, Ontario M1B 5M8, Canada
10 East 53rd Street, New York NY 10022, USA

National Library of Australia Cataloguing-in-Publication data:

Brasch, R. (Rudolph), 1912– .
   A bee in your bonnet?
   Includes index.
   ISBN 0 207 19994 9.
   1. Folk beliefs. 2. Manners and customs.
   I. Title.
390

Cover illustration by Lloyd Foye
Typeset in 10.5 on 13 point Optima by HarperCollins Design Studio
Printed and bound in Australia by Griffin Press on 79gsm Bulky Paperback White

5 4 3 2 1
05 04 03 02 01

For
Ellie, Jake, Eli, Ashleigh and Mila
our great grand nieces and nephew
with love

Foreword

WHY IS IT SO? is a question I am being asked continuously – in letters, on the phone, by fax, in the media, in my capacity as lecturer and visiting professor and by every possible channel of communication. My questioners come from all walks of life, many parts of the world, local and global, and all age groups.

People have contacted me because of their healthy hunger for knowledge, the wish or need to understand the original or real meaning of a name, a word, a phrase, a custom or a tradition, the story behind them and their place in history. Some inquirers might do so merely because of a wager at the dinner table or at a club.

To find the answers to all these many and varied questions presents an exciting and fulfilling experience. Sure, there are people who just take things for granted. They do not realise what they miss.

With the years and the gathering of ever more intriguing and, at times, most unexpected information, I have found out that the more I uncover, the more there is to know, to search for and research. Indeed, the pursuit has become a consuming passion and has given me (and my wife, who shares all my work) unending pleasure.

The material I collect has grown unceasingly and resulted in my writing more and more books. All of them have confirmed my belief in the appropriateness of the title I chose for one of them that *There's a Reason for Everything*.

A Bee in Your Bonnet covers a wide range of the oddest questions I have ever been asked. People have had 'bees in their bonnets' about chamberpots, and why one should not make waves; and what was responsible for the expression 'dressed chicken', really a contradiction in terms. No less odd were requests for my explaining the meaning of such sayings as 'it is cold enough to freeze the balls off a brass monkey' and that 'the show is not over till the fat lady sings'.

Indeed, there is a long list of oddities with which I have been presented through the years. Among the many other examples, you will read in the pages that follow explanations of expressions like 'that's all my eye and Betty Martin', 'a wigwam for a goose's bridle' and 'up to dolly's wax'. Inquirers rightly wondered why 'manhole covers are round', why 'Scotland Yard is situated in London' and why one 'pays a visit'.

This book further deals with the origin and meaning of the paparazzi, the hash key and Mardi Gras. The answers explain why 'the Bill' became a colloquialism for the British police and the 'brass razoo' part of Australian slang. My research has extended to discussing why and how birds fly in V-formation, why a beeline is not straight and why athletes run anti-clockwise. Other explanations explore the reason for speaking of 'daylight robbery', of 'coming home with a wet sail' and whether horse whisperers are real people. One of my British listeners wanted to know the name of Lady Godiva's horse and yet another, also from the Midlands, was mystified by the origin and meaning of the saying, common in that part of the world, that 'there is a dark cloud over Bill's mother's house'.

I am most grateful to all these people, many of whom have become close friends. This book is really due to their alert and questing minds and I hope and wish that you, my readers, share my enjoyment of delving into the roots of things. Perhaps *A Bee in Your Bonnet* might even answer the very question that has been puzzling *you* for so long or that *you yourself* put to me.

The format of *A Bee in Your Bonnet* is not arranged – like my previous books of this kind – according to subject matter or in alphabetical order. For you to share the kaleidoscope of ever-changing themes that come my way, I have endeavoured to follow the very sequence in which I was asked the questions, interspersing them with others that were conspicuous by the frequency with which they were put to me through the years. However, to enable you easily to locate specific topics on which you are seeking information, an Index is provided at the end of the book.

R.B.

Acknowledgments

My sincere thanks are due to a great number of individuals and organisations for providing me with valuable information. Though not all can be listed here, I would like to make special mention of:

Ken Arkwright of Perth, WA

Live J. Alexander

E. Arlsdon of Coventry, UK

Meredith A. Bedell of Gideon International in Australia, Mawson, ACT

Norman Bortz of South Africa

Ronnie Davis of London, UK

Simon Dewer

Eddie Doolan of Birmingham, UK

Peter Gilbert of the US Consulate-General Research Centre, Sydney

George Hayes of the Heritage Centre

Jan O'Hara of the Ritz-Carlton, Double Bay, Sydney

Maureen Kremer

Karl Larson of the Salvation Army, South Africa

Gordon Taylor, Archivist, International Heritage Centre, Salvation Army

Belinda Yuille of HarperCollins Publishers, Sydney

Philippa Armfield of the State Library of NSW

Lydie Bacot, Anne Duffield and Caroline Simons of the City of Sydney Library

Andy Carr of the Mitchell Library, Sydney

Bill Casey of the Woollahra Library, Double Bay, Sydney

Louise Junque of the Goethe Institut, Sydney

Tony Kitson of the Fisher Library, Sydney University

Ingrid Mason and Margaret Rafferty of the Powerhouse Museum, Sydney

Jeff Wyatt of the Sydney Observatory

Australian Broadcasting Corporation, Sydney, Reference Library

The Library of the Royal Australasian College of
   Physicians
The Sydney Conservatorium of Music
The Sydney Morning Herald Library
Major D. James of the RSL Headquarters, Sydney

Daylight Robbery

Why does one speak of 'daylight robbery'? Is it because it is not committed at night?

To offset the cost of forged coinage, which had lost its real value by either being clipped or otherwise damaged, England introduced a window tax in 1696. In 1782 and 1797 the younger Pitt increased its amount. A special edict then exempted from the tax those houses which counted less than seven windows, a number changed to eight in 1825.

To avoid paying the tax, houses were designed with a minimum of windows, whilst the windows that exceeded the tax-free number were bricked up.

It is believed that in protest against this government levy, house owners came angrily to refer to the tax as 'daylight robbery'. Ultimately, it was totally abolished on 24 July 1851.

The Bill For Police

What made people refer to the British police as 'the Bill'?

The origin of the nickname 'Bill' for members of the police force has been variously explained.

When a small squad of 'thief catchers' was formed in England in 1750, this became known as the Bow Street Runners. They did not wear any identifying clothes but nevertheless could easily be recognised by the long tipstaffs they carried. Known as a *'billy* stick', this tipstaff was retained and perpetuated in 'the Bill'!

An alternative derivation links the name not with a kind of weapon but with the era in which the Metropolitan Police Force came into existence, during the reign of King William IV – 'Bill' – and the royal name well suited the guardians of the law!

Special licences issued by the Metropolitan Police for cab drivers were generally known as 'the brief' or 'the kite'. Distinguished and truly conspicuous by their outsize, they seemed like a 'bill'. Soon this description was transferred to the law enforcers themselves. There was also the custom for the police to present a bill to those who made use of their services. Either of these could easily have led to the birth of the nickname.

An apocryphal story, on the other hand, derived the name from a certain East End policeman who was fond of his drink. It was no wonder that he frequented various inns. His daughter, whenever looking for him in one of his favourite watering places, was known to open its doors to call out, 'Has anyone seen old Bill?'

'The Bill' can indeed pride himself on a rich diversity of ancestry.

Horse Whisperers

Who are these people?

Going back to very early days in British life, some individuals were said to be endowed with the gift of a mystical relationship with the equine world. They appeared to possess the supernatural power to communicate with horses, ordering them to follow their instructions.

Horse breakers of such aptitude were highly respected. They made contact with the animal by a whisper, like people who shared some secret, speaking so softly that their words were unintelligible to others. Thus they attained cooperation from the animal that ordinary people were denied, apparently sharing a psychic bond. Being able to obtain obedience in this specific manner, they became known as horse whisperers.

Dishwasher

To whom do we owe this time-saving gadget?

The modern dishwasher owes its existence to the ingenuity of a busy American housewife, as long ago as 1889. She was Mrs W.A. Cockran, of the state of Indiana. Weary with the laborious process of washing her family's dirty crockery, piece by piece, day in and day out, she thought that there had to be some way to mechanise the chore. It took her ten years and much experimentation to make the earliest model of a dishwashing machine!

They were not easy years. Her husband, who was a rich businessman, could have stood by her, at least financially. But he refused to do so. It was only after his death that, with friends coming to her aid, Mrs Cockran was able to see her brainchild become a reality.

Her novel gadget was very simple. It was a wooden tub, and the dishes were placed inside it in a wire basket. Water was then spurted over them by means of a pump, operated by the turning of a handle.

Still preserved is a newspaper report of the time, praising her invention as a novelty 'capable of washing, scalding, rinsing and drying' dozens of dishes 'of all shapes and sizes in two minutes'.

Mrs Cockran would have never dreamt that her invention was to revolutionise the lives of women and – automated and streamlined – one day would be regarded as an essential part of ordinary households throughout the world.

The Four-Letter Word

What does it stand for and what is its origin?

Heading the list of tabooed sex terms for a considerable time, no doubt, was *the* four-letter word 'fuck'. No one really knows its etymological source. Only suggested 'ancestors' can be cited. These include the Latin *futuere* – 'to copulate'; the German *ficken* – a verb describing a fast movement to and fro or meaning 'to push into the pocket', and in German vulgarly applied to intercourse; and the French *foutre* – 'to spurt'.

Added to the mysterious origin of this four-letter word are the circumstances of its first literary evidence. This goes back to a poem attributed to a former Franciscan friar, William Dunbar (1460–1525), who was also a court bard and famed as 'the rhymer of Scotland'. Entitled 'Brash [bout] of Wowing [wooing],' it was published in Allan Ramsay's *Ever Green* in 1724. It deals, as the title indicates, with the wooing of a maiden by her lover:

> *He clappit [fondles] fast, he kist and chukkit*
> *   [bobbed under the chin]*
> *Yit be his feirris [gestures, sexual desires]*
> *   he wald [would] have fukkit;*
> *'Ye brek my hart, my bony ane [pretty one].'*

Following this first occurrence of the word in poetry, it reappeared in numerous Scottish folk songs and seemed to gain wide popularity. However, towards the end of the sixteenth century, its employment suddenly stopped and no respectable work dared use it. Thus, for reasons that can only be guessed, a word of common usage became befouled and disreputable. It is an early example of (linguistic) pollution. Hundreds of years later, attempts by James Joyce and D.H. Lawrence to resurrect it were unsuccessful. For many decades still in the twentieth century the four-letter word remained an obscenity which many a government declared punishable to use in print. All writers could do was to suggest it by the use of innocuous dots.

The explanation of fuck as an acronym for '*f*or *u*nlawful *c*arnal *k*nowledge' is merely a modern rationalisation.

Scoring In Tennis

How did the odd scoring in this sport come about?

Playing tennis, some wits have suggested, goes back to the Garden of Eden, when Eve 'served' an apple to Adam: the first 'fault'.

Scoring in tennis, so different from all other sports, has mystified many. Its units of '15' and '60' for game in fact stem from paume, an earlier game from which modern tennis evolved. In French, its name referred to 'the palm of the hand' (*paume*), with which it was played prior to the introduction of the racquet.

In paume, as in present-day tennis, the field was divided by a net. Each half was subdivided into 15 sections individually numbered. As still nowadays, ordinarily the ball was not permitted to bounce more than once. However, if the player could not return the ball on the first bounce, he was still allowed to do so on the second, so long as he was able to hit it into a sector of his opponent's field of a lower number. For instance, if he returned the ball from his sector 7 he had to make sure it landed in a sector not higher than 6.

The scoring in the sequence of 15, 30, 40 and game, which tennis also adopted from paume, fundamentally is a legacy of Babylonian culture of thousands of years ago, when no one ever dreamt of a game like tennis. The Babylonians introduced to the world the sexagesimal system which has left its impact in diverse ways. Babylonians believed in the cosmic significance of the figure 60 (*sexaginta* later in Latin), which made people divide every hour into 60 minutes. Subdivided into quarters, it made 15 a popular unit generally.

It was for this reason that fourteenth-century France chose it as the basis of its monetary system. A coin was valued at 60 sous. By means of an embossed cross, the coin could be divided into four quarters, each worth

15 sous. It so happened that at the same time the 'game with the palm' had become a favourite pastime of the French. They played it for money, mostly for a 60 sous piece which, prior to the game, they either handed for safekeeping to a spectator friend or placed under the net. No wonder, having the beckoning prize in mind, they did not score in simple numbers – 1, 2, 3 and game – but in the 15 (sous) units for each quarter, totalling 60 (sous) for the game.

Maybe psychology played its part as well in the rather inflated scores. To gain 1, 2 or 3 points sounded not very much. But to be able with one hit to obtain a score of 15 was something worthwhile and was an extra incentive to a player.

It was a practical reason that eventually reduced the 45 score to a mere 40. In calling out the figure (whether in French, English or, for that matter, in any tongue) forty was so much more euphonic and rolled more easily from the tongue than the ponderous forty-five.

Flavour Of The Month

What do we mean by this saying?

To be the flavour of the month is to be in fashion, in vogue. The description can be applied as much to an individual as to an object. It was first created in the world of commerce, with its fierce competition and constant endeavour to attract new customers.

American ice cream vendors were well aware of people's love of trying out new things, not least in the way of gastronomic enjoyment. This gave them the idea of regularly producing a special flavour, not obtainable elsewhere. They advertised it as 'the flavour of the month'. To encourage would-be customers further to purchase the offered treat, they even reduced its price. The catch phrase achieved its purpose and, becoming popular, soon caught on to become – metaphorically – part of everyday language.

As Cool As A Cucumber

Has this expression any scientific foundation?

The phrase 'cool as a cucumber' was first coined around 1700, though it was then used in the slightly different form of 'cold as a cucumber'. It has now been proven scientifically that on a hot day the centre of the cucumber is significantly cooler than the air surrounding it.

Don't Make Waves

What is behind this strange warning?

People liable to cause trouble or threatening to upset things are admonished not to make waves. It is an odd expression indeed. Apocryphally its origin has been linked with a joke, certainly not one in the best of taste.

This tells how a man who, having just passed away, immediately is sent to hell. Hearing the hubbub of voices in the distance, he makes his way towards it to locate the source. He finds that it comes from a large pool crowded with people who are standing in it up to their chins. The contents, however, instead of water, were nauseating excrement. Trying their utmost not to move, they reminded each other at the top of their voices 'not to make waves'. The reason was obvious!

The Bee's Knees

Do bees really have knees? And why do we praisingly speak of a person using this term?

In its present-day usage, to speak of someone as being the bee's knees points to their being something special, exceptional in their excellence. However, it was only in modern days that the phrase acquired this meaning, first so in American slang. It was used for 'the best', possibly in the way of some sort of rhyming slang, or as a pun: the bee's knees was 'the business'.

Also feasible is another explanation, derived from the observation of nature: the way bees contribute to the pollination of flowers. To gather the pollen, they wisely bend their knees to make it stick to them, then carry it out either to the chosen plant or back to their hives, and deposit it there.

Oddly, prior to this modern use of the 'bee's knees', though no later than the 1700s, the phrase was applied in the exact opposite sense to 'the best'. To speak of the bee's knees then portrayed something exceedingly small, of little effect or value. People and things were described as the bee's knees when they were of no consequence – as weak as the bee's knees, or so small that they could not even be compared to the diminutive size of the insect's joints.

The Friction Match

Who invented it?

Although the use of matches has been for many people superseded, they are still used and there is no doubt as to the significant contribution they have made to modern life. As applies to many inventions, the friction match was created by mere accident. Its inventor was John Walker (1781–1859), an English pharmaceutical chemist of Stockton-on-Tees.

At the time, Walker was engaged in experiments to improve the flintlock pistol, trying to do so by producing a new type of combustion. Whilst making his tests, he used a small stick to mix his various concoctions, one of which consisted of antimony sulphide, potassium chlorate and sulphur.

It so happened that some of the substance got stuck to the tip of his stirring stick. On trying to scrape it off, it ignited. Being a person of alert mind and initiative, he forgot all about his immediate project, the pistol, and concentrated on trying to discover the circumstances that had caused the minor 'explosion'. He did not leave it at that, but embarked right away on searching for ways in which he could apply his findings for the improvement of everyday life.

In no time he hit upon the idea of producing a new type of striking match, which would serve a most useful purpose. Going ahead at once, appropriately he called his invention the 'friction light'. To start with, he marketed it himself. The earliest surviving sales record shows his sale of 100 matches to a Stockton solicitor on 7 April 1827. He received for them one shilling (10 cents), with two pence (2 cents) extra for their tin container.

Public-spirited Walker refused to patent his invention, which he regarded as a service to the community. It took a mere two years before others exploited his altruism for their own benefit.

Coca-Cola Bottles

Why do the traditional bottles have such a peculiar shape?

Coca-Cola was first bottled in 1894, though its best-known bottle was designed only in 1913. Its inspiration and model, so it is told, was a mannequin in a department store who wore the then fashionable hobble skirt (a long skirt cut narrowly at the ankles). No one nowadays realises that this has been perpetuated – in glass!

Lady Godiva's Horse's Name

What was the steed's name on which she is said to have ridden naked through Coventry?

Various suggestions have been put forward as to the name of Lady Godiva's horse, on which she rode naked through the city of Coventry. They include Belshazzar, Baltasar, Drummer, Aethelnoth and 'Milk White Thora'. None of them, however, can stand up to the light of day.

Although the story of Lady Godiva (or Godgifu, her real name) goes back to between 1040 and 1080, it was not recorded until two centuries later! Taking into account the absence of modern means of communication at the time, it stands to reason that it is totally unreliable. The oldest version in existence is that related by Roger of Wendover (d. 1236).

Leofric, Earl of Mercia, Lady Godiva's husband, had imposed exceedingly high taxes on the people of Coventry. Concerned with their wellbeing, she had begged him to reduce the amount. Possibly to stop her nagging, he agreed to do so, but only if she would ride naked through the town. Obviously, he hoped that she would reject the condition. However, to his surprise, she concurred, though to preserve her modesty she cleverly used her beautiful long hair to cover her nudity.

On her compliance, Leofric issued an edict ordering the citizens not only to stay indoors during her ride but to also keep the shutters of their windows closed. All obeyed, with the exception of one man – Tom, the tailor. He could not resist the urge to peer through a window, with the result that he was immediately struck blind (or, according to some versions, even dead). He became known as the proverbial 'Peeping Tom'. It is interesting to note that it was not until during the reign of King Charles II (1630–1685) that this part of the story was added to the legend.

The full account was eventually written down in Latin by two monks at St Alban's Abbey, Hertfordshire. All these circumstances make it obvious that any name given to the horse is mere fiction.

Gone For A Burton

Who has gone where?

In English slang 'gone for a Burton' means that someone is lost or has died. During World War II, the English air force, the RAF, used it to describe an aviator who had not returned from his mission and was presumed to have been shot down.

Several explanations exist as to the origin of the expression. The township of Burton-upon-Trent, in Staffordshire, was renowned even in medieval times as the centre of brewing. In the nineteenth century, Michael Bass, who was to become Lord Burton, carried on the tradition. Soon his beer, called by his name, was promoted all over Britain. A special advertising campaign on hoardings cleverly employed a sequence of large posters.

The first one in the series showed a workman asking, 'Where is George?' It was renewed so many times that eventually no one could help but take note of it and start wondering what it was all about. Who was this George and why was he missing?

At long last, the public was given the answer on yet another placard. This explained that George was absent and not doing his job because he had 'gone for a Burton'. Without the foreman's permission, he had slipped out for a drink. To have a Burton (ale) was well worth taking the risk of a severe reprimand if not of losing his job ...

Thus, 'going for a Burton' entered English phraseology and was adopted by the airmen. Reluctant to voice the gruesome fact of the death of one of their mates, they referred to their missing friend as 'having gone for a Burton'.

There is an alternative version, also linked with the brew. During the war, the beer was in short supply. Whoever went out for a Burton could not get it. He had 'had it'. Adopted into the RAF jargon, it meant that he had been killed. Oddly and almost eerily, the expression fitted many a tragic case. Airmen shot down over water often drowned in the 'drink', the colloquial name for the sea.

There is also a naval tradition that claims the phrase actually came from customs at sea and that the air force had only appropriated it from sailors. As early as 1704, the term 'burton' was used for a light hoisting tackle, employed to set up the rigging of the mast as tautly as possible and on occasion, to haul a load as well.

If an officer discovered that a sailor was missing from his assigned station, his mates covered up for him by explaining that, in pursuit of his duties, he was looking for a pulley – he had 'gone for a burton'.

Englishmen traditionally associated the name of Burton not only with a drink, but with Messrs Montague Burton, a well-known firm of tailors. Through mere coincidence, their name came to play a significant role in airmen's talk. The airforce's wireless operators used to be trained in Blackpool, and it so happened that the very room in which they had to pass their intermediate test was situated just above the local branch of the firm. Candidates who failed in the examination were debarred from continuing the course. Rather kindly and metaphorically, it was said of them that they had 'gone for a Burton' (suit) – to replace their uniform.

A Mother Kangaroo And Her Pouch

How does she keep it clean?

A kangaroo mother carries her offspring in her pouch for quite some time before the little joey can jump out and move around on its own. This creates a special problem in keeping her pouch clean. After all, like all other living creatures, the joey has to expel its waste products. However, it must be realised that, whilst still in the pouch, the joey's faeces is soft and therefore enables its mother to lick it up. Once old enough to leave the pouch and eat grass, the faeces hardens and the joey will do its business outside. Any dirt left in the pouch, the 'roo', just as before, will simply lick up.

Kriss Kringle

Who was Kriss Kringle?

The story of Kriss Kringle is as confusing as is the name, which is the corrupted version of the German *Christkindl*. This itself should be *Christ-Kindlein*. *Kindlein* is the German for 'a little child' (*Kind*) and being applied here to the young Jesus, created his description as Kriss Kringle, the 'Christ child'.

It became the custom on the evening of the feast of St Nicholas (6 December) for someone impersonating the saint to visit every home in which there were children. After inquiring what good they had done during the year, and what they had learnt of their faith, most importantly, he also asked what kind of gift they desired for Christmas. On Christmas Eve itself, lit candles were placed in the windows of those very homes to guide the Christ child who was thought to be actually bearing the gifts.

From Europe the legend eventually reached Germans and German-speaking Swiss who had settled in Pennsylvania in the United States. With the passing of time, other features were added, further expanding the story. Among them was even the expectation that the Christ child, 'the Babe of Bethlehem', would enter the home through its keyhole. It is thought that when English-speaking settlers joined the German communities in that part of the world, they transformed the 'Christkindl' into 'Kriss Kringle', a change that greatly anguished some theologians, who saw the transformation and novel description as 'gibberish of the vilest kind'.

Ultimately, the place of Kriss Kringle was taken by Santa Claus and his story and visit on Christmas Eve were identified with all that was known of the figure of St Nicholas, the fourth century bishop of Myra.

Still, the fantasies surrounding the Christ child live on in the minds of some German children who also believe that apart from bringing the presents, it decorated the Christmas tree.

Marriage At Gretna Green's Smithy

Are these nuptials legal?

The tradition that an eloped couple can get married in the Scottish village of Gretna Green by a blacksmith over an anvil, however romantic it sounds, is based on mere fiction.

It all started not in Scotland but in England and, of all places, London's (future) Fleet Street prison! Couples in a hurry to get married could have their wish fulfilled there, without any fuss or officialdom.

Touts and pseudo-priests hanging around 'the Fleet', without asking any questions, would tie their knot, doing so for the small consideration of half a crown (25 cents) per couple. The first such clandestine marriage took place in 1613.

The news spread fast and wide, and 'the Fleet' became the very centre of such unauthorised and often disreputable marriages. Their number increased to such an extent that, in 1753, a Bill was introduced in parliament which declared any marriage contracted in 'the Fleet' illegal. Henceforth, according to what became known as the 'English Marriage Act', a marriage, to be legal, required the previous publication of banns, the issue of a licence and its solemnisation in a Church of England. It was this very Act that brought Gretna Green into the picture.

Located just inside the Scottish border, English legislation did not apply there and according to ancient Scots law, all that was necessary for two single people to become husband and wife was to declare their desire in the presence of two witnesses. It did not matter who these witnesses were. They could be landlords, coachmen, toll keepers or ferrymen. The marriage could be contracted at any time of the day or night.

The mere fact that three busy highways, leading from the east, the south and the west, joined at the small village made it a most accessible venue, which further contributed to attracting runaway couples from, as it were, all directions.

The tradition that this unique place of solemnisation was a smithy is a mere legend. The site was an inn, elaborately expanded and refurbished for the very purpose. Among the special 'amenities' offered was the 'hidden chamber'. It was reserved for any couple anxious to take refuge from angry relatives pursuing them, in an attempt to stop their union. Its window was so positioned that it allowed the fugitives to watch the approach to the inn. Ingeniously, it would also serve them as an emergency exit, if circumstances so demanded. Indeed, anyone entering the room without permission was regarded a trespasser, duly to be punished by law.

That the inn was a smithy in which the blacksmith forged the marriage link over an anvil is also a myth. It developed out of a sign which one of the 'celebrants' had fixed outside his residence. This depicted a smithy with a young man and woman joining hands over the anvil and the blacksmith bringing down his hammer to forge their union. However, apart from this picture, 'marriages over the anvil' are merely a modern commercialisation of this colourful signpost.

Nevertheless, the famous saga of Gretna Green made the legendary smithy a veritable marriage mill. Thousands of eloped couples, as well as those wanting to add further romance to their union, found their happiness there. It made Gretna Green not only a byword for marital bliss, but also provided the pseudo-blacksmith exploiting the myth with a fortune.

Things became more difficult when, in 1856, the Scottish authorities made 'immediate marriage by declaration' illegal, stipulating that at least one of the parties had to have a residential qualification. Ultimately, in 1940, it all came to a sudden end. From that point on, the law demanded that, for a marriage to be valid, it had to be contracted before an ordained minister of religion or an officially appointed registrar.

The smithy is still in existence and continues to be a popular tourist attraction, with the legendary anvil its central showpiece.

Father Christmas And The Chimney

Why does he come into a home via the chimney, remembering that he is pot-bellied and beautifully garbed and the chimney is narrow and sooty?

The chimney would seem to be the very last point of entry for Santa to choose! Apart from possibly getting his rotund body stuck in the narrow passage, the soot would ruin his outfit!

The idea of entering a home via the chimney dates from prehistoric times, when people actually dwelt underground. The smokehole – which was later replaced by the chimney – doubled as the entrance and the exit. This explains why, in present-day French, the words for both 'chimney' (*cheminée*) and 'path' (*chemin*) have the identical root, just as the Italian *cammino* communicates both meanings.

It Is Cold Enough To Freeze The Balls Off A Brass Monkey

What is the explanation of this very odd and suggestive saying?

To describe icy weather as 'cold enough to freeze the balls off a brass monkey' is not obscene, as some might imagine. It is straight naval talk. 'Monkey' used to be the nickname for a young cadet assigned with the duty of fetching the ammunition. The description was then transferred to the large brass plate on which the cannon balls were placed, accordingly called a brass monkey.

The practice created a problem. As the rate of contraction of the brass plate differed from that of the iron cannon balls, it so happened that in extremely cold weather the balls would roll off the much faster-shrinking plate. Quite correctly, therefore, on such occasions the sailors could observe that it was 'cold enough to freeze the balls off a brass monkey'.

Another derivation gives the same basic interpretation. However, it recognises in the 'brass monkey' a seventeenth-century sailors' nickname for the ship's cannon. When the temperature dropped far below freezing point, the iron balls, contracting at a different rate from the brass cannon, put it out of action!

Whichever way, the words were ambiguous. To avoid any misinterpretation, those anxious not to endanger their reputation slightly changed the saying, remarking that it was 'cold enough to freeze the ears off a brass monkey'.

That's All My Eye And Betty Martin

This phrase sounds nonsensical. What does it mean?

To describe anything as utter nonsense by saying, 'That's all my eye and Betty Martin' is certainly mystifying. Various explanations have been proffered, two of them tracing the phrase to the misinterpreted words of a prayer.

Most commonly, a British naval crew is given the doubtful credit for the expression. When their ship docked at an Italian port, some of the sailors attended the local church service. Among the prayers said was a supplication appealing to St Martin of Tours. Hearing it pronounced in Latin – a language totally foreign to the men – they misunderstood the words. To their ears the invocation to the saint, *O mihi, beate Martine* (meaning 'Oh grant me, blessed St Martin...'), sounded just like 'All my eye and Betty Martin'.

Equally bizarre and rather more involved is another claim advanced by L.A. Waddell. This links the expression with the visit of ancient Phoenicians to Cornwall in Britain, from where they imported tin. While there, they had introduced the people to the worship of Britomartis, the Cretan mother goddess. Cornishmen, listening to their prayer to the alien deity – *O, mihi, Britomartis* ('Oh, (help) me Sweet Maid') had imagined those Latin words to say in English, 'All my eye and Betty Martin'.

Rejecting such far-fetched theories, Eric Partridge in his *Dictionary of Catch Phrases* suggests that in fact the expression is indigenously British. It started with a favourite exclamation by an eighteenth-century English actress, Betty Martin. She loved to call out on every possible and impossible occasion – perhaps as a gimmick or affectation – 'my eye' or 'all my eye'. Soon the words were associated with her name.

Birdie In Golf

One under par in golf is called a 'birdie'. What is the origin?

The first 'birdie' was a mere fluke, and appeared, as it were, out of the air. It all happened on a beautiful day in 1903 in Atlantic City, USA. A.B. ('Ab') Smith enjoyed a good game of golf, but he also knew that there was room for improvement. Therefore, when on that morning he made a shot that enabled him to sink his ball into the hole with a score of 'one under par', he was rightly overjoyed.

Giving expression to his feelings, spontaneously he called out at the top of his voice, 'That's a *bird* of a shot!' And the bird caught on. In the course of time, players learnt fondly to refer to it as a 'birdie'.

The eagle and albatross were an almost logical sequence. To attain 'two under par', of course, is much less frequent, just as to see an eagle is not so common. To encounter an albatross on land was as rare an event as scoring 'three under par'.

The Upper Crust

Why were the wealthy and members of the aristocracy so called?

Speaking of the 'upper crust' makes one immediately think of people at the top of society, constituting what was once called the 'upper class'. Actually, to start with, the expression was used very literally. It goes back to medieval banquets, when dinner plates were still unknown and round loaves took their place. Cut in half, each part served as a plate. Once the guests had consumed the food heaped on their bread 'plates', they finished up the meal by eating them as well. There were no leftovers and no need to wash up.

As the upper crust of the loaf was by far the best one, it was reserved for the most honoured and important guests. Though a long-forgotten custom, it is recalled in daily conversation, without having become stale, so to speak! It is used whenever people refer to those making up the elite of society as the 'upper crust'.

Donkey's Years

What is the reason for colloquially referring to a long time in this way? After all, donkeys don't live any longer than horses.

For things to last 'for donkey's years' is obviously a misunderstanding. Donkeys, after all, do not live all that long. However, they are distinguished by their extra long ears, which were stretched into 'donkey's years'. To add insult to injury it was all due to being misheard!

Blue For Boys And Pink For Girls

Baby boys are dressed in blue and baby girls in pink. What accounts for the choice of colour?

Dressing baby boys and girls in different colours is linked with their sex. Babies all look alike, and what better means of identifying them readily than by colours – blue for boys and pink for girls? This colour scheme has been adopted all over the world. But who would ever suspect that the colour blue is connected with the haunting fear of anxious parents, deeply concerned for their baby's future?

From the days of antiquity it was believed that evil spirits hovered menacingly over the nursery. It was thought furthermore that the evil ones were allergic to certain colours, of which the most potent was blue. It was considered that the association of blue with the heavenly sky rendered satanic forces powerless and drove them away. Even nowadays Arabs in the Middle East continue to paint the doors of their homes blue to frighten away demons. Thus, the display of blue on a young child was not merely an adornment but a necessary precaution.

Girl babies were regarded as vastly inferior to boy babies and it was assumed that evil spirits would not be interested in them. That is why blue was reserved for boys. Any distinctive colour for girls was deemed unnecessary.

Possibly later generations, unaware of the reason for 'blue for boys' but very much conscious of the neglect of girls, introduced for them the new pink look.

European legendary tradition suggests another beautiful explanation of the colour scheme for babies. This tells that baby boys are found under cabbages whose colour – on the Continent of Europe – is mostly blue. Baby girls, on the other hand, are born inside a pink rose.

American Way Of Eating

What is the reason for the difference of the use of knife and fork by Americans?

Americans particularly appreciate the value of time. Masters in the study of time and motion, they have learnt to streamline life in many ways. Incongruously, though, they waste time whenever they sit down for a meal. They follow a peculiar custom that is conspicuous to outsiders. First, they cut up the meat holding the fork in their left hand and the knife in their right as Australians would do. They then put down the knife and change the fork over to their right hand to pick up the individual pieces and the vegetables. An involved procedure, it makes Americans stand out in any crowd.

The origin of the American way of eating shows how traditions of the past are perpetuated, even if their once-useful reason no longer holds true. In the early pioneering days, knives were in short supply and it often happened that a family possessed only one knife, whereas forks were much easier and cheaper to produce. It was therefore only natural that, when sitting down for a meal, the head of the house was privileged to use the knife first. After having cut up his food, he passed the knife on to the next member of the family who in turn, after having used it, handed it on. With the knife thus making the rounds, each individual had only a fork left. Obviously, this was now held in the right hand. The habit became so ingrained that even when knives became plentiful, the early mode of eating was never abandoned.

Bridegroom Breaking Glass At Jewish Weddings

Why does the groom break a glass at the end of the ceremony?

A peculiar custom at a Jewish wedding occurs at the very end of the ceremony, when the bridegroom breaks a glass – and does so rather noisily. The glass itself originally had to be a valuable one, not of the cheap kind. The material loss and the 'racket' were thought to divert the attention of the potentially evil forces from the happiness experienced by the couple at that moment. Otherwise, the evil spirit might be so roused in its envy that it would be determined to spoil the good luck, and the marriage would never succeed. That, too, is the original reason why the assembled congregation accompanies the breaking of the glass by shouting loudly *mazzal tov* – 'good luck'.

This explanation, however, has long been discarded and replaced by a diversity of modern interpretations. Husband and wife use the glass to consecrate their marriage. In order that it should never be used for other (especially more mundane) purposes, the bridegroom breaks it.

Personal joy must not deaden awareness of the trials and tribulations of others. When happiness has entered their lives, the couple must not be blinded to the fate of the less fortunate or forget the Jewish people's calamity. This is why, as a reminder and a spur to compassion, the glass is broken. It speaks of the destruction of the ancient Temple in Jerusalem and the vanished glory of the ancient Jewish state. But especially it is meant to lead their thoughts to those who have lost their way in the world. At the moment of their joy they should open their souls in sympathy and charity.

Opposites are easily associated. When speaking of one idea, the contrasting thought immediately arises. Black suggests white; high, low; and day, night. Similarly the breaking of the glass reminds one of the unbreakable bond of wedlock. Man and wife feel that they are bound together. Much may change and pass, but their love will remain, and 'aught but death part you and me'.

Finally, the custom is a timely warning. Light has its shadows and happiness has its anxieties. Love must be prepared to accept both the joys and the sorrow of life. It must see the difference between ephemeral joys, as breakable as thin glass, and perpetual happiness which nothing can ever destroy. Such richness of symbolism is found in that simple and only too often misunderstood custom of breaking the glass.

Round Manhole Covers

What is the reason why the 'underground service access covers' – their modern, gender-neutral name – are always round?

A manhole cover, as a description, no longer exists: the 'man' in the hole is sexist. To call it a 'person hole' just does not seem right and might be subject to misinterpretation. Hence in its modern terminology it has been referred to – rather ponderously – as an 'underground service access cover'.

Hardly ever noticed or commented on is its shape, which invariably is circular. There is a reason for everything. A round cover can never fall into a round hole of the same size.

Washers Under A Nut Or In A Watertap

Why is it called a washer?

Intriguing is the question why the flat ring of metal or rubber, placed under a nut or inside a tap (or 'faucet' in America) to tighten a joint or distribute pressure, is called a washer. Plausible and least involved is the suggestion that it was so named because early washers were made of *wash*-leather, a soft kind of leather, mostly of sheepskin, so named because of the 'washing' involved in the process of manufacture.

Its description, however, may have no connection at all with water. It may go back to an old Anglo-Saxon word for straw, stubble or grass – *ways* (pronounced 'waize') – and be explained by a practice of fishmongers at the famous Billingsgate fish market in London. To ease the pressure of the heavy baskets of fish the market workers had to carry on their heads, they cushioned them by means of a ring of straw. It acted as a buffer between head and basket.

This wreath or wisp of straw, the *wayzer,* did not take long to deteriorate in speech to become a 'washer'. And as the ring in the watertap looked like a miniature replica of that improvised buffer, it was called after it. To begin with, in fact, the washer under a nut actually consisted of straw wound around the screw. Its name was therefore very much to the point.

The washer thus found its way from on top of a head to inside a tap. No matter where it was found, however, its purpose was the same: to ease a load or to prevent friction.

Being On Cloud [No.] 9

This describes the state of being deliriously happy – why is that so?

There is a suggestion that this figure of speech expressing rapture and ecstasy might be derived from the science of meteorology. Weather experts numbered the various cloud formations and in their numerology, 'No. 9' referred to a thundercloud. To sit on top of it would certainly put a person up very high. In fact, they would be out of danger of being struck by lightning which, it was assumed, always struck downward. A person thus positioned was sure to enjoy the full benefit of the warmth and brightness of the sun.

Also very likely, 'cloud [no.] 9' was specially chosen as a figure of speech because people in the heaven of perfect bliss felt so uplifted that they would associate their state of mind with the most perfect number, the holiest figure – the trinity of trinities (three multiplied by three).

Peacock Feathers

Why are they supposed to be unlucky?

People have always kept their eyes open and carefully observed everything around them. They have asked questions, wondering about a myriad of whys and wherefores. They were convinced that everything in life had a purpose and that there was nothing without a cause. So when they saw peacocks strutting about with their gorgeous tail feathers spread out, they were sure that the feathers' countless eyes must have been placed there for some significant reason.

Greek myth gave its own interpretation to the eyes on the peacock's tail, linking them with jealousy among the very 'human' gods. Hera (Juno to the Romans) was distressed over the constant unfaithfulness of her husband Zeus (or Jupiter), and she knew of the affair he was having with his latest mistress, Io. To conceal Io, Zeus changed her into a heifer. He hoped the innocently grazing 'animal' would not rouse Hera's suspicions. But he had not reckoned on a wife's jealousy, for she could not be deceived even by the cleverest scheming and subterfuge.

Hera, knowing the true identity of the heifer, enlisted the help of Argus, the hundred-eyed giant, to keep watch on the 'animal-mistress' and thereby prevent any tryst between her and the amorous Zeus. Argus was the best choice for the purpose. He was renowned for keeping open at least two of his eyes at all times.

Hera unfortunately could not outwit Zeus, who remained master of the situation. He commanded his son Hermes (Mercury) to put Argus to sleep by the sound of his magic flute and by songs so soporific that not even the faithful Argus could resist dozing off. The moment his hundred eyes had closed, Hermes slew him by severing his head.

In her grief and rage, Hera transferred the eyes of her loyal servant to the tail of her favourite bird, the peacock. It is one of the strangest living memorials. Renewed with each generation, the colourful, brilliant display of the male peacock perpetuates the death of a vigilant hero for the sake of the goddess of monogamy.

The peacock thus became sacred to both Greeks and Romans, who revered and cared for it as the treasured guardian of their temples, wifely virtues and conjugal rights. The numerous eyes on its tail were regarded as symbolising the gods' never-resting watchfulness. Thus the bird became part of holy sanctuaries. Only priests were allowed to handle the sacred bird. For an ordinary mortal to do so was a sacrilegious crime punished by death, and to possess even one of its feathers was to defy sacred tradition.

However, it was the fear of the devil and of the evil eye that was primarily responsible for the assigning of magic power to the bird. The numerous wide-open eyes on the tail intrigued the ancients. When haunted by fears they assumed that the eyes belonged to the devil or were a perilous manifestation of the evil eye. To live constantly under their stare would expose the entire household to the malevolent influence of the power of darkness.

The belief was reinforced centuries later by a Moslem legend that held that the peacock had opened the gate to Paradise to admit Iblis, the devil, thus enabling him to cause the fall of humans. The bird's early association with the Evil One has never been forgotten. No one could ever trust the peacock again. Worse still, the devil might take advantage of its spectacular plumage, tempting people to take it home and thereby place themselves within the power of an ever-vigilant traitor.

As time went on, the peacock became a symbol of immortality and resurrection. People noticed that its feathers did not fade or lose their lustre. This might have given rise to the fallacious notion that the bird's flesh never decayed either. Because of the flesh's assumed incorruptibility, it became customary to use the bird's plumage at funerals, to indicate that the deceased person was not really dead. Their spirit survived and their eventual rebirth was assured. The presence of the feathers would actually help the deceased in their life in the hereafter.

The custom had a bad side effect, however. Because of their use at funerals, the peacock's feathers became closely linked with death. People, forgetting their former protective association and symbolism, started to dread the presence of peacock feathers in their home. The feathers were no longer an assurance of immortality but an omen of doom as they had been to the ancients – a telling example of how ignorance of the past can confuse and lead to sad misunderstandings.

Fairies

What made people refer to gay men as such?

In its etymology the word 'fairy' referred to 'enchantment' and can be traced to the Latin for 'destiny' and 'fate'. This might well be an explanation of the modern 'fairy' – the male homosexual. It is his 'fate' to be such.

However, there is another theory that associates this use of the word with the stage. In productions of Shakespearean plays, it was found that the part of fairies was performed most convincingly by homosexual actors. And this choice in the casting of plays eventually led to the identification of the fairy with homosexuals.

Top Dog And Underdog

How did these designations come about?

It is not uncommon for dogs to engage in a fight – whether as a (mostly now outlawed) sport or merely in street bouts. The winning dog always ends up on top of the losing one, leading to the descriptions 'top dog' and 'underdog' respectively, terms subsequently applied metaphorically to humans as well. A person with superior power or winning in a fight thus is referred to as the top dog, whilst the losing party in a contest or anyone occupying an inferior position appropriately is known as the underdog.

An alternative explanation of the terms has no relationship with the canine world. It comes from the early days of saw milling, prior to the invention of the circular saw and relates to logs requiring to be sawn lengthwise. This was then done by hand and by two men. With the log placed on a frame, one of them stood on top whilst the other was positioned in the saw pit below. He was nicknamed the 'underdog'. After all, his was the less pleasant job, with sawdust raining down on him.

It has been suggested that the saying originated in Australia, where people will always support or barrack for the underdog.

An Albatross Around One's Neck

Is it not usually a millstone which, after all, is so much heavier? Why this bird?

The albatross has been the companion of sailors on the high seas far back into history. When all other birds had left off following a ship, this largest of web-footed birds kept on circling it, now and then alighting on the ocean, perhaps dropping back for a while, but always reappearing. In a sense, it became a member of the crew, who regarded it with superstitious fondness.

Anxiously they looked out for its presence. This alone could explain the objection to killing the albatross. It was such a steady and loyal friend, whose company helped to relieve the monotony of sailing.

Imagination runs high on the lonely watches at sea. It is not known who the sailor was who first began to fancy that there was something mysterious about the way the bird clung to the company of a ship and showed such stupendous power, flying long distances against the wind, apparently without ever using its wings as a means of propulsion. From his musing sprang the haunting legend that the bird embodied the soul of a drowned sailor, clinging close to his own kind. From there it was only a logical step to believing that the killing of an albatross was unlucky.

Perhaps, after all, thoughts of mere self-preservation could account for the superstition among sailors. The bird was so strong that tales were soon current that it had lifted up ship-wrecked sailors out of the sea and brought them to safety. To kill a potential rescuer was tantamount to suicide.

Making use of the tradition, the English poet Samuel Taylor Coleridge (1772–1834) in 1798 wrote a poem entitled *The Ancient Mariner*. It relates how, whilst at sea, the old mariner killed one of the great birds. A curse fell upon him and the dead bird was hung around his neck. The ship became becalmed and ran out of drinking water before being able to reach port.

The account of the incident led to the custom of referring to anything that causes trouble or worry, as well as a problem that is difficult to solve, as the condition of 'having an albatross around one's neck'.

The Fly In Men's Trousers

What is the explanation of this odd description for the front opening of men's trousers?

Flies have the ability to find their way into everything. But people have rightly wondered how the 'fly' found a permanent place as the opening in the front of men's trousers. Etymologists have been puzzled and recorded that its 'origin [is] obscure'.

However, to associate flying with a man's trousers is not as out of the way as people might think at first. Flying itself belonged to the occult and particularly to witches. They were supposed to fly to their Sabbaths (or meetings) using the devil's erect phallus (at least symbolically) as their horse.

Flying has been closely linked – not in air space but in the realm of speech – to actual copulation, as psychoanalysts have pointed out. And the original trouser 'fly' was introduced by the Turks into eighteenth-century Europe not to make it easier and quicker for man to relieve his bladder, but to facilitate his various kinds of erotic enjoyments.

The Tightfisted Scot

What gave him the reputation of being mean with money?

Scottish people have suffered many a misrepresentation. Qualities deserving admiration have been misjudged and, at times, even quoted to denigrate them. Their acumen and ability to make a little go a long way have been misinterpreted as miserliness. They have been called tightfisted.

The term certainly applies to them, but not in the sense in which it is now used and understood. If a Scotsman clenched his fist, he did so not to retain the little money he possessed but to make sure of his next meal!

In days gone by, many a Scotsman used to carry oatmeal in his sporran (the purse worn at the front of a kilt) – and very wisely so. It enabled him to prepare a snack for himself at almost any time in any place. All that was necessary was to roll the meal into balls and then cook these in the hot ashes of a fire. To bind the oats, however, he had first to wet them. He did so by taking a handful and dipping them into a brook or river. This created a problem: the running stream tended to wash away the cereal. To prevent this from happening, the astute Scotsman made a tight fist around the oats. It was this simple but ingenious practice that gave him the reputation of being 'tightfisted'.

Vichyssoise

Who created this potato and leek soup and why was it so named?

The very name of Vichyssoise, that popular creamy leek and potato soup that mostly is served cold, has misled many to assume that, like other gastronomical treats, it was first created in France. However, this is only partially correct. In its present form the dish was invented in the United States. Yet Louis Diat, who introduced it, came from Vichy in France and by giving it the name wanted to honour his home town. He well remembered how his mother used to serve a typical peasant soup, inexpensively prepared from leeks and potatoes, nourishing and plentiful at the time. Refining the recipe, he would create something truly novel and delightful to the palate, worthy of the establishment he worked for – the elegant Ritz-Carlton Hotel on Madison Avenue, New York.

According to information supplied by the Australian Ritz-Carlton, Sydney, there are several versions as to the date and specific circumstances of the soup's invention. One of them suggests that it goes back to the auspicious opening of the prominent New York hotel in 1910. Alternatively, it is said to have occurred in 1917. In that year a new roof garden had been added to the hotel and its opening was to be celebrated by a gala dinner. Diat, the chef then in charge of the kitchen, remembering a soup of his mother's at that time totally unknown in the States, decided to add it to the menu as something extra special. But in the excitement of the occasion, when the dinner was about to be served, he was horrified to notice that his staff had forgotten to heat up the soup. Not prepared to omit his treat, on the spur of the moment, he decided still to serve it, but to make it most palatable by keeping it ice cold and adding cream and chives. It is one of the many examples of how a mishap became responsible for the enrichment of life. The dish not only caught on, but the delighted guests spread its fame far and wide. In almost no time, an originally local peasant food became a world-renowned delicacy.

Blue Jokes And Blue Movies

The colour blue has been chosen to suggest something sexually risqué. Why is that so?

'The Blue Boar' was the name of a popular eighteenth-century London tavern, the haunt of prostitutes. Many a man picked up a bout of venereal disease from there. No wonder that this soon became identified with the inn's name. In fact, anything risqué and 'off-colour' came to be described as 'blue'. That is why, according to one tradition, people still speak of the blue joke and the blue movie.

A different theory derived the application of this colour to anything sexually improper from the stage, from an earlier period of permissiveness. Whenever an indecent scene was enacted, the spotlight was dimmed, which was mostly done by adding to it a blue filter. In no time blue thus became associated with the sexually tainted.

A Bull In A China Shop

What accounts for this odd expression?

It is said that people who are clumsy and lack finesse act like 'a bull in a china shop'. The phrase is really self-explanatory, as it can well be imagined that the powerful animal, if let loose in a china shop, might easily wreak havoc among the delicate breakable goods displayed.

The saying goes back to 1834, when it first appeared in the novel *Jacob Faithful*. Frederick Marryat, its author, was also a captain in the Royal Navy.

Almost exactly a century later, it is claimed, a lost bet between Fred Waring, a renowned bandleader at the time, and the actor Paul Douglas again featured this proverbial bull. Losing the wager, Waring had to guide a bull through a well-known china shop on Fifth Avenue in New York City with the understanding that any damage done by the animal in the process would be made good by him. However, luckily for the bandleader nothing happened and the bull dexterously wound its way through the aisles. Not even the swishing of his tail dislodged a single object. Oddly though, it was Mr Waring, the winner, who knocked down a table with precious china, thereby, as it were, invalidating the popular saying.

There have been other explanations of the origin of the phrase. One relates to an early nineteenth-century effort on the part of the British and Americans to promote trade with China. To achieve this aim, a British representative was dispatched to the States, but dismally failed in the mission. By his lack of diplomacy he destroyed any possibility of success. The popular personification of the American as Uncle Sam and of the Englishman as John Bull, led people to comment that the clumsy (John) 'Bull' had wrecked the hoped-for opening up of China to the world market. Another tradition links the debacle with an abortive attempt to break up the existing trade monopoly of the East India Company.

The Carillon

Why is this set of bells so called?

A carillon (pronounced 'carillion' – influenced by the original French word) is the name given to a set of bells, mostly suspended in a tower, or of the actual tune or chime played on it, either manually or mechanically by hammers or clappers. Derived from the Latin *quatrinio* (via the Old French *carignon*) it literally referred to the 'four' bells which originally constituted the instrument.

Particularly popular in Belgium and Holland, from there carillon playing spread worldwide to become an art of its own taught at special schools, with even a university offering courses as part of its musical syllabus, and training of the carillonneur, as a carillon player came to be known. Though maintaining its name referring to the original four bells, their number was vastly increased – sometimes amounting to seventy. The melodies played came to supply an entertaining and most varied repertoire. Johann Sebastian Bach (1685–1750) even wrote some specific music for the instrument that was published in 1898.

A fascinating story is told about the origin of the carillon. It goes back to the early days when the chiming of the town clock, recurring each hour, played an important part in daily life. Unfortunately, people became so used to the clock's sound that they no longer listened to it and thus were not aware of the passing of time. To overcome the problem, some ingenious artist conceived the idea, prior to the actual striking of the hour, of drawing people's attention by chiming a particular melody. The variety of tunes used and eventually specifically written for the purpose became so popular that, divorced from their original practical function, they became an art form of their own, solely devoted to the carillon, with its unique attraction and beauty.

The Colly Bird

What is the colly bird mentioned in the popular folk song 'The Twelve Days of Christmas'?

Many have been mystified as to the identity of the colly bird, made popular by the carol 'The Twelve Days of Christmas' (although some versions call it the 'calling bird'). The Old English name for the blackbird, 'colly' refers to coal, and obviously was chosen because of its colour. The same reason accounts for the name of the collie, the shepherd's dog. When bred in Scotland in the seventeenth century it was black like coal and then very appropriately referred to as a 'coaly'. Soon, however, this justified description was changed into collie, a linguistic streamlining as it were, obscuring the origin of the canine's name.

First Cousin And First Cousin Once Removed

What is their difference and relationship?

A first cousin is of the same generation, the son or daughter of one's uncle or aunt (one's parent's brother or sister). It is an obvious relationship. A 'full cousin', he or she is sometimes also referred to as a 'cousin germane' (meaning 'related'), on occasion mistaken as a 'German' cousin.

In the case of a 'first cousin once removed', however, the term 'removed' indicates that he or she belongs to a different generation, and is removed by one degree. Whilst the 'germane' first cousin belongs to one's own generation, the first cousin once removed is a member of either the preceding generation or that following. They are either the daughter or son of one's first cousin or the grandchild of one's great-grand-parents. As it were, in the family tree in their position a horizontal relationship is replaced by a vertical one.

There Is A Dark Cloud Over Bill's Mother's House

What is the meaning of this observation?

A variety of explanations has been given to the observation that 'there is a dark cloud over Bill's mother's house'. The saying is mostly used in the Midlands of England, where it originated. To begin with it might merely have indicated the direction of a threatening thunderstorm. However, there are other more likely derivations. It might well have had its beginnings during World War I, when a certain Bill, who lived with his mother in Birmingham, served with the British forces in the Dardanelles. When he was killed in action, the tragic news was conveyed to his home by the War Office, which indeed, metaphorically speaking, brought 'a dark cloud over Bill's mother's house'.

There is also the suggestion that Bill was not a personal name but a corruption of Bilston, a township not far from Birmingham renowned for its industry. Its steel works and coal mine belched forth a pall of black smoke. Seen from afar, people could rightly say that there was a dark cloud over Bilston's houses.

Least likely is a fourth possibility, going back to the music halls of the Victorian era and a popular comedian who was travelling from place to place. He was renowned for the peculiar way in which he tried to capture his audience's immediate attention. The moment his turn had come, he commenced his act by shouting out aloud, 'There's a dark cloud over Bill's mother's house'. And of course there must have been many a Bill present.

The Coast Is Clear

To express that no one is about or watching, this phrase seems so obvious that to ask any question should be redundant. And yet, its very origin is intriguing.

When speaking of 'the coast is clear', it implies that no one is about or watching. The saying, now applied merely metaphorically, in the beginning was meant literally. It goes back to the sixteenth century, when it was used by smugglers who were about to land to discharge their contraband. To do so unobserved they had to make sure that the coast or inlet they had chosen for the purpose was safe.

Plastics And Bakelite

What is the origin of these significant products?

A multitude of products and materials serving modern society are made of plastics. The name is derived from the Greek for 'to mould' and reflects the very process of their synthetic creation.

Credit for the first introduction of plastic goes to the American inventor John W. Hyatt and was the result of strange circumstances. Hyatt invented the substance in the 1860s to gain a prize, promised to whoever was able to find a material for the moulding of billiard balls that could replace the ivory used for their manufacture at that time, which had proved too scarce and expensive.

It is odd to realise that the game of billiards prompted his history-making chemical discovery. Using a substance he called celluloid (from the Greek for 'having the form of cellulose'), he won the prize, which led to a most significant scientific advance.

Celluloid soon proved to have a drawback: it was flammable. And it was this disadvantage that led to the invention of bakelite. Its name, sometimes wrongly presumed to stand for 'baked light', recalled the name of Leo Hendrik Baekeland, who first evolved it. A Belgian-born chemistry teacher, he had migrated to the United States in 1889, where he patented his invention in 1909. To begin with, he called it by the German name 'Bakelit', joining the first part of his name with the chemical suffix '-it'. He did not realise at the time that his name would be permanently linked with the modern development of plastics and the industrial revolution they would bring about.

A Dressed Chicken

Why does one speak of a chicken as 'dressed' when in reality it is plucked and gutted?

It seems paradoxical that a plucked and gutted chicken should be called 'dressed'. After all, it is far from clothed, indeed totally bare.

The term comes straight from the abattoir. After an animal had been slaughtered, its carcass was prepared for the market. De-hided and with its intestines removed, it was cut into quarters or halves. This process became technically known as 'dressing' – explaining the apparent incongruity when speaking of a 'dressed' chicken.

Flog A Dead Horse

No one in their right senses would do so. Why then is the expression used?

Some statesmen of renown who helped in shaping the history of their nation also enriched the loom of language by their gift of tongue. Many of their achievements may be forgotten, yet some memorable phrase they coined or remark they made has survived to become a popular quotation. A typical example is the portrayal of a futile effort in pursuit of a certain aim, by comparing it to the 'flogging of a dead horse'. There is no use in whipping it. It won't get up and pull the cart, no matter how much it is beaten.

The simile was made by John Bright, the famous English politician and member of parliament. The occasion was the fight for the democratisation of electoral rights, which at the time were restricted to certain classes and individuals. A Reform Bill to this effect, introduced into parliament in 1867, seemed still-born from the outset. Members' apathy showed that there was little interest in seeing it enacted.

John Bright's own party, the Liberals, appeared totally indifferent. Bright, known as a man of conscience, with a deep concern for the welfare of the entire nation and not caring for popularity, was determined to see the Act passed nevertheless. To rouse his fellow members, he strongly rebuked their lack of interest. He called the entire Bill 'a dead horse' which no flogging would bring to life again.

Surprisingly, Bright was proved wrong and his comparison did not apply on this occasion. Contrary to his expectations or even possibly as the result of his challenge, on 15 August the parliamentary *Reform Act* was passed. It extended suffrage to a wide circle of formerly unprivileged citizens.

It is possible, however, that the phrase might go back to earlier times and might have originated among merchant sailors. It was then the custom to pay them in advance for their working time on board ship, a period oddly called by them a 'dead horse'. The attempt to get extra work out of the mariners whilst they were working off the 'dead horse' they described in their slang as to 'flog a dead horse'. The saying caught on and soon was adopted more generally. It was useless trying to revive interest in a job which had already been paid for. Further extending the application of the phrase, it was interpreted to mean that trying to enthuse anyone on an issue already done with or resolved was like 'flogging a dead horse'.

Yellow For Cowardice

Why is this colour associated with a lack of courage?

Why of all colours has yellow been chosen to depict cowardice? Sometimes expanded to 'yellow-bellied', the origin of the association can be traced to America, where slavery was a highly contentious subject even prior to the Civil War. The two opposing sides did not stop at anything in voicing their mutual antagonism, not least in scurrilous circulars they published anonymously! They printed these 'flyers' on rough, unbleached paper of a yellow hue. It did not take long for people to find out that newspaper writers were involved in the publication. Their lack of courage in not admitting their part in spreading the lies and insults made people dub them 'yellow journalists'. To equate yellow generally with cowardly acts was but a small step from there.

The Unlucky Wattle

What gave it this reputation?

The wattle is related to the English acacia and mimosa. It is said to have received its Australian name from the colony's early English settlers, who used its timber and twigs for building their 'wattle and daub' homes. They had brought from the old country the custom of using thin, flexible twigs of a tree to secure the thatch on a roof, and of intertwining the twigs with mud to build a wall. This process was known to them from back home as 'wattling'. Looking for the most suitable tree to supply the branches, they found the Australian acacia which grew abundantly everywhere. Eventually identifying the tree with the practice, they called it a 'wattle'.

Because a wattle in bloom was a beautiful sight, it was seen as an Australian national emblem. Nevertheless, in many rural areas it was regarded as unlucky to have a flowering wattle indoors. One possible reason was the notion, supported by experience, that wattles caused hayfever. Another more morbid suggestion is that the smell of the blossoms reminded settlers of an imagined odour of the dead.

To Put The Kibosh On Someone

What does this mean?

Several reasons, most of them very far-fetched and unsupported, have been given for the expression that speaks of 'putting the kibosh' on something or someone. It is used in the sense of making something fail or jinxing it.

Most likely it goes back to the Gaelic *cie bais* (pronounced 'kibosh'), meaning 'cap of death'. In other words, it is reminiscent of a judge who, when about to pronounce the death sentence, puts on a black cap. Equally it could refer to the hood slipped over the head of the condemned person just prior to being executed.

Another totally unsubstantiated theory suggests a Yiddish expression as the source of 'kibosh'. It was used at auctions to offer an increased bid – of eighteen pence, an exceedingly small amount. No convincing proof of such claim has ever been brought forward, however.

Kibosh has also been linked with an English word, 'bosh', meaning 'rubbish' or 'nonsense'. Yet another suggestion sees in the word a corruption of the Italian word for a 'tin lid', used when ice cream street vendors were being told to replace the lid on the container – to 'put the kibosh [back] on'.

The Hen Cackling After Laying An Egg

What makes her do so?

An animal's early instinct, particularly in the wild, to preserve its life and that of its offspring, becomes so deeply ingrained that it is never lost. It survives even in the tamed and sheltered domestic livestock or pets.

Cats, for instance, to protect themselves, will rarely sleep in the one spot for any length of time. The only exception might be when, for their own comfort's sake, they will sleep in their owner's bed, where they feel safe.

The same precautionary measure applies to fowl. No amount of cross-breeding has ever stopped the domestic chicken from cackling after having laid an egg. The practice has been traced to its forebears, wild jungle fowl from India and Malaysia, and to their concern for safety. It was their habit to live in groups, each made up of a cock and six to eight hens. When one of the hens was ready to lay an egg, she would leave the others to find a secluded spot, safe and secure from any interference.

Once she had laid the egg, she was ready to rejoin the group. The group, however, had meanwhile moved on and she had to cackle to locate their new whereabouts. The cock, on hearing her call, duly answered, letting her know where she could find them. This was the initial reason for hens to cackle.

It is believed that the hen's cackling on the occasion of laying an egg had an additional purpose. Proud of her achievement, the bird wanted to broadcast it as far as the sound could carry. It is not only humans who are apt to boast.

The term 'cackle' is onomatopoeic in origin, trying to reproduce the sound made by the hen.

Housewarming Party

What makes people give such a party even in the height of summer?

A 'housewarming' nowadays is a social get-together arranged to introduce friends to a new home. Originally it was done not for the entertainment of the guests invited, but out of deep concern with the spirit world.

In every epoch and culture there has been a focal point in the home around which people have gathered. Today it is the television set. In front of it the family sit in silent communion not with each other but with the TV screen.

In earlier times the source of attention was the hearth, which symbolically and literally formed the very centre of the home. The flames of the fire burning in the grate have always mystified people. The shapes they take on and their constant flicker seem to reveal a live force, a supernatural being dwelling within.

The ancient Greeks and Romans believed the fire itself was part of the divine sun. Thus for them the hearth became the humble, earthbound temple occupied by their domestic gods. These house gods were worshipped throughout the year as the keepers and guardians of the household and its food supply. In their honour the fire was kept burning in the hearth. Soon the fire itself was regarded as sacred and as representing life, and it was never allowed to go out.

Even as the original notion of the divine nature of the hearth became less clear, its influence on people's lives continued. The Roman and Greek house gods were replaced by fairies, brownies and other spirits who were thought to have taken possession of the hearth and on whose good will the family's life and luck depended. The entire family was cared for by these spirits of the hearth. To please them in every possible way and to keep them warm would make everybody happier. To neglect their welfare would displease them and one would have to face the inevitable consequences. Hence, prior to going to bed, people especially tidied up the grate. To keep the fire burning and thereby the goblins well satisfied, they put on a new log or fresh peat.

In certain regions tending the hearth was the duty of the woman of the house and was conducted with deep reverence, accompanied by special invocations asking for protection.

It followed that when people moved into a new home, they were truly concerned that it might lack a protecting spirit and that the spirits that had looked after them would stay behind in the old house. It is not just by way of metaphor that one continues to speak of a home having or lacking a special atmosphere.

Therefore when people moved from one place to another, they took live embers from the old grate, to start a fire at once in the new hearth. By this 'housewarming' they ensured continuation of their good fortune. They had brought with them the very spirits that belonged to and had looked after their family for so many years previously. And that is how housewarming parties have their roots in the occult and it is in this 'spirit' that they survive.

Sleeping Like A Log

Logs don't sleep. Why then does one say so?

Witches seem to have crept into the most unexpected places. People completely at rest and so much at ease that nothing would rouse them are said to 'sleep like a log'. Who would ever guess that this now common phrase was truly 'bewitched'?

It was told that witches when leaving for a nightly tryst went out of their way to make their absence from home inconspicuous and unnoticed. Anyone who found a witch's bed unoccupied would become suspicious and start asking questions. To avoid this, the witch placed a log in her bed. At times, to make the deception still more realistic, she would top the log with a nightcap. Whoever then looked at her bed in the dim light would think that she was asleep so soundly she did not stir.

A witch had to be careful at all times. Consequently, when meeting one of her own kind and wanting to discuss a coven she had attended the previous night, she had to do so with great caution. If overheard, she would endanger herself and her group. For this reason she would say that last night she had slept 'like a log'. This said everything to those in the know.

Eventually the phrase was adopted as a telling password among witches. However, when the outside world somehow got hold of it, all the magic went out of the log and it lost its original function as a secret codeword.

Discarded by witches, it was taken over by the world at large. And if one now happily sleeps 'like a log', it is done unperturbedly, and truly without consciousness of the occult 'root' from which the log grew.

To Foot The Bill

How did this saying come about?

It was the custom for anyone presented with a bill not to settle it on the spot, but rather to sign their name below the totalled-up amount – at its 'foot'. This signature was their promise to pay the account in due course. Its specific placement thus created the phrase 'to foot the bill', and eventually expanded to the settlement of any debt.

To Get In One's Hair

What is it that gets into people's hair to annoy them?

'To get in someone's hair' may seem an odd way to describe the experience of people giving a person persistent annoyance. The expression goes back to early times, when many a phenomenon, now easily understood, mystified people and led to strange beliefs. One of them was the mysterious crackling of one's hair, now known to be normally the effect of static electricity which, of course, at the time was totally unknown. It was then assumed to be caused by some evil spirit that was about to take its abode in the hair, or had already done so. In Muslim mythology this evil spirit was known as a Jinni. Possessed by supernatural power, it could take on a variety of forms. Among them was that of a male being who would attempt to 'get into a woman's hair'.

Much more plausible and reasonable to enlightened society, the expression might well also be derived from the unpleasant experience of some irritating bug or insect being caught in one's hair. This was not uncommon in the days when a stable or barn was attached to the house and people were growing their hair long. The hay and straw often housed crab lice which easily found their way into the home and then into people's hair, resulting in extreme irritation.

The Garden Of Eden

Where was this site of paradise located and what does its name signify?

Many attempts have been made to identify the exact geographical location of the Garden of Eden, the traditional site of Paradise. The biblical account, indicating that rivers were in the region, suggests that its site was part of the area of the former Mesopotamia, present-day Iraq.

'Eden' is not a Hebrew name but is Sumerian, and designates a fertile plain, a further pointer to its approximate location.

The name has also been linked with the Old Persian word for a garden which, three millennia ago, was specifically applied to a walled garden, enjoyed as a place of retreat. Whatever the linguistic root of its name, paradisal Eden is seen as an abode of bliss and supreme happiness.

The Greenhorn

What created this nickname?

Fruit and some not yet ripe vegetables are mostly green. Typical examples are green apples, green bananas and green tomatoes. It was almost a foregone conclusion that this natural phenomenon made people apply the colour to humans as well, in their case to the young, the inexperienced, the gullible and the naive. The earliest recorded date for such association, in this case with immaturity, is 1300. It can also be found in the writing of Shakespeare, who in *Hamlet* (Act 1, Scene 1) made Polonius, the Lord Chamberlain, reprove his daughter Ophelia for her naive acceptance of assurances of affection: 'You speak like a green girl,' he tells her.

A similar natural background accounts for the use of the term 'greenhorn' for the same type of people: those easily taken in, newcomers to a country unacquainted with its customs, raw recruits – in fact all those who make fools of themselves through their ignorance. This description was derived from the still-green horns of a young steer or deer, which they had difficulty in handling due to their underdeveloped intelligence.

Flowers In Hospital Rooms

Why were these traditionally removed at night?

If healthy people were exposed to dangers during darkness and forced to take due precautions, it followed that at night anyone sick was even more vulnerable to attacks by evil spirits. Already weakened, the patient offered a minimum of resistance to unearthly intruders who would take advantage of their condition.

Aware that entry during the night would be difficult with the windows shut, the fairy spirits used a devious means to gain access to the room prior to 'closing time' and before the sun had set when they were still powerless.

Friends visiting patients would show concern and cheer them up by bringing flowers. The visitors did not realise that their gifts carried harmful and dangerous entities. For flowers, according to ancient belief, were not only beautiful plants but could serve as a hiding place for spirits anxious to get to the weak.

Once night had come and the lights were out, the spirits would pounce on the sick persons, attempting to take possession of them and to inflict all the harm they could. That is why all flowers were traditionally removed from a sickroom before nightfall. The usual explanation given – that this was done because the flowers would use up vital oxygen during the darkness – is not only fallacious but a rationalisation of the original occult belief in fairies and their potentially lethal attack during the dark of night.

To Put Paid To It

What is the explanation for this phrase?

Many a phrase now used in everyday life comes from the world of commerce. A typical example is the practice of indicating the completion of a purchase by either stamping or writing on the bill the simple word 'Paid'. Equally, anyone who 'puts paid to' something indicates that it is the end of the matter. Whatever the circumstances, it has been settled once and for all. There is no chance of any further development or, as in the case of an appointment, hope for promotion. Nothing further can be done.

Fortune Cookies

Is it correct that, as it is often claimed, they are a Chinese creation?

Diners at Chinese restaurants welcome and in fact expect the fortune cookies served to them at the end of the meal. The enclosed little scrolls with their meaningful and frequently thought-provoking messages are interpreted to be particularly addressed to the recipient. The custom, followed worldwide, makes people assume that it was part of the ancient Chinese way of living and eating.

Actually, it is of recent origin, going back to 1916 and not to China at all. It was introduced through the business acumen of a Chinese immigrant to the United States. He was David Jung, the founder of the Los Angeles-based Hong Kong Noodle Company which supplied a wide range of Chinese restaurants.

Aware of the long period it often took for guests to be served their food and their consequent impatience and dissatisfaction, he sought some means of overcoming this problem, something that would make them forget the delay. Most likely he conceived the idea of the fortune cookies thanks to his knowledge of the ancient practice among Chinese rebels of exchanging information by hiding it in buns.

Apparently a man of faith, to start with, Mr Jung felt that for his purpose some spiritual message would be the most appropriate choice. As it were, it would enrich the minds of his guests, who, by discussing it, made the waiting period shorter. A Presbyterian minister he engaged was given the job of selecting appropriate passages from Holy Scripture, which he inscribed in condensed form on slips of paper to be enclosed in small, hollow cookies.

His idea worked and, enlarging on it to make it appeal to every type of person, he decided to secularise it. This would make it all the more attractive and entertaining. For this purpose, abandoning the spiritual realm, he replaced the clergyman with the wife of one of his salesmen, renowned for her alert mind. It was her special task to produce countless succinct messages, following the way Confucius had written his aphorisms. In no time these caught people's imagination and became a popular part of every menu. However, when the initial delay no longer occurred, the presentation of 'fortune cookies', as they came to be known, was not abandoned. Now they were served at the end of the meal.

Wedlock

What accounts for referring to marriage as 'wedlock', suggesting a state of captivity?

When speaking of wedlock one imagines that a marriage is something that locks people up and chains them together like prisoners. The original *lock* is no lock at all but the Anglo-Saxon for 'gift', as *wed* means a 'promise'. Wedlock thus pledges the finest of all gifts: the happiness of a man and a woman.

Son Of A Gun

What is the reason for calling someone by this mild pejorative term?

The original 'son of a gun' may well have been born on a vessel of the Royal Navy. Women were not always banned from coming on board, at least while the ship was in port. On occasions, they even sailed with their men, although they were kept well out of sight and out of the way. For this reason they were made to take up their quarters between the ship's guns, often protected and hidden behind canvas screens. Some of the women were or became pregnant and gave birth next to the guns. A boy who was born in that situation, particularly if his paternity was uncertain, was listed in the log of a ship as the 'son of a gun'. In many cases he was, indeed, a bastard in the technical sense of the word. Memories of his illegitimate birth lingered on, to render the 'son of a gun' a general term of abuse and contempt.

An alternative suggestion denies any relationship between the son of a gun and the Royal Navy and does not believe that he received his name, so to speak, from his gun-cradle. It traces the phrase back to Hebrew-Yiddish slang in which a thief was known as a *gunnef*. Somehow the word was mutilated and all that was eventually left of the *gunnef* was the 'gun'.

Not much good could be expected from the son of a *gunnef* who grew up in an environment of dishonesty; he is tainted by his father's pursuit. Nevertheless, people who call anyone by that name nowadays do so more in a jovial sort of way.

Horse Latitudes

What are they and why are they so called?

In the days of sailing ships their progress depended on the wind. Regions located in the North Atlantic between 30 and 35 degrees latitude were notorious for becalming them. The reason was either atmospheric conditions or the fact that in this zone, near the equator, the trade winds from the southeast and northwest met, neutralising each other.

Many have wondered why the area became known as the 'horse latitudes'. Several explanations have been proffered for the choice of this peculiar name. In colonial times, when ships carried horses from Europe and New England to the West Indies, the animals often succumbed to the stifling heat caused by the becalmed sea and their bodies were subsequently thrown overboard.

Alternatively, it has been suggested that, having run out of feed and with the water supply also reaching a low mark, the sailors were forced to dispose of their live cargo, and did so in like manner.

Yet another line of thinking attributes the naming of the horse latitudes to the Spaniards, at a period when their ships transported troops with their mounts to the New World. Becalmed for long periods, their vanishing supply of feed and drink forced them to abandon the horses, which they had dumped into the sea. However, these theories are most unlikely. After all, the soldiers had a strong instinct for survival and would never have thrown good edible horseflesh overboard. In fact, there is even a tradition that, after slaughtering them, they drank the horses' blood to supplement their ever-diminishing supply of drinking water.

In spite of modern motorised shipping and the fact that the early reasons no longer hold true, the now-obsolete name for the horse latitudes has not been changed.

Seeding In Tennis

What is the meaning of the term?

The question of who plays whom in tennis could be determined by drawing lots and be left completely to chance. It was realised early on that this was not the way to make games in a tournament exciting. On such occasions, it was much better to arrange the matches with forethought, avoiding having ranking players or teams meet in the early rounds.

In 1911, this system of allocation of games was first described (in the United States) as 'seeding'. Opinions differ as to why this particular term was chosen. Some believe that no other word could have described more adequately what was being done. In its original application in agriculture, 'seeding' denotes the separation of the seeds from the straw – and is not that exactly the procedure followed in the matching of players and teams?

Others, however, deny any connection between the seeding in tennis and that practised in the agrarian field. The term was the result of a fault, they say; not in the game but in speaking. Originally this method was very simply called the 'conceding' of a position to certain players or teams. Slovenly speech made people drop or swallow the first syllable. As the remaining 'ceding' made no sense in the circumstances, it was soon confused with 'seeding' and, sounding alike, eventually spelt that way.

To Tie The Knot

Why does one speak of getting married as 'tying the knot'?

'Tying the knot' certainly is a descriptive metaphor of marital union. However, like so many phrases that nowadays appear to be solely figurative, once upon a time it applied literally. In ancient Babylonian days, threads taken from the garments of both the bride and the groom were tied into a knot. This was not a symbolic practice but was believed to act as a magic means of ensuring the oneness of the couple.

Ancient superstition was convinced that by tightly making a knot a man could magically secure something he was anxious to keep. That could also be the reason why the bride and groom still, metaphorically speaking, 'tie the knot'. It also explains why the ribbons decorating the bridal bouquet are often knotted. This was originally meant to capture the moments of great happiness and love on the bride's wedding day and make them permanent.

A Frog In The Throat

Frogs live in swamps. How did they become part of this metaphor for a hoarse voice?

Those speaking with a croaky voice are said to have a frog in the throat. Although apparently an appropriate and innocuous figure of speech, its origin might not be so straightforward.

Its most common explanation recalls the days when, to quench their thirst, people drank from the nearest pond or well. In the process, they could easily swallow a frog or its spawn and it was truly believed that such an unfortunate occurrence accounted for the loss of voice. Gruesomely, it was further imagined that the frog in the throat had eventually moved down into the victim's stomach and was slowly devouring its host!

The expression might also be derived from a practice in medieval folk medicine. The prescribed cure for what is now diagnosed as a throat infection or thrush in the throat was the application of a live frog. The patient was asked to keep the frog inside the mouth without eating or swallowing it, and the frog was thought to extract and exhale the disease with its breath from the human throat. The frog's healing function could be compared to an exhaust pipe!

The treatment has long been abandoned and people have learnt to drink only water that is unpolluted. Nevertheless, the 'frog in the throat' survives in everyday speech, whenever people refer to a croaky voice.

To Take A Raincheck

What is the background of this saying?

Baseball has become more and more an integral part of the American way of life. Its vivid slang and terminology have entered everyday speech. This even includes the 'giving [or taking] of a raincheck'. It originated, so it is said, in the custom of issuing spectators with a ticket for another game if the baseball match for which they had paid was interrupted or cancelled because of rain.

Gargoyles

What is their function?

Gargoyles are grotesque waterspouts projecting from the roof gutters and other parts of churches and other notable buildings. Mostly carved in the shape of the bizarre heads of monsters and other mythical figures, many go back to the twelfth century or earlier. At the time downpipes and drainpipes leading straight from the gutter into the sewer were unknown, with the result that rainwater cascaded from the roof to the ground along the walls of the edifice, in the process damaging the masonry. Gargoyles were meant to avoid this, as by jutting out they made the water fall far enough away from the walls to avoid as much damage as possible.

Their name comes from the French *gargouille* meaning 'throat' or 'gullet'. It was an appropriate choice, as the gargoyles spurted the water out of their throats.

According to a seventh-century French legend, however, the word perpetuates the name of a ferocious dragon. From the River Seine, its abode, it had viciously attacked and looted the city of Rouen. Coming to the victims' aid, the then bishop of Rouen had slain the beast. And yet, somehow it survived – in the gargoyle. In its stone form, it now paradoxically served a utilitarian purpose. The decorative work of skilled craftsmen, it fulfilled a significant preservative role.

True masterpieces of all kinds and shapes, possibly most famous of all were the numerous gargoyles on top of the cathedral of Notre Dame in Paris. They spouted the rainwater clear of the sanctuary's walls.

In spite of their beneficial function, some clerics opposed the existence of the gargoyles. They feared that they would attract people to stay outside the churches to study their many intriguing features, instead of joining the congregation inside in prayer!

There was another, positive role that gargoyles came to play. The superstitious believed that their frightening grimaces would act as a devil repellent and as guardians against evil demonic spirits. Catching sight of them, they kept well away!

It is interesting to note that the English word 'gargle' etymologically has the same root as 'gargoyle'. An example of onomatopoeia, it is imitative of the sound made by the flowing water or the noise of gurgling.

The Paperclip

Who invented it?

Tracing to its very beginning such an apparently simple object as a paperclip shows how some modest products, now taken for granted, are the result of enormous effort and many modifications. The paperclip goes back thousands of years to the early stages of literacy, when scribes first felt the need to keep together several sheets of parchment.

Initially they did so by making a slit or hole in one of the corners of the individual sheets, through which they threaded a string or a ribbon. This they then secured with sealing wax. An arduous task, it soon showed flaws. In no time the holes deteriorated and in the process often tore the parchment or paper, so that the sheets became detached.

The modern pin seemed finally to answer the problem and offer an ideal solution. After much experimentation, its ultimate shape and quality appeared to ensure that the loose sheets were 'pinned' together securely and permanently. However, it did not take long for this method to reveal snags as well. In no time, the small pin holes also grew in size and the pins were loosened and fell out. Even if this did not happen, the pins became rusty, ruining the document.

There were other unwelcome side effects. The pin could get stuck in other things or prick those using it. Most of all, in the early days, pins were not cheap. They were so precious that women needing them for their clothes were given as a special allowance from their husbands, a gift appropriately called 'pin money'.

Having experienced these many difficulties, it was realised that something totally different had to be provided to serve the purpose. The vast development of trade and the ever-increasing volume of correspondence made it all the more necessary to find some simple means to join together a multiplicity of documents.

Who was actually the inventor of what came to be known as the paperclip has been the subject of controversy, between not only a great number of people, but countries as well. Britain, the United States and continental Europe have been among the chief contenders.

Generally, however, it is believed that it was a Norwegian, Johann Vaaler, who invented the paperclip in 1899. Unfortunately at the time he had to face an unexpected problem. His own country had no patent laws. This forced him to have his novel device protected by the Germans and then, in 1904, by the United States, where his invention, referred to as 'the paper clip or holder', was given a detailed description. This stated that his product was made from a 'spring material, such as a piece of wire, that is bent to a rectangular, triangular, or otherwise shaped hoop', and it said that the end parts of the wire pieces 'form members or tongues lying side by side in contrary directions'.

Ever since, numerous improvements have been added to the clip. They have made it more serviceable, non-slipping, unlikely to scratch or tear paper, streamlined in appearance, not too bulky and – being mass produced – easily available to everyone.

Greenbacks

American paper money is so called. Why?

In the United States paper notes of all denominations are green in colour and referred to as 'greenbacks'. It goes back to the Civil War when, because of a shortage of gold and silver coinage caused by the need to finance the war, Salmon P. Chase, the then Secretary of the Treasury, issued the first paper currency in 1862. The green ink used for the back of the notes (or 'bills', as they are known in America) made him call them 'greenbacks'. There is also a tradition that not Chase himself but Union soldiers, who were among the first to receive their pay in the form of the new bills, were responsible for their colourful name which, whoever so dubbed them, has been maintained ever since.

A Left-Handed Compliment

What does this mean?

Many features that once belonged exclusively to the ritual of the Church have become so much part and parcel of everyday life that their religious source is forgotten. Such is the case with the 'left-handed compliment'. Ambiguous in its praise, the irony implicit in such a compliment is meant to hurt.

When class distinctions were still rigid, an unbridgeable gap separated the nobility from the 'common people'. They lived in different worlds and, in some places, even worshipped God in separate churches! It was a policy of 'apartheid', not between races, but social classes.

For a member of the upper class to marry a commoner was just not done. Love, however, knows no bounds and, in spite of the unwritten law, such misalliances did happen. To discourage them, an invidious practice was adopted, intended to give public expression to society's disapproval. A man of noble birth who had dared to choose a woman 'below his station' as his bride was not permitted to follow the usual custom at the solemnisation of their marriage of giving the bride his right hand. He had to offer his – inferior – left hand.

This manner of indicating the low standing of such alliances gave rise to the habit of calling them 'left-handed'. And this verbal expression of contempt for the union was not the only mark of disapproval imposed. The unfortunate low-born wife was never recognised as having joined the ranks of nobility. For the rest of her life she remained a commoner. So did any children born of 'left-handed' wedlock. None of them could ever share or inherit their father's title or property.

Thankfully, such obnoxious class distinctions are now a matter of the past. But 'left-handed' compliments are still paid, using an expression that is the linguistic residue of a long-obsolete part of the marriage ceremony.

An Ill Wind That Blows Nobody Any Good

What is the meaning of this saying?

The saying that it is an 'ill wind that blows nobody any good' comes from the days of sailing ships when vessels crossed the seas in all directions. It is quite possible that a wind blowing from east to west, whilst obstructing one ship, proves most favourable for the progress of another going a different way. Therefore the saying should really be changed to 'it is an ill wind that blows somebody some good'.

It is a common experience for somebody to profit from the misfortune of others. A house badly damaged by fire certainly proves an ill wind for its owner. However, it might well benefit a number of other parties, such as the builder repairing it, the stores supplying new furniture and the tradespeople restocking destroyed goods. Likewise, a car involved in a smash is bad luck to the owners but not so for those restoring it.

Bonking

What is the origin of this term for sexual intercourse?

'Bonking' has become part of the twenty-first century vocabulary as a colloquialism for 'having intercourse'. Its earliest literary mention has been traced to a 1975 magazine feature. Although everyone now knows what the term stands for, its origin is still uncertain.

According to one suggestion, it developed out of an early slang word for 'hitting'. Others discovered in the word, as it were, an echo of 'banging'. In both cases, bonking would refer to violence, which, not rarely (and in many languages), has been associated with the sexual act, as in 'to knock up' and 'to screw'. Some, however, have seen 'bunk' as the cradle of bonking: a couple beds down to copulate.

Reversing direction, so to speak, there is also a hypothesis recognising in 'bonk' the 'knob', a well-known slang word for the penis, read from back to front, perhaps to camouflage it. A variety of possibilities, they are as mysterious as sex itself.

A Mummy

Why is an Egyptian embalmed corpse called a mummy?

According to ancient Egyptian belief, shared by many other cultures, death is only a stage in life's progress. However, survival in a future world was not inevitable or automatic. It necessitated the preservation of the body and it was this assumption that accounted for the Egyptians' special way of embalming the body. Known as mummification, it was responsible for the very description of the body so preserved as a 'mummy'. The word actually recalls the application of bitumen in the process, known in Arabic as *mumiyah,* which, in turn, was derived from the Persian *mum* for 'wax'.

A complicated and costly procedure, it was only natural that its full treatment should be reserved for royalty and members of the nobility. Cheaper methods in various forms were applied to people of lower status.

Mummies have fascinated the mind ever since their being first discovered and unearthed in modern times. They tell much of early Egyptian technology, but even more significantly relate humanity's ancient belief that death does not conclude existence.

'Grass' For Police Informer

How did this odd name come about?

Generally, to 'grass' on someone means to act as an informer, usually for a reward. Specifically, it is applied to doing so to the police or prison authorities. The term is said to owe its latter application to the policeman himself, whose description in Cockney rhyming slang refers to the 'copper' as a 'grasshopper'. Criminals were not slow, as it were, to cut the 'grass' for their special use.

In Drag

Why does one speak of a man dressed in women's clothes as being 'in drag'?

The practice of men wearing women's clothes goes back to the early days of the stage, when women's parts were taken by men. As the dresses they wore often 'dragged' along the ground, in the jargon of the theatre such roles became known as 'drag roles'. It was but a small step for people to refer to the actors taking the parts as being 'in drag'. Eventually the term was applied to everyday life as a description of those who, in search of extra sexual stimulus, don the clothing of the opposite sex.

A Gone Coon

Which circumstances originally created the term 'a gone coon'?

Anyone or anything ruined or caught in an irreversible, hopeless situation is said to be 'a gone coon'. The term – an Americanism – was adopted from the animal world.

'Coon' is the shortened form of 'raccoon', an animal at one time hunted for its fur. Trying to escape from its pursuers, it would climb up a tree, not realising, of course, that from there it had no chance to get away. Indeed, it was 'a gone coon'.

There is a variety of other explanations of the origin of the phrase. Best-known among them is the story of an American spy during the Revolutionary War (1775–1783). Anxious to observe a British encampment, he had donned a raccoon's hide and, so disguised, hid in a tree, where a British rifleman spotted him. However, mistaking him for the real animal, he aimed his rifle at him. Before he could discharge his weapon, the camouflaged spy shouted, 'Don't shoot, I know I'm a gone coon!'

Similar is the story told in the form of a fable by Captain Frederick Marryat, an English officer and novelist who spent some time in America. His account involved Martin Scott, a captain serving in the US army who was an accomplished sharp-shooter. One morning he came upon a raccoon resting high up in a tree. The animal instantly recognised Scott as the renowned hunter who never missed his mark. It begged him not to shoot. Fully realising that it was 'a gone coon', it would come down from the tree by its own volition.

The identical incident has been linked with David (Davy) Crockett, another famous rifle shot, though it has never been established who was the first to attempt to shoot the animal.

Horns Of A Dilemma

A dilemma is bad enough. Why has it horns as well?

Whoever is 'on the horns of a dilemma' is in an unenviable, awkward position. Having to decide an issue in such case, one has only two (*di*) choices for a 'proposition' (*lemma*). The term is derived from Greek and Latin roots.

Either alternative is equally undesirable and obnoxious. Being stuck on an issue is like sitting on the sharply pointed horns of an animal, a metaphor indicative of the discomfort it implies. Whichever way one chooses, one will be tossed about, getting nowhere or merely changing one disadvantage for another. Neither of the alternatives available promises a satisfactory course of action or one superior to the other.

A Gravy Train

What does it mean?

In the original sense, gravy is the tasty juice exuding from cooked meat and is often obtained with little effort by those preparing a meal. This might well be the reason for the colloquial application of its name for money easily come by, not really earned or even deviously acquired. In American politics, it would mostly take the form of graft.

Using the word in this sense, people came to speak of those getting excessive pay for little work as 'riding the gravy train'. It has been suggested that actually, before being adopted in general speech, the expression originated on the American railroad. It was applied there to crews who got good pay for little work. Not inappropriately it could be said of them that they had a ride on a gravy train.

It was in Benjamin A. Botkin's *Lay My Burden Down*, published in 1945, that the phrase first appeared in print.

A Windfall

Why is an unexpected gain referred to as such?

A good fortune unexpectedly coming one's way is referred to as a 'windfall'. Originally, the term really meant what it said. It had its beginnings in Britain and goes back to British members of the nobility, whose estates often included large tracts of forest. In spite of their owning them, they were not permitted to make free use of their trees. Much less so, of course, could any commoner.

To protect forests is not a modern phenomenon. Long before the ecological concern shown by conservationists and environmentalists, royalty pursued and enforced an identical policy. However, they did so with a totally different aim in mind. They were prompted by considerations of national defence.

At the time, Britain's rule and defence greatly depended on its fleet. To maintain a sufficient number of ships was paramount. For this reason, it was decreed that no tree could be felled or timber cut except for the purpose of building vessels for the Royal Navy.

There was one exception. Trees uprooted by storms or branches blown down by a strong wind were free for the taking. In every sense of the word, they became a 'windfall'.

Go Troppo

What is the origin of this description of people who become unbalanced?

Those acquainted with the world of music know 'troppo' as a term mostly applied in a negative sense. From the Italian for 'too much', it might thus be used to admonish the performer against some excess, such as *allegro ma non troppo* – 'quickly, but not too much so'.

However, there is another 'troppo' as well. An Australianism, and of a totally different meaning, it is an abbreviation of 'tropical'. In this sense it is applied to those who, unused to tropical humidity and heat, have become mentally unbalanced.

Unknown prior to World War II, the word was then coined by soldiers serving a long stretch in the Pacific zone which because of its unusual climate eventually affected the mind of some. Identifying the tropics as the source, Australian servicemen used the words to describe this unfortunate condition. To be called 'half troppo', obviously, meant 'partially mad'.

To Steal The Thunder

What was responsible for the choice of this metaphor for misappropriating another's recognition?

Varied indeed was the career of John Dennis (1657–1734). A saddler's son, he was educated at famous Harrow School and Cambridge University. One college expelled him for stabbing a man. Eventually he became a playwright and critic.

All of his plays proved failures, and yet one of his tragedies, *Appius and Virginia*, written in 1709, made him famous. It was not because of any inherent merit or success of the play, but through a gadget he had invented for it. This produced better sounds of thunder than anything had done before. The show soon folded up. But when, shortly afterwards, Dennis visited the same theatre to watch a performance of *Macbeth*, he discovered that his thunder machine was being used. Outraged that someone should have 'stolen his thunder', he exclaimed, 'My God, the villains will play my thunder but not my plays!'

Dennis himself is forgotten but echoes of his outcry can still be heard, whenever people speak of someone 'stealing the thunder'.

Scotland Yard

The London headquarters of the Metropolitan Police are so called. What is the explanation of this odd 'misplacement'?

Scotland Yard (now New Scotland Yard), the famous headquarters of the London Metropolitan Police, was originally the name of a palace. It was so called because in Saxon and later times it served as a residence for the kings of Scotland, whenever they came to London to pay their respects to the kings of England whose vassals they were.

After unification of England and Scotland the palace, having lost its purpose whilst maintaining its name, was converted into offices which then in 1829 became the centre of the Metropolitan Criminal Investigation Department, briefly referred to as the CID. When, sixty-two years later in 1891, this came to occupy new premises, this time specially built for it in what was termed 'the Scottish baronial style', it became known as 'New Scotland Yard' – thus still recalling the early days of its existence and as a memento of British history.

In [The] Seventh Heaven

Are there a number of heavens and what is the reason for describing someone who is extremely happy to be in the seventh one?

Anyone who says that 'I'm in [the] seventh heaven' feels deliriously happy.

The words are not a mere metaphor, chosen to express the intensity of one's euphoria and bliss. They are based on an ancient belief in the actual existence of not merely one, but seven heavens. Possibly going back to Babylonian mythology, this plurality of heavens not only played a prominent part in Jewish mysticism, particularly so in the *Kabbalah*, but was also adopted by Christian writers of the first centuries AD, and widely popularised by Moslem teaching.

Each heaven was separate, with distinctive features. These surpassed those of the one preceding it. No wonder that speculation and accounts of their individual names, substances, contents and promises abounded. Growing through the generations, they gave a wide range to the fantasies, expectations and diversity of interpretations of the devout. However, all shared the belief that the seventh heaven was the ultimate one. Superior to all the others, it was the holiest of all. A region of pure light and the abode of God, it was beyond human power to describe it.

Whether in the ecstasy of the moment or after a person's death, their soul would leave the body to ascend into one of the heavens. Which of the seven was determined either by the merits they had gathered and perfection they had attained or the intensity of their faith. The worthiest, of course, in their migration would enter the very acme of the galaxy of heavenly realms: the heaven of heavens.

Paper Patterns

Who first thought of making these aids for home sewers?

Of all people, an American shirt maker, Ebenezer Butterick from Sterling, Massachusetts, was the first to conceive the idea of producing paper patterns for the 'home sewer'. It seemed paradoxical that someone who made his living from selling shirts should provide people with the means if not to replace him, at the very least to minimise his own business. Somehow, however, he must have guessed that his innovation, if it caught on, would bring him a fortune, far surpassing what he was earning at the time.

It was almost a foregone conclusion that the first of the paper patterns he designed, in 1863, was that of a shirt, which he then produced in a variety of sizes. Jointly with his wife, he cut the patterns from tissue paper, selling each set with sewing instructions and a picture of what the finished article should look like.

The idea proved such a success that, in no time, he was able to enlarge the range of his patterns to include children's wear and then ladies' fashions. Within four years he had opened an office on Lower Broadway in New York City!

The demand for the Butterick paper patterns grew constantly and reached such proportions that sales ran into millions. The firm soon spread abroad, with offices in Europe and Britain catering for clamouring customers. Apart from proving such a successful business venture and even more importantly, his paper patterns gave women a new and constructive pursuit which they could follow at home and which they took up enthusiastically.

That Rings A Bell

What is the background of this odd expression for remembering something?

This expression comes straight from the croquet lawn of former days. At one time, a player in making the winning stroke actually caused a bell to ring. The game was completed when the winner hit, not the stick used now, but a combination of two hoops which crossed each other at right angles forming a dome from which a bell was suspended. The game was over when the player drove the ball through the hoops and thereby rang the bell.

Able To Sleep On A Clothesline

What is the background of this strange figure of speech chosen to depict a very sound sleeper?

Insomniacs envy people who can sleep anywhere and at any time, even if 'pegged out' on a clothesline. The phrase is not simply a figure of speech but goes back to nineteenth-century England and concerns a real rope.

Destitution and poverty then abounded in the country. It was estimated that in London alone there were 100 000 homeless people. Workhouses were overcrowded. The rent charged by so-called lodging houses was exorbitant, far beyond the means of those ordinary men and women able to earn just a pittance. Down-and-outs regarded themselves as lucky if able to bed down on the bare floor of a stable, or in a sewer.

More 'fortunate' were those who were permitted by a landlord to spend the night sitting on a hard bench in one of his rooms. Invariably they had to share this with many others. A rope, stretched in front of them, served as a makeshift support on which they could lean. But even for this convenience they had to pay – two pennies (two cents) per person. At daybreak their host removed the line and they were jolted back into reality.

It is a strange paradox that the tragic need of those who had to literally 'sleep on a clothesline' is recalled by a phrase that has acquired a totally new meaning. It is now the happy gift of those who are able to nod off anywhere – even, metaphorically speaking, stretched out on a clothesline.

The Safety Pin

Who invented this most useful everyday object?

Safety pins of one kind or another have been in existence for thousands of years, already being used in the Bronze Age. Homer's *Odyssey* tells how Queen Penelope was offered an embroidered robe to which twelve golden pins 'with well-bent clasps' were attached. In classical Greece and Rome, women used to fasten their clothes with richly ornamented metal brooches, specially shaped for that purpose and known in Latin as *fibulae*.

A forerunner of the modern safety pin was patented by Thomas Woodward of New York in 1842. Rather pompously, he called it 'the Victorian shielded shawl and diaper pin'. Having no spring, his pin easily came undone, particularly so if the material it was meant to hold together lacked bulk.

Seven years later, in 1849, Walter Hunt, also of New York, became the inventor of the real safety pin. In fact, he has been credited with many other 'firsts', which include a paper collar, a repeat-firing rifle and, not least, a sewing machine.

At the time, Hunt was at an all-time low financially. Deeply in debt, somehow he had to raise money, and do so quickly. In his case necessity was indeed the mother of invention.

Hunt reasoned that there had to be something badly needed by people, but which was not in existence – yet. If only he could identify the missing object and then make it. Luckily, with his ingenious mind, he found the answer – near at hand. There was nothing that could hold together articles of cloth or other material, and do so securely. After having pondered the problem for a mere three hours, he had the solution. It was a pin that, protected by a clasp, was safe – the safety pin as we know it today! By cleverly twisting a wire, in no time he produced the first model. Lacking the funds to manufacture the novel 'gadget' himself, he sold its patent (No 6281) for a paltry sum, for others to cash in on his idea and inventiveness.

Going Down The Gurgler

What is the origin of this saying?

To 'go down the gurgler' is an Australian slang expression. It says exactly what it means: to 'go down the drain' – to be finished!

Interestingly, the saying recalls the gargoyle, the waterspouts carved in the shape of the head of some grotesque mythical creature. They can be seen on the parapets of European cathedrals and churches, some universities and other notable buildings. They were not just fancy projections from their roofs, but fulfilled a significant role – to let the rain flow down to the ground without damaging the walls of the edifice – and thereby greatly contributed to the preservation of many historic landmarks.

Sure As Eggs Is Eggs

What explains the presence of eggs in this affirmation?

To confirm a certainty by stating something is 'as sure as eggs is eggs' is not only grammatically faulty, it also makes no sense. Paradoxically, the original observation contained not a single egg. A mathematical expression, originally it used 'X', the symbol of algebraic propositions. To underscore the validity of something said, it was very appropriate to apply the formula that it was 'as sure as X is X'. The 'eggs' is merely a corrupted 'X'. To add to the oddity of the phrase, it uses a symbol standing for an unknown quantity as an assurance of an irrefutable fact.

Whistle Blower

Why are informers so called?

To sound an alarm police used to blow a whistle. Referees continue do so, in their case to stop a game because of some fault or infringement of the rules on the part of a player or a team. For whichever purpose, the practice made 'to blow the whistle' an apt description of concerned people's determination to stop a wrong by revealing its existence.

The phenomenon of whistle blowers has become part of modern industrial, political and economic life. Their revelations, however, are a dangerous undertaking, as they expose themselves to retaliation by those whose wrongs they disclose. Unless mere spite or self-interest is their motive, whistle blowers show great courage, as they are well aware that what they do, although it may be right and proper, might be to their own detriment.

A Wigwam For A Goose's Bridle

What is the explanation of this abstruse saying?

Many people have been puzzled by the saying that 'it's a wigwam for a goose's bridle'. The words do not make any sense. There is no such thing as a goose's bridle, hence to provide a wigwam (a dwelling place of North American Indians) for something that does not exist only adds to the confusion.

A jumble of words, mere verbiage and gibberish, the expression says nothing at all. And this is exactly its intention. When asked a question to which they do not know the answer, or when unwilling to supply it, people will not say so outright. Instead, either to cover up their ignorance or to avoid having to reply in the negative (whether to an adult or a child), they say something that sounds so incomprehensible that, awestruck and flabbergasted, the questioner does not dare pursue the quest further. They accept the answer as final.

Up To Dolly's Wax

Who was this dolly and what was the wax for?

Not a few expressions have found their way into everyday speech from the nursery. An Australian coinage is the description of having overindulged in food as being (full) 'up to dolly's wax'. Rather puzzling words, they only make sense if put back into their proper context.

Dolls have always been one of the most favoured of children's toys. Not mere objects to them, children treat them like human beings. Using a doll as an example, therefore, was once considered the best way to teach children a lesson.

Whilst the body of dolls used to be made of cloth or some other material, their heads were frequently of porcelain or wax. To impress on a child how inappropriate it was to be greedy, with the child's love of a doll in mind it was told that the food reached up to the dolly's wax (head).

The saying caught on, to be applied in the adult world when speaking of any glut or excess as 'up to pussy's bow and dolly's wax'.

Shopping Trolleys In The Supermarket

What is the story of their introduction?

The shopping trolley (or 'shopping cart', as it is called in the United States) presented a major development in the history of merchandising. It was first introduced in the 1930s by Sylvan Goldman, the owner of a supermarket in Oklahoma City. His initial motive was not merely to help shoppers to carry their purchases but also to increase the volume of goods sold. Watching his customers carry the baskets into which they put their shopping, he noticed that they stopped buying the moment these were full or too heavy. It greatly limited the amount of items sold. Somehow he had to overcome this problem.

His imaginative mind set to work and he ingeniously made use of an existing object to create a totally new contraption, one which would change the entire process of shopping.

Travelling salesmen at the time carried with them folding chairs for their own convenience. Why not make use of these, Goldman thought. He mounted the legs on wheels and raised the seats, placing on them one or two baskets. This would make it possible for shoppers to wheel away goods which, in volume and hence in value, would far exceed any amount ever sold before.

To his disappointment, however, his endeavour seemed to prove a failure. Business did not increase. Shoppers were reluctant to make use of the trolley, fearing that it might get out of control and hence be dangerous.

Goldman did not give up. Well aware of how easily people could be influenced, he employed a ruse. He re-advertised the innovation and, surprisingly, this time it appeared to be most successful. Crowds of shoppers began to wheel carts, fully laden, outside of his store. Would-be customers, seeing them, were convinced that the carts would not after all present any hazards. No longer hesitant, they went inside to be offered – by a woman specially positioned at the door for the purpose – one of the vehicles ...

They did not realise that they had become the victims of a stunt. Goldman had hired people, some of them actors, to impersonate those customers happily pushing the loaded carts out the front! It took no time for the trolleys to prove their worth and, using the words of the title of Terry Wilson's biography of Goldman, to become *The Cart that Changed the World.*

Having patented his idea, Goldman founded the Folding Carrier Corporation in 1936, to manufacture his trolleys and to take up the building of supermarkets and shopping centres. He died in 1984 at the age of eighty-six, two years after having retired as the head of Goldman Enterprises. Leaving a fortune estimated to amount to US$200 million, even more significant was the legacy he left to the world: his shopping trolley.

Head Shaking For 'No' And Nodding For 'Yes'

What created this expressive body language?

Charles Darwin gave an interesting explanation as to why people of most cultures shake their heads to express 'no' and nod them for saying 'yes'. He suggested that the gestures go back to the language of babyhood. Infants who are breast-fed, when they have had enough of their mother's milk, move their heads away and from side to side. On the other hand, when hungrily looking for the breast, they make a forward movement. Hence this widespread part of human body language is a survival of infantile nursing habits: the babies' breast-seeking and breast-refusing gestures.

The observation that babies born both blind and deaf still follow that same instinctive pattern duly confirmed Darwin's theory.

Act [Or Play] The Goat

Why would anyone wish to do so?

The goat has played a significant and varied part in history. In some early cultures it was regarded as the familiar of a witch or even the devil himself. Others offered the animal as a sacrifice for the atonement of people's sins.

Conspicuous features displayed by the animal were responsible for the phrase 'to act [or play] the goat'. People 'playing the fool' could easily be likened to goats, seen frolicking and jumping about without rhyme or reason. The goat was also known as a lecherous animal and of men who were lascivious it could be said that they 'acted [or played] the goat'.

Yuppie

What is the origin of the word?

The popularity of acronyms has made people soon forget what they 'initially' represented. A combination of initials in reality, they are often mistaken for proper words. Their number is now so great that special dictionaries list and explain them.

The 1980s created the 'yuppie'. Yuppies are members of the ambitious and affluent but reckless young working generation. They love the good life and anything money can buy. They wear fashionable designer clothes, sport expensive watches and jewellery and fill well-paid jobs in their professions. They drive fast and flashy cars and live in showy homes, located in suburbs renowned for wealth.

So distinguished, they were given their own label. A member of this group was identified as a '*y*oung *u*rban *p*rofessional', popularly shortened to yuppie. In people's minds, the slightly pejorative nickname reflected their conspicuously wealthy lifestyle and ostentatious place in society.

A Horse Of A Different Colour

What is the reason for this equine comparison?

To convey the fact or opinion that something is a completely different matter, it is said that it is 'a horse of a different [or another] colour'.

The origin of the phrase has been traced to the English village of Uffington in Berkshire. On a hill just south of the village can be seen the outlines of a galloping white horse of gigantic dimensions. Covering an area of almost 0.8 hectares (2 acres), it is 112 metres (374 feet) long and, on a clear day, can be seen from as far away as 18 kilometres (12 miles). Thomas Hughes made it the scene of the opening chapter of his 1857 classic, *Tom Brown's Schooldays*. 'And what a hill is the White Horse Hill!' he wrote. 'There it stands right up above the rest ... the boldest, bravest shape for a chalk hill you ever saw.'

The horse probably dates back to the Iron Age. For the ancient Celts it was a shrine in honour of a deity. It was inevitable, however, that with the passing of time fresh vegetation and weeds overgrew the figure, which thus became 'a horse of a different colour'. To retain it for years to come, it became the custom periodically to 'scour' the horse and thereby restore its original hue.

An alternative claim attributes the white horse to totally different circumstances: not to ancient mythology but to the history of the English people. Apparently Alfred the Great, the Saxon king, placed it there after his victory over the Danes at nearby Ashdown in AD 871. This led to the enemy's eventual complete withdrawal from English soil.

The horse was to serve as a perpetual monument to the Saxons' casting out of the foreign invader. As the traditional emblem of the Saxon people, the white horse proclaimed from on high the message of Saxon supremacy. This would be threatened if ever it became 'a horse of a different colour'. To prevent this from happening, the population regularly went up the hill to restore the horse to its original white.

Different again is a third explanation. This links the saying with medieval tournaments, those jousting matches in which armoured knights competed against one another on horseback. Whilst it is the modern method to distinguish the various racehorses by the colours their jockeys wear, at that time it was the colour of the horse that identified its rider. If a favourite knight was expected to win a race but did not succeed in doing so, his supporters, and particularly his lady, would sadly remark that it was 'a horse of a different colour' that came first.

Shakespeare must have been familiar with the phrase when, in *Twelfth Night* (Act 2, Scene 3), he made Maria say to Sir Toby Belch, who shared her opinion on a certain matter, that 'My purpose is, indeed, a horse of that colour'.

Philtrum

What is a philtrum and why is it so called?

Oddly enough, even the terminology of human anatomy has preserved the 'love potion'. 'Philtrum' is also the name of that mysterious groove or channel between the septum of the nose and the centre of the upper lip. No one really knows its purpose. Perhaps that is why, situated so closely to an erotic zone, it has been named so 'lovingly'.

Another possible explanation is that a drop of perspiration, easily caught in this diminutive 'cup', might be sucked up by a passionate kiss. As an excretion from the lover's own body, it would act like a love charm and exciting sex stimulus. In poetry, indeed, this dimple forms part of the upper lip and its Cupid's bow. In fact, it gives the Cupid's bow its shape and thereby perhaps conveys its message of love and gave it its name.

Anatomically, however, the philtrum is part of the juncture between the two halves of the face. The blasphemous might even suggest that a seam left thus showing may reveal bad workmanship.

Diamonds For Engagement Rings

What is the reason for the choice of this specific gem?

Traditionally, a diamond adorns the engagement ring. History claims that, in 1477, Emperor Maximilian I of Austria was one of the first to give a diamond ring to his fiancée, Mary of Burgundy. The choice of a diamond was not just due to its intrinsic value or conspicuousness, but was also based on a combination of long-held beliefs.

In earlier, more superstitious times, people imagined that invisible, malevolent forces continually tried to destroy human happiness. No doubt a couple engaged to be married would be a prime target. It was further assumed that those evil spirits, belonging to the world of darkness, would shun light, and that therefore anything bright would scare them off. This made a diamond in a ring the perfect safeguard, its reflected light warding off any devilish forces near by. Thus the couple's love would no longer be threatened and nothing would break their engagement.

Another, even more fanciful assumption that was once prevalent was that the diamond possessed procreative power! For instance, it was widely held that two stones set in one ring would multiply. And, by association, some of the diamond's supposed sexual potency would be transferred to the wearer. The presentation of a diamond to one's fiancée, therefore, had a very practical meaning and purpose, as well as a symbolic one. To be effective, it was further believed the stone had to be set unbacked, so that it was able to touch the skin.

The diamond was known to be one of the world's hardest substances, which no other stone could cut or scratch. It was therefore also imagined to give constancy and permanence to the forthcoming marital union. Its transparency made the diamond a symbol of purity, innocence and sincerity. Apart from indicating the wearer's virtue, it also expressed the pledge on the part of both the man and the woman never to deceive each other.

The Italians used to call the diamond 'the stone of reconciliation'. They were convinced that if a disagreement ever threatened a couple's happiness, a diamond would magically restore harmony. Hence its presence in a ring ensured a lasting and happy relationship between husband and wife.

Sleepwalking

Is the practice dangerous?

Sleepwalking has been a phenomenon that has mystified, if not frightened, people through the ages, though it is now known that there is no need to worry about those who suffer from this affliction.

Of much more concern however, even from earliest days, has been the question of whether it was wise to wake anyone who wanders about in their dreams, unconscious of their actions. People are afraid that it might shock the sufferers and inflict on them serious mental damage.

The fear goes back to the belief held in primitive society that during sleep a person's spirit left their body. It was a superstition easily explained by the vivid experience of dreams, in which dreamers find themselves in far-off places, a situation that might well apply to sleepwalkers, who travel literally to other places. In their case, it was assumed that to wake them up would mean to do so whilst their spirits were still separated from their bodies, with no opportunity of both being reunited, resulting in the person's death.

Soft Drinks

Who thought of bottling them first?

Joseph Priestley (1773–1804) is most famous for his discovery of oxygen and his naming of rubber. Hardly known is the fact that he started his career in a totally different field – as a Unitarian minister. As a mere hobby and as 'a relaxation from other studies', he embarked on experiments in a laboratory.

When he was serving a congregation in the Yorkshire city of Leeds, England, chance willed it that his parsonage should be adjacent to a brewery. The beer mattered little to him, but his curiosity was roused by the fumes diffused by the fermenting grain. In search of their source, he was led along the very track that in 1772 made him give soda water to the world. As the first to create the carbonated drink, he has rightly been called 'the father of the modern soft drink industry'.

Electricity

Why was it so named?

The ancient Greeks were among the first to note, as early as the seventh century BC, a special property of amber. If rubbed, it would become magnetic, attracting light objects, such as woollen fibre and small feathers. Doubtless, there were other substances of equal capacity, but none seemed so outstanding and conspicuous in this faculty. Another fascinating feature of the element observed by the Greeks was that friction caused it to produce sparks. This made them call it *elektron,* for 'a beaming sun'.

Both practical and romantic, the ancients soon imagined that the amber could serve them in another capacity. Worn in the form of an amulet, its magnetic power would be sure to attract love.

In his study of magnetism, the English scientist William Gilbert (1540–1603) took note of the Greeks' findings. Confirming amber's ability to attract other objects, he adopted and adapted their findings in connection with the fossil resin. He did so in his major work, published in 1600, which contained the results of his experiments in magnetism, the first comprehensive study on the subject. Writing in Latin, he used its equivalent of the Greek word for amber, the 'beaming sun' – *electrum.* When, subsequently, he rendered his historic work into English, he created the modern term 'electric' which in turn became responsible for the name of electricity. Adopted universally, it resulted in Gilbert's becoming known as 'the father of electricity'.

X For A Kiss

Why an X for a kiss?

That X – a mere cross – came to represent a kiss has its own story to tell. Some have seen in the choice of that figure from mathematics a most appropriate symbol. It may signify nothing at all, a mere 'zero', or stand for (an) infinity (of delight). On the other hand, it can 'multiply' joy and love.

However, the prosaic explanation for this affectionate sign may be twofold. Originally it represented the formalised, stylised picture of two mouths – > < – touching each other – X. But then the kiss became connected to the cross by a chain of events and really owes everything to men's lack of education.

Early illiterates signed documents with a cross. They did so for an obvious reason. A cross was so simple to draw and yet, being also a sacred symbol, implied the promise of truth. To solemnly confirm further the veracity of what he had endorsed, the writer kissed his 'signature', as he was accustomed to do to the holy book. And that is how, finally, by its very association, the cross came to be identified with a kiss.

Come Home With A Wet Sail

What does this imply?

It is generally assumed that this phrase comes from sailing races. The expression 'a wet sail' might suggest that in its progress a boat had capsized. On the other hand, it may also imply that by the crew's making every effort to come first, a lot of spray wet the sail. Either of these factors might well be responsible for the idiom now used without any idea of its origin.

There is also the suggestion that the words go back not to sporting events but to commercial competition. During the days of sailing ships trading vessels were anxious to land their goods before others. In attempting this they proceeded with such speed that they came home with their sails wet.

Throwing Of The Bridal Garter And Bouquet

What is the significance of this custom?

It used to be the custom for the bride when 'going away' to throw her garter to the groomsmen, who would scramble for its possession. Having been so close to her body, and particularly so high up on her thigh, it was thought to have absorbed special sexual potency which would be transferred to whoever came to own it. At times it was difficult, if not embarrassing, for the bride to remove the garter, and the men struggling for it became very rough. Therefore, it was no wonder that she much preferred to present her 'pursuers' with flowers.

Considerations of propriety thus made the bride replace the garter with the bouquet which, appropriately, she now throws to her own attendants. It is caught by one of the bridesmaids with the hope that she will catch the bride's good fortune and be next in line to be married.

The custom of throwing the bouquet has also been seen as an expressive, though little realised, symbolic gesture. It has been described as a visual pun referring to her imminent deflowering.

Cobber

How did a cobber get this name?

A variety of explanations has been given for the origin of 'cobber', considered an Australianism for a true mate, a close friend or a companion. The most popular etymology derives the name from English dialects: from the verb to *cob,* used in Suffolk for 'to like someone' or 'to form a friendship', or from the related Cornish *cobba.* English convicts or migrants then introduced it to their new domicile in Australia.

There are several other hypotheses, however. One traces the cobber to Hungary, where in the form of *chever,* pronounced 'hovver', it was used as a slang word, mainly in Budapest. The cobber has also been linked with the Hebrew *chover* or *chaver* for a 'close companion'. Although far-fetched, if true it would be symbolic of the close companionship and friendship of the Australian Jew and Gentile.

Yet another etymological claim recognised in the term the Aboriginal *cobbra,* for 'head'. This would make the cobber truly indigenously Australian.

Brandy

Who first distilled and named this alcoholic drink?

The name of brandy is the shortened form of the Dutch for 'brandy-wine' *brandewijyn,* made up of *branden* for 'burn' and *wijyn* for 'wine'. This alcoholic drink was produced by distilling 'burnt' wine.

An unidentified Dutch apothecary is said to have been the first to introduce people to the simple process of distillation. Boiling the wine in a still, he caught the resulting vapour in a vessel in which, cooling down, it condensed into the intoxicating drink.

It was in the seventeenth century that brandy first came onto the market, according to unconfirmed reports, to make use of a bad year's wine! It is not surprising that the Netherlands was its birthplace, as at the time this country was the leading producer of spirits in Europe.

The so-called Napoleon brandy has no historic foundation. Without any real link with the emperor, it made use of his fame merely for promotional purposes. The stars on a bottle, likewise, give no indication of its age or quality. Theirs is simply a decorative role.

Blue For Police Vehicles, Uniforms And Stations

What is the reason for the choice of this specific colour?

It is commonly believed, though wrongly so, that the police force adopted blue lights for their cars to differentiate them from the red lights of fire engines (obviously linked with flames), ambulances (associated with blood) and other emergency vehicles. Although a very plausible explanation, it does not tally with the facts.

Initially, red identified the police as well. No doubt they had adopted it from the Bow Street Runners, a body of men previously employed to catch criminals. Going back to as early as 1749, the Bow Street Runners were renowned for their efficiency. They were nicknamed 'Robin Red Breasts', and for a very feasible reason. It was the colour of the red waistcoats they wore, chosen to make themselves especially conspicuous.

It was therefore almost a foregone conclusion that when in 1829 the modern police force was established, taking over the duty of those 'runners', it also appropriated their distinctive colour.

However, red was not to last. It reminded people of the Red Light District, and to be associated with prostitutes in any way (other than by taking them into custody) was not in keeping with the dignity of the police force. Hence red was replaced by blue to identify a police station, a police vehicle and a policeman's uniform.

It is interesting to learn that for a short period in the 1880s, at Queen Victoria's request, the blue was abandoned. A frequent visitor to the opera at Covent Garden, Victoria had to pass the police station in its vicinity and, for reasons of her own, disliked the colour blue. Why she did so is not certain. It has been suggested that it is linked to an incident in which she stepped on a blue opal, crushing it underfoot. At her behest, the blue of the police was changed to white, at least locally. Soon after the queen's death, however, it was changed back to the original blue, which it has remained ever since.

There is another totally different suggestion to account for the change of colour. It was an attempt to thwart the cunning minds of criminals caught in their endeavour to escape from pursuing police cars. Taking advantage of the fact that they shared the conspicuous red colour of fire engines and ambulances, they claimed that they had never tried to flee from the forces of the law. On the contrary, they had sped away to clear the way for these emergency vehicles, displaying the identical red lights as those of the police. In such case indeed, if they had failed to do so they would have been asked to pay a minor fine. To avoid any such subterfuge, this theory claims, the police force adopted blue instead of red.

Driving On The Right And Left Sides Of The Road

Why do some countries drive on the right and others on the left?

In the early days of travel, traffic was sporadic. Although roads, if they existed at all, were narrow, no one had to worry very much about colliding with a rider or vehicle travelling in the opposite direction. Traffic rules then dealt only with specific situations. These included the breaking down of a loaded waggon; the procedure to be followed when a faster vehicle wanted to overtake a slower one; and which of two vehicles travelling in opposite directions had to give way by drawing up by the roadside.

In some parts of the world traffic laws reflected the class-consciousness of the time. The number of horses permitted to pull a person's carriage was determined by his or her social standing. A mere count of the horses thus would reveal the importance of their owner and whether this person had the 'right' of the road. The practice certainly anticipated the modern cult of high-powered cars with a maximum of horse(!)-power as a status symbol.

Once traffic had become relatively heavy, moving almost continually both ways, to avoid accidents and, not least, head-on collisions, its flow had to be controlled. The obvious thing to do was to widen the roads and then to legislate that traffic had to keep to one definite side for each direction. The question now was to which side.

It is an intriguing if not puzzling fact that to this day countries are divided into two groups: those who keep to the left and those who prefer the right. This choice of the right or the left does not reflect the politics of a nation. It was the result of a combination of many factors: practical considerations; people's innate wish to do things the easy way; national and religious antagonism; exigencies of war; and plain logic.

The English and those who follow their example – such as Australia, New Zealand, Japan and Thailand – keep to the left. Their persistence, there is no doubt,is due not least to English conservatism. They preserve regulations which, when introduced, made good sense, though their motivation has long become redundant.

It all goes back to the days when the horse dominated the road. For thousands of years it served people as their only means of fast transportation. Riders everywhere mount a horse from the left. It was the natural way for right-handed persons, the majority of the population, to grasp its mane and the reins with their left hand and then to swing their right leg across. Therefore it became a universal practice.

It was the first step along the road. The next followed almost inevitably. By mounting their horses from the left side, riders would naturally keep to that side of the road. That is how the horse first 'pointed the way' and taught people how to travel. Accordingly, special mounting posts provided for riders on early English roads were always on the left.

The introduction of the coach did not change matters. In fact, it reinforced the rule of the left. Good horses made good miles. At times they needed some prodding. As mere vocal exhortation proved insufficient, coachmen used a whip. But to do so they needed ample room. Heavy carts and some carriages were pulled by several teams of horses. To reach those in front, the driver had to have still more freedom of movement for his whip.

Worse still, they could easily have hit and injured pedestrians on that side of the road. On country lanes, the whip would have been caught in the hedges and trees flanking them. The adoption of left-hand travel was the logical choice, and for many years it remained the universal European custom.

The earliest known official 'keep left' regulation was issued in 1756 for vehicles crossing London Bridge. Scotland was the first country – in 1772 – to make left-hand travel a national law, applying to all city traffic. (Offenders were fined 20 shillings – $2 – a substantial amount then.) England and Wales followed suit in 1835.

Coaches and traffic could thus run as smoothly as could be expected at the time. An apparent contradiction did not go unobserved. Henry Erskine put it in rhyme, when he wrote:

The rule of the road is a paradox quite,
Both in riding and driving along;
If you keep to the left, you are sure to be right.
If you keep to the right, you are wrong.

Views still differ as to why this general and practical rule of the road was altered, leading to the present world confusion between the right and the left, traffic-wise.

One theory credits warfare with the change in sides. Traditionally, a battle was started by an attack on the enemy forces from the left. For this purpose the troops advanced along that side of the road. But Napoleon shrewdly reversed the sides. He foresaw that the enemy army trained in the standard way would thus be taken completely by surprise. Unable to switch quickly, from the outset of the battle they would be at a great disadvantage.

His new strategy of launching attacks from the right necessitated that his marching columns should proceed to their battle stations on that side of the road as well and therefore no longer from the left. Napoleon carried his new 'order of march' wherever he went in his conquest of Europe. Inevitably, all other traffic had to adjust itself to his way.

This military explanation of right-hand driving is greatly supported by the fact that two countries Napoleon did not reach – Britain and Sweden – kept to the left. (Sweden switched to the right in 1967.)

Another theory attributes the reversal of sides to religious antagonism. For centuries, papal authority felt that the wellbeing of the entire person and not merely their soul was the Catholic Church's responsibility. Thus it regulated everyday life over the vast area of Catholic Europe, including the issue of road safety. The Pope made it mandatory for all traffic to travel along the left side of the road.

Robespierre, the French revolutionary and atheist, was determined to break the power of the Church in Rome.

He set out to display French freedom and independence from the Church and the Pope who represented it wherever he could. For no reason other than to be contrary and to show his contempt, he reversed the order of things. That is how, it is suggested, he abolished the Papal traffic law and made the French people change sides on the road. Later, with Robespierre gone, traffic in France continued to move in the new direction. It became the state law in 1835, the same year in which England legislated for the left. When it became fashionable to copy all that was French, many other countries adopted their rule of the road as well!

Americans chose the right side. Some have wondered why. After all, America is a former British colony. It was certainly not done as a gesture of defiance or expression of independence, nor in imitation of the French. The most likely reason is linked to the postillion who usually was in charge of the many horses necessary to pull large transports. To have maximum control over them, he had to be mounted on the left horse in the lead. It was more natural for him to mount on the left-hand side, and riding on the front horse he could steer all of the others. Thus mounted, his left leg was slightly sticking out, easily to be caught by a tree or hedge or even to be squashed by a wall, if he kept on the left side of the road. (At the time sidewalks for pedestrians, which could have acted as a buffer zone, did not exist.) And so, for the protection of the postillion, traffic in America kept to the right.

Paparazzi

How did the paparazzi enter the modern vocabulary?

Freelance photojournalists of a specific type have become known as 'paparazzi'. Their job is to obtain off-guard pictures of some celebrity, if possible in an embarrassing and compromising situation. If necessary they do so at all costs, then try to sell them to the highest bidder.

Tracing their name to its present-day 'professional' meaning reveals a combination of diverse circumstances. It goes back to an insignificant observation an English novelist made during a trip to southern Italy. *By the Ionian Sea,* published in 1901, was the only travel book of George Gissing, the English novelist. His entire life was haunted by misfortune, generally reflected in the gloomy and pessimistic outlook communicated by his works. But this book was praised as a real gem, 'full of masterpieces of prose writing', clear analysis combined by the scholarly student with the description of travel. During a brief sojourn at Catazaro in the deep south of Italy, a printed notice displayed in the bedroom of the hotel in which he stayed especially intrigued him. It was an appeal by the proprietor to his guests. He had learnt with extreme regret that some of those enjoying his hospitality did not patronise his restaurant, but took their meals elsewhere. This not only hurt his feelings, but also harmed the reputation of the establishment. He assured the visitor that he did his very utmost to maintain a high standard of culinary excellence. Imploring his 'honourable guests' to dine in his restaurant, he personally signed the notice 'Cariolano *Paparazzo*'.

It is the only reference to the name in the book. No one could have guessed that sixty years later it would become part of the modern vocabulary when this very name was given to a character in Federico Fellini's masterpiece *La Dolce Vita,* a film (first shown in 1960) that was to gain worldwide fame. While the screenplay writer Ennio Flaiano was writing its script, he was also reading the Italian translation of Gissing's travel recollections and was taken by the innkeeper's 'prestigious' name, which made him choose it for one of the characters. The movie portrayed the high living of the

Roman 'smart' set and depicted the decadence of modern society generally. Fellini himself considered it 'a documentary film about life'. Paparazzo's role in it shows him accompanying the central figure, a gossip columnist searching in vain for the fulfilment of his venal desires. Paparazzo is shown as a ruthless intruder into the personal lives of other people.

Thus the world-renowned film gave the name of the Italian innkeeper its new meaning, making it part of the modern vocabulary. It finally gained the widest and most unexpected publicity on the occasion of the tragic death of Princess Diana on her fateful car ride through a Parisian tunnel in 1997.

Many attempts have been made to explain the etymology of the word, including the misguided suggestion that the root of the name was 'paper'. However, *paparazzo* (*paparazzi* being its plural) is of Sicilian origin. It spoke of buzzing insects, like bees, gnats and mosquitoes, which, with their noise and sting, proved a great nuisance and harassed those they pursued. What word could better describe the sensation-seeking, intrusive modern press photographers mercilessly hounding their quarry?

Curiosity Killed The Cat

Cats are nosy creatures. But why should this prove fatal?

Cats are notoriously nosy and in their eagerness to find things out can endanger their own lives. This would explain why it is said that 'curiosity killed the cat'. The expression is used to warn people who want to know things that are none of their concern not to be so inquisitive.

However convincing, the saying is not authentic in its present wording but is the result of an early substitution. Originally, the expression did not relate to curiosity at all but to care, in the sense of 'worry'. Worry can be a killer, to be avoided at all costs.

To emphasise the point, the cat was used as an example. Believed to be resistant to all types of dangers, the cat was said to have nine lives. Even so endowed, care (worry) could wear it out. The implications for humans were much more serious. For them, anxiety could prove lethal!

Quotations from early writers confirm this association of care and the cat. 'Let care kill a cat. We'll laugh and grow fat,' boasted the *Shirburn Ballads* in 1585. In *Much Ado About Nothing* (1599), Shakespeare wrote, 'Though care ki'd a cat, thou hast mettle enough in thee to kill care.'

With the passing of time, people misunderstood the word. Well aware of a cat's nosiness, they corrupted the original 'care' into 'curiosity', and that was how 'curiosity killed the cat' was (mis)conceived.

Nose Running When Crying

What causes it?

When crying, tears not only flow out of the eyes but also drain through a duct that connects the eyes to the nose. This, which could be called an 'overflow', causes the nose to run when shedding tears.

Fit As A Fiddle

How can an inanimate object be fit?

To be as fit as a fiddle sounds rather odd and 'out of tune'. It has been explained by saying that the phrase speaks of persons who always live at 'concert pitch'. 'Highly strung', they are able to produce the very best.

Originally, however, there was no fiddle at all in the saying. Instead, it spoke of someone 'as fit as a fiddler', which immediately makes much more sense. Whoever first made the comparison must have thought of some specific fiddler whose task was particularly strenuous and who therefore had to be in prime condition. Two possibilities offer themselves.

At Irish feasts a fiddler served as the sole source of entertainment. He led the dance which, almost without a break, extended into the early hours of the morning.

To provide such uninterrupted fun amounted to a veritable endurance test. Admiring his stamina, people came to speak of being 'as fit as a fiddler'.

The second type of 'fiddler' who might have suggested the phrase lived in a different world. He was a sparring partner in the boxing ring. His aim was to wear out his opponent. He did so by engaging him ceaselessly, without respite. The constant movement reminded people of a fiddler playing the violin. Requiring tremendous staying power, they could well refer to him as being 'as fit as a fiddler'.

Bar Codes

How did they start?

Bar codes are now taken for granted. They can be found not only on grocery items in supermarkets but on nearly all merchandise.

Their beginning can be traced to San Francisco, USA, where on 4 January 1973 eight men gave birth to the idea. Members of a 'symbol selection committee', they created what was then called a 'Universal Product Code' (UPC), the future bar code. It consisted of a cluster of black stripes of various thicknesses on a white field with ten numbers at the base. They supplied electronically every essential detail about the specific product they marked, and could easily be identified by a laser scanner.

Their introduction achieved an unparalleled degree of progress at the checkout counter of supermarkets, as they fulfilled a dire necessity at the time. Profits had slumped to an all-time low. The reasons for this were the high wages paid, and particularly the time-consuming procedure at the till. Mechanising the entire process by modern electronic means not only streamlined it, but also made it possible to reduce the number of staff. It also cut down on losses caused by inaccuracies at the cash register due to human error. The novel technological advance eliminated the need for extra packers as well, then employed to put the purchases into bags, because the checkout person was now able to do this. Additional bonuses for the shoppers were the resulting reduction of their waiting time in the queue and their no longer having to check the accuracy of the bill.

It did not take long for the bar code to prove its inestimable value and to be adopted worldwide. Now a generally accepted feature of daily trade, it provides the maximum degree of efficiency and benefit to all parties concerned.

Gone To The Dogs

What is the explanation of this and other canine sayings?

Throughout history and all over the world, the dog has been the constant companion of humans. Loyal and brave, the dog has contributed to humans' welfare in the most varied ways: as a guard, a lifesaver, hunter and pet. Surprisingly, however, its influence on everyday phrases mainly reflects the seamy side of its life – and death.

In some countries and at various times dogs have been feared and shunned. And not without reason. Because dogs often carried rabies and tetanus, their bite could prove fatal. Starved, the poor creatures attacked the unwary. Reproducing fast, they were considered a nuisance, if not a threat. Chased away, they began to roam the outskirts of villages and settlements seeking food wherever they could find it, in dumps and among refuse, leading to more infection. Not looked after like treasured pets, their life was a constant struggle.

In their desperate fight to survive, they became bedraggled, diseased and ferocious. To 'go to the dogs' and join such contemptible creatures certainly was a misfortune and a disgrace. Dogs were little cared for, in every sense of the word, and it is no wonder that those described as 'going to the dogs' were to be pitied. They were to become like the neglected creatures, of little worth and despised for their vile habits. Indeed, dogs were no example of moral behaviour either, and 'to go to the dogs' could also imply that those joining them equally were lacking ethical standards.

It was this harsh canine existence which – paradoxically – enriched the English vocabulary with a number of metaphors. The depraved were called 'dirty dogs'. Those who had fallen on bad times were said to 'lead a dog's life' or, worse still, to have 'gone to the dogs'.

Reminiscent of the ultimate fate of such an abandoned canine, the most destitute and forgotten of person was said to 'die like a dog'.

The Four-Leafed Clover

What made it a luck-bringer?

The precise origins of the belief that a four-leafed clover is lucky are lost in antiquity. Only a biblical legend that offers an explanation survives. This relates that when Adam and Eve were expelled from Paradise, Eve took a four-leafed clover with her, which flourished in the Garden of Eden. She wished to retain at least something that would remind her always of her happy existence in the now-lost paradise. That is how its presence in one's own garden came to be looked upon as an omen of good luck.

Two Minutes' Silence

How long ago did this custom start?

Silence that means not just the stopping of talk but pausing in all of one's activities has been a custom dating back to classical times. Most religious faiths observed it, in one way or another, and the ancient Egyptians even had their own god of silence. To quote a modern writer, 'to be alone with Silence is to be alone with God'. A time of meditation and introspection, silence also serves to pay honour to individuals or occasions recalled.

Best-known is the two minutes' silence solemnly observed on 11 November at 11.00 a.m. The date and time mark the exact moment – the eleventh hour of the eleventh day of the eleventh month – when, in 1918, the armistice between the Allied and Central Powers took effect and all hostilities of World War I came to an end. Four years of war had cost the lives of over ten million soldiers and it was in their honour that the silence was first kept in 1919 and later extended to pay homage to the victims of other wars.

Opinions differ as to who introduced the custom. Some claim that it was Edward George Honey, a colonial journalist. Others, however, name Sir Percy Fitzpatrick, a well-known South African and the author of *Jock of the Bushveld,* as the initiator, a view more generally accepted and shared by King George V. Shortly before Sir Percy's return to South Africa from Britain, the king's private secretary informed him that 'the King desires me to assure you that he ever gratefully remembers that the idea of the two-minutes' pause on Armistice Day was due to your initiation'.

A Goose Egg

What accounts for the goose egg and other egg-related expressions in sport?

A zero stands for nothing and the world of sport has created its own terminology deriving from the shape of the cipher. As its very outline was that of an egg, this led to the obvious choice of the egg as the metaphor for the nought mark on the scoreboard.

It was an egg of any kind. In their logical way the French used it in tennis, calling it just 'the egg' – in their tongue *l'oeuf* – which on English tongues sounded like 'love' for 'no hit' or 'zero'. The British, always practical and specific, applied it in cricket first in 1863 in the form of a duck's egg (or just a 'duck') when a batsman had scored no run in an innings. Following the British example, the Americans around 1886 selected a bigger variety of egg. For 'no score' in an innings in their national sport of baseball, they used the goose egg. No wonder that to 'lay an egg' (of any kind) came to denote a failure.

The Unlucky Opal

How did this superstition begin?

The superstition that the wearing of an opal may bring bad luck is the result of a combination of circumstances and long-held beliefs. It is associated with false reasoning, the sickness of an Italian woman, Spanish royalty and the fictional character of a world-renowned writer.

One-third of Europe's total population died of the Black Death that ravaged the continent in the fourteenth century. At the time, Hungarian-mined opals were a favourite adornment. A Venetian woman who had caught the fatal disease continued to wear the stone even on her sickbed. Those looking after her remarked on its brilliancy.

Soon after her passing, they noticed that the opal had lost all its fire and lustre. They imagined this pointed to some strange connection between the wearing of the gem and her death. In the tortuous reasoning of their minds, it did not take them long to assume that, in fact, the opal had caused the death. Some malignant power inherent in the stone had killed the patient! Doing so, it had spent all its energy, which 'explained' why the opal looked suddenly so dull and lifeless.

Point the finger at anything and, sooner or later, people will believe it or at least say that 'there must be something in it', and the misdiagnosed cause of the Italian woman's death spread the superstition of 'the unlucky opal'.

Oddly enough, people had been right in what they had seen; it was just their interpretation that was at fault. Modern knowledge supplies the true reason for a phenomenon quite correctly observed at the time. Changes of temperature affect an opal's appearance. The unfortunate victim of the plague had been feverish and her overheated body had made the opal shine so extraordinarily. Soon after her death, her body naturally turned cold. The variation in temperature no doubt had caused the fire in the opal to die as well, at least temporarily.

The story is told that Alfonso XII, King of Spain (1875–1885), on his wedding day had presented a beautiful opal ring to his bride Maria. Two months later she died. At the time, it did not enter the king's mind that there could be any connection between the stone and her passing.

After the funeral he gave the precious heirloom to his sister, who died a few days later. Still unsuspecting, Alfonso now passed on the opal to his sister-in-law and with it, so it seemed, her death sentence. Within the short period of three months, she, too, passed away.

When the stone was returned to the king, he decided to keep it for himself. He had it made into a tiepin which he wore with pride – and with the identical fatal effect. Two weeks later Alfonso was buried.

Playing safe, the Queen Regent now donated the opal to a Madrid church where, protectively, it was suspended from the neck of the statue of the Virgin of Almudena. But the damage had been done to the name of the opal.

Nevertheless, the belief in the opal's death-dealing quality was based on mere circumstantial evidence. Many of the quoted dates and data cannot be substantiated. Rumours grow in the telling. Soon a mere myth was taken to be an undeniable fact.

Modern fiction reinforced the doleful reputation of opals. In his novel *Anne of Geierstein*, Sir Walter Scott (1771–1832) told the story of Lady Hermione, a charmed princess. She arrived quite suddenly on the scene, from no one knew where. Conspicuously, she wore in her hair an opal which, like herself, seemed enchanted. Somehow it was bound up with her life, reflecting her various moods. Thus it sparkled when Hermione was happy; her anger, however, caused red beams of piercing light to shoot from the stone. Holy water would immediately extinguish its lustre.

The phenomena were as mysterious as the woman herself, who eventually vanished as unexpectedly as she had first appeared. Collapsing, she was carried into her room and placed on her bed. Next morning, all that could be found was a small heap of ashes. The spell was broken and the enchantment was at an end.

People are always intrigued by the mysterious and soon, not least because of Scott's popularity, the novel was avidly read. Readers are only too apt to believe in anything as factual, once they have seen it in print.

A mere confusion of words has also been suggested as the reason for the superstition. In Elizabethan times, the opal was spelt 'ophal'. It appears as such, for instance, in a list of the queen's jewellery. Those knowing Greek soon were reminded of a striking resemblance with the Greek *ophthalmos* for 'eye'.

And did not, in fact, some opals look very much like an eye? Fascinated by the stone's mysterious 'lights', it did not take long for people to imagine that some ominous link existed between the eye-shaped stone and the 'evil eye'. That is one explanation of how they came to shun the stone.

Not supernatural causes, but very much down-to-earth reasons may have contributed to the opal's bad reputation. At the famous Australian opal-mining centre of Lightning Ridge, so the story goes, two men were determined to buy up all stones mined there. To do so at the lowest possible price, they cunningly spread the rumour that bad luck was associated with all opals. Consequently, miners worried about getting stuck with their treasures, let them go for very little money. A bad name, once given to anything, sticks and no logic can ever wash it off.

Lapidaries and jewellers, on the other hand, have also been blamed for the superstition. And for some very valid reasons. Experience had taught them how brittle the opal could be. Many a time, when asked to set a stone, it fractured. Naturally, that was bad luck for them and their customers. They loathed thus to have anything to do with opals. Their well-founded prejudice then attached itself to the stone generally.

It is really no wonder that the opal became an object of so much fear. Of exquisite beauty, it had the distinctive faculty to change its colours swiftly and so mysteriously. Even Shakespeare was aware of this quality of the opal, which he used in *Twelfth Night* (Act 2, Scene 4) to express fickleness: 'For thy mind is very opal'.

Mystery creates awe and the inexplicable, fear. That is how the opal acquired its ominous quality, no matter what its explanation.

Parking Meters

In which country and by whom were they introduced?

With cars having become ever more affordable and thanks to continued population growth, traffic into the inner cities grew to such an extent that the cars not only came to choke the streets, but parking them also became a problem. Something had to be done to control it.

In 1933, Carlton C. Magee, the then editor of the main newspaper in Oklahoma City, came to the rescue. A man of ingenuity, he had the idea of introducing what was to become known as the (coin-operated) 'parking meter'. As its name indicated, it timed the period a car was permitted – for a fixed fee – to occupy a space.

In order to execute the scheme properly he established the Dual Parking Meter Company, which was the first to manufacture his meters. Called 2-R Meters, they were so named for the twofold purpose they served: the Regulation of traffic and, simultaneously, the provision of Revenue, to be collected by the municipality. The latter was a clever idea, as it roused the interest of the City Council, which immediately ordered 150 of his meters, the first in the world. They were installed in July 1935, which was the very year in which Magee patented his invention.

What had started as an experiment proved so successful that the American example was followed in Britain, first so in London, with almost all countries following suit.

In some cases the meters created difficulties. In Alaska, for instance, they had to withstand a harsh climate, with exceedingly low temperatures prevailing in winter and deep snow covering the streets. To facilitate the movement of snow ploughs and protect the meters from being knocked down by them, these were put up not, as elsewhere, nearest the curb but right up against the walls of buildings. In Bogota, Columbia, another problem had to be met that did not remain confined to that city. Thieves not only stole the money collected but, when unable to do so easily, wrenched out the entire meter from its concrete base, to remove the coins undisturbed at some isolated spot far from all traffic, and then to dump the ruined meter.

Put A Flea In One's Ear

How did this saying originate?

The flea is Anglo-Saxon, at least in the origin of its name. Very descriptively this recalls one of the insect's outstanding gifts: its ability to 'jump'. Feeding on the blood of humans and beasts, it can leap thirty times its own height. This fact was first established in Greek days by Socrates, the philosopher.

Others have discovered a close affinity between the *flea* and *fleeing,* as this lively creature always seems to be able to get away.

Usually, a flea – like its bite – metaphorically points to something trifling, a thing of really no importance. And yet, to actually put a flea in one's ear can be a serious thing. It becomes most annoying and can drive one almost mad.

Commonly the phrase has been explained as the result of watching a dog with a flea in its ear. It makes him so restless that sometimes he flees in terror.

However, humans have long been flea victims. As far back as AD 700, Saxon nobles complained bitterly of its bites, though only a few of the over 500 different species of fleas choose people as their host.

Fleas became especially aggravating at the time of the medieval knights. In chain mail from head to foot, those valiant men soon discovered that almost more worrying than the adversary they had to face outside was that small glutton that had invaded the inside of their suit of armour, which now shielded the flea as much as its wearer.

At first the flea enjoyed a good feed, truly having a field day. Jumping about freely without the knight's being able to hinder its progress, it bit him where it pleased. No one could stop it from sucking the man's blood.

Sooner or later the flea felt it had had enough of the gentleman. Trying to leave its dark prison, it just could not find a way out. In its search for an escape route, it eventually got into the knight's ear.

There it settled – sometimes for hours – intermittently biting and jumping. This caused the helpless knight unending frustration, aggravation and even torture. That is how, when speaking of putting a flea in someone's ear, unknowingly those former days of chivalry are recalled, when the knights in shining armour experienced alarm and distress through these wingless insects which unwittingly had become their prisoners.

Good Wine Needs No Bush

An odd saying. What does it mean?

Inn signs are now an accepted feature of the trade. They differ from one inn to the next and each has its own story. But in days gone by, all inns displayed the identical symbol. It was like a signpost to help thirsty travellers easily find their way to the nearest inn. Just as doctors in some countries indicate their place of practice, their office or surgery, by a red lamp, so did saloon keepers by a bush. Their choice was motivated by Greek mythology. The bush was sacred to Bacchus, worshipped as the god of wine.

A tavern serving the finest of drinks was so popular that everyone knew its whereabouts. It really needed no sign. Hence, 'good wine needs no bush'. Quality is its own advertisement.

Throwing A Pinch Of Salt Over The Left Shoulder

What is the reason for doing so over the left shoulder and not the right one?

The superstitious person who has accidentally spilled salt will immediately take remedial action to cancel out any unfortunate after-effect by throwing a pinch of salt over their left shoulder.

There are significant reasons why they do so. As the result of the 'upsetting' incident, the superstitious believe that the devil is about to pounce on them. But being a most cunning creature, he will do so not only from the rear where he cannot be seen, but also from the left or the weaker side.

Salt is loathsome to the devil. It is linked with God and his power and was used in the divine ritual. It signified all that was incorruptible and immortal. A substance used as a preservative would be inimical to any evil force out to destroy. Hence to hit the devil in the eye with a pinch of salt would not only temporarily blind him but also make him turn tail at once with his mission unaccomplished.

A Pretty Kettle Of Fish

What is the origin of this phrase?

To understand the phrase 'a pretty kettle of fish', it must be remembered first of all that 'pretty' is sometimes used ironically, to describe a nasty sort of situation. And to speak of 'a pretty kettle of fish' referred to exactly that: awkward circumstances, a real mess. The kettle itself has been explained in several ways.

One tradition links the kettle with Scottish picnics, at which much of the fare was improvised. Camping near a river, the people heated up a huge kettle, putting into it salmon they caught on the spot. At times, they were unlucky and, for one reason or another, the meal did not turn out the way they had hoped. With the outing spoiled, they spoke of it as 'a pretty kettle of fish'.

Another explanation eliminates the kettle altogether and sees in the word a corruption. Originally, the fish were not in a kettle at all, but where they truly belonged, in the water of a river. Unfortunately though, they had lost their freedom, as they had been caught in a 'kiddle'. This was a sort of net or a basket placed in the water to catch fish. The right to do so was strictly controlled and often granted as a privilege to certain selected people. Poachers who discovered such traps duly raided them. When, later on, the rightful owner of the traps found them empty, he lamented their loss by the exclamation, 'What a pretty kiddle of fish!' Indeed, it was a sad state of affairs.

Language has a life of its own and even word usages grow old and eventually die. And that is what happened to the kiddle. When later generations no longer knew what a kiddle was, they replaced it with the kettle and thus created the really senseless 'kettle of fish'.

Yet another school of thought, agreeing on the mispronunciation, links it with slightly different circumstances. It was the poachers themselves, it says, who put the kiddles into protected waters, to catch precious trout and salmon illegally. They did so very ingeniously lest their mischievous pursuit be discovered. When the traps were found nevertheless, possibly crowded with fish, the warden or master of the manor cried out, either in wrath or even in admiration of the substantial haul of fish caught by the felons, 'What a pretty kiddle of fish!'

The Honeymoon

Why does one speak of a honeymoon when describing the immediate period after a marriage?

There are several opinions as to the origin of the word 'honeymoon'. Its true meaning depends on whether it is taken very literally or merely as a beautiful picture.

The moon gave birth – on the loom of language – to the 'month'. In ancient days (and still today among Arabs and Jews) the duration of a month coincided with the period of one revolution of the moon. One had only to look at the moon to ascertain the approximate date. A new moon always signified the first day of the new month. Hence the 'honeymoon' was the first month of marriage, when all was sweet.

Other lunar observations turned away from the sunny side of the moon – and life – and noted their ever-changing character. The moon never appears the same. It is always different. According to this dismal way of thought the honeymoon refers not so much to the period of one month as to the eventual waning of love, after the first white heat of passion. Indeed, not a few misanthropes explained that the honey was bound to change – like the moon – but to water and gall . . .

But of all the lunar things that change,
The one that shows most fickle and strange,
And takes the most eccentric range,
Is the moon – so called – of honey.

Thomas Hood

However, the most likely origin of the phrase is an old Scandinavian and generally northern European custom of drinking honeyed wine or other kinds of diluted and fermented honey as an aphrodisiac during the first month of marriage.

Honeymoon Destination

Why is it kept secret?

Many a newlywed couple do not like to reveal, even to their closest friends, the place where they are going to spend their honeymoon. They really do not know why they keep it a secret and mostly, superstitiously, believe it to be for good luck. The practice has also been rationalised by the explanation that they want to be left alone and, by the added air of secrecy, make the occasion all the more romantic.

Actually, the custom originated in the days when the man used to capture his bride-to-be. There was every reason, therefore, for the couple not to make known their whereabouts, lest the girl's family catch up with them and create unpleasantness or, at the very worst, take her back. Once the honeymoon was over, the young couple hoped, tempers would have cooled and the new situation would be accepted.

Big Ben

What accounts for its name?

Big Ben is not, as is frequently and erroneously assumed, the clock or clock tower of the English Houses of Parliament at Westminster. It is the name of the huge bell that strikes the hour, of which it could well be said that it is the most famous of bells in the world.

Actually, when cast in 1858, it was christened St Stephen's. The choice of its ultimate name, so tradition has it, was the result of a hilarious incident during the parliamentary session, when the very question of its name was discussed and one of the members suggested – at the top of his voice – that it should be called after Sir Benjamin Hall, the then Chief Commissioner of Works. His proposal was met with roars of laughter. And not without reason. Everyone immediately understood what had prompted his choice. Sir Benjamin was conspicuous by his outstandingly tall and rotund figure, responsible for his generally being known by the nickname of 'Big Ben'. No other name was more fitting for the new bell, so conspicuous by its large dimensions. The idea was immediately supported by the press and captured the public's fancy, with the result that the original St Stephen's became Big Ben!

Weighing 13½ tons, the bell is struck by the hammer at the completion of each hour. In fact, this had been one of the conditions made when the bell was first ordered. It was demanded that on each such occasion the first blow should occur within a second of the actual moment of time. The new hour was to start exactly at the end of its chimes, which adopted the tune of the following song:

> So hour by hour
> Be Thou my guide;
> That by Thy power
> No step may slide.

The Full Monty

What accounts for this characterisation?

'The full Monty' means 'the whole lot', 'all of it'. A colloquialism, it was hardly known or used till 1997 when, all of a sudden, it received extraordinary popularity and acceptance. The reason was the release of a movie of that title that became an overnight success. There is no doubt that the specific circumstances in which the picture used the phrase were responsible for its sudden worldwide adoption. The title words applied to the film's very climax: a strip tease by six retrenched factory workers of a steelworks in the English industrial city of Sheffield. They performed it to raise direly needed funds. In their act they went 'all the way', with even their G-strings being taken off. So to speak, they showed 'the full Monty' – the lot. No wonder that the sexual context caught people's fancy and promoted a previously rarely used term, giving it the widest circulation. Indeed, the phrase proved a well-paying choice for the producers of the movie.

How and when the expression 'the full Monty' was first used as a description is still a subject of controversy. A diversity of origins has been suggested. Interestingly none of the hypotheses put forward have the slightest sexual association, which was the very thing that gave the words their sudden repute.

The name Monty prompted experts to claim that it recalled Field Marshall Viscount Montgomery of El Alamein, the renowned military figure of World War II and regarded as the greatest general since Wellington. He was popularly referred to as 'Monty' and famous for his extraordinary principles and eccentricities. For instance, even during the most decisive fighting and no matter what the circumstances or emergency, he would retire early every night and no one – not even a Churchill – was permitted to interrupt or cut short his rest. His equanimity, likewise, was said to have been unparalleled. Nothing could upset him. Whilst serving in the North African campaign far away from home and all its comforts, he made sure to be served a full English breakfast every morning. That is how, it was claimed, this breakfast came to be referred to as 'the full Monty', words that subsequently were applied more generally.

A totally different derivation links the expression not with a person called Monty, but with the township of Monte Carlo. Situated in the principality of Monaco and famous for its casino, it is also the location of what has been regarded by some to be, from the spectators' point of view, the most thrilling car race in the world: the Monte Carlo Rally.

The day prior to the actual race, the individual owners of the cars were permitted to drive around the circuit themselves, a practice called the 'half Monte'. The name was chosen to differentiate it from the 'full Monte', the race proper, in which the professional drivers competed. The English soon changed the 'Monte' into what was to them the much more familiar 'Monty', thereby adding 'the full Monty' to their vocabulary.

Yet another theory linked the full 'Monty' with 'Monte', not as part of the name of the Monacan town, but as the name of a Spanish gambling card game. The name had been chosen for it for a very valid reason. *Monte* is the Spanish for 'mountain' and the pack of cards distributed among the players resulted in each participant having a small heap or mountain in front of him on the table.

'The full Monty', indeed, became associated with many parts of the world. From the North African battlefield, via Monte Carlo and Spain, it also found its way to London. There Montague Burton, the city's one-time most fashionable firm of tailors, were claimed not only to be responsible for the saying 'Gone for a Burton', but were also credited with having created 'the full Monty'. In this case it was applied to the three-piece suits they made for the well-dressed – their 'full' outfit!

Have A Bee In The Bonnet

How did this insect get there?

The eccentric who is obsessed with or crazed by a particular idea or subject is said to 'have a bee in the bonnet'. It is buzzing around their heads.

Originally the saying spoke of having 'a head full of bees'. Robert Herrick has been credited with having introduced or at least suggested its modern version in 1646 in his poem 'The Mad Maid's Song'.

Preoccupying the mind, some special and often idiosyncratic thought excludes any different consideration or possibility. Like buzzing bees such thoughts prevent any clear thinking and give no room for alternate attitudes. Having likewise a one-track mind the droning insects deafen their victim to any other and more feasible view or course of action. Or, worse still, the monotonous humming acts like a hypnotic influence on the mind.

Imaginatively, although to some rather far-fetched, the shape of the human head reminded people of a bee hive. The bonnet tightly tied around it trapped all it carried within and prevented anything from the outside from entering.

To Screw

What is the background of this sexual vulgarism?

Copulation is an act which has been described in many ways, very bluntly so or euphemistically as 'making love'. To 'screw' is one of its vulgar versions.

The term combines a variety of sources, two of them going back to ancient Rome, and their subsequent contraction into one word.

First of all, this kind of screw can be traced back to the sow, *scrofa* in Latin. However, it does not relate to the animal itself, merely to its curly tail, somehow reminiscent of sexual relationship. Also, in Roman times, common people compared the vulva to a 'ditch', which was *scrobis* in Latin.

In Middle English, on the other hand, *scrue* meant to 'dig', and was responsible as well for the naming of the screw in joinery, which digs into the wood ever more deeply, just as the penis does during intercourse into the vagina. All three words – *scrofa, scrobis* and *scrue* – by a process of assimilation, were then joined to create in English 'screwing' as part of the dictionary of once strictly tabooed sexual terms.

666, The Number Of The Beast

What explains this cataclysmic figure?

Periods of political upheaval and cataclysm often have been regarded as the work of satanic powers. It was thought that no human could cause such disastrous conditions, leading the world to the very brink of destruction. For almost 2000 years, the evil-bringing force has been identified with the apocalyptic 'Beast'. To add to the mystery, it has been said that its number is '666'.

The origin is a passage in the Book of Revelation (13,18) that gives some indication as to the meaning of the puzzling numerical reference:

> *He that has understanding, let him count the number of the beast: for it is the number of a man; and his number is Six Hundred and Sixty Six.*

The number specifically refers to a person – not a supernatural demonic force such as Satan or the Antichrist, as is sometimes assumed.

The Book of Revelation, the last book in the New Testament, is largely a series of visions. They deal with the terror and disaster at the end of time when, in the last battle with the forces of evil, the divine power will triumph, to establish a New Heaven and a New Earth.

The book was written during a period of great worry, when people still vividly remembered the terror of the fall of Jerusalem and the suffering that Nero's persecution of the Jews had caused. Saint John no doubt wrote his Apocalypse (by which name the Book of Revelation is also known) to give courage and comfort to the young Christian community. When human power was at its wits' end, divine intervention would save the world by establishing a new era, cleansed from evil and ruled by the divine spirit.

To understand the relevant passage, it is necessary to realise that John was well acquainted with Jewish tradition and, no doubt, with a particular characteristic of the Hebrew language. As in Greek, the letters of the Hebrew alphabet double up as figures. Therefore, every name (or word) has a numerical value as well, easily ascertained by adding up the letter-figures of which the name consists.

Applying this method to a common name of today, the number for Smith (with the name spelt out in Hebrew, in which the 'i' is not a vowel but the consonant 'j', worth 10), would be 124, the total achieved by adding up the value of the S (60), the M (40), the I (10), the T (9) and the H (5).

S M I T H
60 + 40 + 10 + 9 + 5 = 124

Experience throughout history further clarifies the employment of this method of coding in political circumstances. Ruthless dictators have frequently outlawed any criticism of their regime. Whoever dared to criticise would be punished by imprisonment, exile or execution. However, freedom-loving people then, as now, would not be silenced. Unable to voice their opinions openly, they learnt to use secret symbols or cryptograms. The peculiar faculty of the Hebrew alphabet easily lent itself to such a code. People just replaced the name too dangerous to be mentioned with its numerical value! Contemporaries had no difficulty in identifying who the 'figure' represented.

Present-day readers can only guess which tyrant was meant by '666'. The Book of Revelation was written during a tumultuous period when many tyrants were trying to gain the upper hand. Identifying who was meant by '666' is a hazardous task that may easily lead to error or misinterpretation. It is no wonder that the number of the beast has been said to refer to, or to prophesy, many people throughout history. These have included Emperor Hadrian, the Pope, Napoleon, Martin Luther and even some twentieth-century heads of state!

However, the most plausible suggestion points to Nero Caesar. Spelled out in Hebrew characters (in which initially only consonants were used), the letters of his name add up to 666.

$$N \quad R \quad W \quad N \quad K \quad S \quad R$$
$$50 + 200 + 6 + 50 + 100 + 60 + 200 = 666$$

There is another, much less complex explanation. Traditionally, '7' was regarded as a sacred figure. It was 'the perfect number'. But when reduced by one it changed into its opposite. With one digit less for each number – 666 – it was thought to represent 'the man of sin' – the Antichrist.

Birds Flying In V-Formation

What accounts for it?

Nothing perhaps demonstrates more the wonders of nature than the flight of birds. Its most conspicuous feature is the V-formation in which flocks migrate at the change of season to milder climates or regions more favourable for them at that time of year. There is nothing haphazard in the way they fly and the V-shape they form. They are the result of what could be regarded as the perfect adaptation to air currents and the laws that govern flight.

To start with, it is believed that the migratory habit evolved through the birds' need for sufficient nourishment. Among other significant reasons, no doubt, was their procreative urge, so essential for the birds' survival.

The flight pattern facilitated progress and did so in a diversity of ways. It increased the range of vision of each bird and demanded less effort on its part. Birds flying in V-formation thus saved a great amount of energy. In fact, as has been calculated, a bird flying on its own may expand up to seventy per cent more of its body than twenty-five birds flying in the V-pattern. The reason is the so-called 'up-wash' (in lay terms 'updraft') created by the neighbouring bird. It reduced the need for essential effort and consequently made progress easier. Technically the phenomenon is known as the 'wingtip vortex'. Indeed, the birds' progress in V-formation is governed by the same aerodynamic principles that have been recognised and taken advantage of in the development of the modern aeroplane and are well known by every pilot.

The question that may well be asked is how the bird leading the V-formation does not get exhausted long before the rest as, apparently, it lacks the others' support. However, it has been established that this bird, too, provided that it does not fly too far ahead, still gets the benefit of the up-wash. Therefore it takes good care not to fly too much ahead, in which case it would instinctively fall back. As the same principle applies to all the birds, it may account for the fact that they will hardly ever stray out of the V-pattern.

Buttoning Clothes In Different Directions For Men And Women

What explains this fashion?

How to secure one's dress has always been a problem of human existence. Even Adam and Eve must have wondered at first how to fasten their fig leaves!

The bulk of early clothing merely used to hang down from the shoulders, but later the folds were secured by laces and braces. A further development was the button.

This was adopted as early as the thirteenth century, when it first became part of people's dress to serve either practical or decorative purposes, perhaps still hidden away or, on the contrary, conspicuously displayed. In men's clothing it came to play a significant role. It helped to secure a man's fly, introduced into the breeches in the days of King Charles I.

It might be thought that even though men and women wore different types of garments at least they would share the same method of fastening them. But, as everyone knows, this is not so. Men button their clothes, from pyjamas to everyday jackets, from left to right, while women do exactly the opposite.

The origin of this peculiar fashion and its variation in the case of women is not due, as cynics have sometimes suggested, to a woman's stubbornness and her traditional way of being contrary – but to the fact that most men and women are right-handed.

It was practical, but now forgotten and obsolete, considerations that led to this little-noticed but nevertheless marked distinction in buttoning a garment.

Men were always independent, at least in their manner of dressing, which they did mostly without any assistance. Women, however, and noble ladies especially, were dressed by their maids. Therefore, in the case of women, it was a convenient process to reverse the sides of the garment on which the buttons were secured because the maid, who faced her mistress during dressing operations, used her right hand and so found it easier to button the garment from right to left.

Women had to carry a baby, usually supporting it with their left arm. When it became necessary to breast-feed a child in public – and it quite often did among the masses – the left breast was used as being most convenient. To shelter the infant from wind and cold while it was feeding, they covered it with the right side of the dress or coat and thus designers of those days made women's clothes so that they would button up from right to left.

Another possible reason for the difference is that a medieval man always had to be prepared for a fight and therefore walked about armed. So that he could readily grasp and effectively use his sword, it was essential for him to have his right hand ready for combat and not stiff from cold. To ensure this, he would thrust it into his coat to keep it warm. To be able to do so, his coat had to open from left to right. In the early days men also wore a loose cloak which they grasped with their left hand, throwing the left side over the right so as to keep the right hand free. This, too, contributed to the introduction of overlapping from left to right for men's clothes.

All these motives no longer apply. Yet habits do not die easily, and men and women still carry on the now apparently senseless fashion of buttoning up their garments in opposite directions.

Spirit Level

What explains this term?

From the ancient Egyptians onwards people were aware of the importance of the horizontal level for a variety of tasks. To ascertain or obtain it, in their constructions not least, they devised specific tools or gadgets. Prominent among them was what was described as the 'A-frame'. This, in fact, sometimes with slight alterations, was retained in Europe and elsewhere till the 1850s.

An alternate method for determining a horizontal line or surface was the use of water. It was prompted by the realisation that a liquid's surface would always be perfectly horizontal. This led to the design of a tool, either in the form of a simple trough or of a more complicated combination of hoses and tubes, each of them containing water. In the end, however, neither proved ideal.

Ultimately, these various gadgets were replaced by what became known as the 'spirit level'. This consisted of a hermetically sealed glass tube filled with spirit, responsible for the name, which contained an air bubble. If the surface on which the 'level' was placed was perfectly horizontal, the bubble would be exactly in the centre.

Melchisedech Thevenot, the Frenchman renowned for his work in the fields of science and technology, has been credited as the inventor of the spirit level. In fact, the first reference to the novel instrument has been traced to his correspondence with Christian Huygens, the Dutch physicist, mathematician and astronomer, himself known to have discovered the planet Saturn's rings and largest satellite and to have applied the pendulum as a regulator of a clock for the first time. Significantly, their relevant exchange of letters took place between 1661, the very year of his invention, and 1662.

To start with, the novel gadget was used in telescopes, subsequently to serve as part of the surveyor's instrument. It was only as late as the mid-nineteenth century that it became the carpenter's and builder's indispensable tool, which it has remained ever since.

Wind Up A Company

Should this not instead speak of 'winding it down'?

When a company is liquidated and its assets distributed, it is said to be 'wound up'. Would it not be so much more appropriate to speak of it as being 'wound down'? After all, when a clock is wound up, it works. Wound down, it stops.

The term might have originated in early mining. When all the coal had been brought to the surface and the mine, having been exhausted, was about to be closed, the last bucket was hauled to the top. It was 'wound up' by means of a rope around a windlass – and that was the end of the mine.

On the other hand, the apparently paradoxical use of

the phrase may come from hand spinning and the practice of taking the 'loose ends' from a fleece of wool to wind them up into a tidy ball. Winding up a company frequently implies the unravelling of the tangled mess in which it has ended up. The similarity of situation equally could have been responsible for referring to the closure of a firm as being 'wound up' and not wound down, just like those loose ends of woollen thread.

In a similar vein, a speaker winds up a talk or a chairperson a discussion. Either of them does so by gathering in – summing up – the various strands of thought or points of view expressed and, with it, concludes the discussion or discourse.

Sweet Fanny Adams

Who was she?

The phrase 'sweet Fanny Adams', specifically used in naval and military circles, is English slang. It denotes 'nothing at all' and expresses worthlessness.

The saying has a gruesome origin: the cruel murder in 1867 of an eight-year-old girl at Alton, in the English county of Hampshire.

On 24 August of that year, just after one o'clock, little Fanny Adams was playing with her younger sister and a friend in a meadow near a church adjacent to the River Wey when a well-dressed young man approached. After treating the girls with some apples, he managed – for a gift of a halfpenny (half a cent) – to make Fanny, a pretty girl, accompany him into a field of hops close by. When at seven o'clock at night she had not returned home, a search party was sent out. It led to the discovery of one of the most horrendous murders. Fanny had not only been brutally killed but, sadistically, her body had also been dismembered. *The Standard,* reporting the ghastly case, commented that 'no tiger of the jungle, no jackal roaming famished about a city of the dead, could so fearfully mutilate its victim'.

It did not take long to identify and apprehend the murderer, Frederick Baker. There was a history of insanity in his family. At the inquest, which was held on the day after the murder, Baker's diary was produced. In it he had recorded on the day of the crime, 'Killed a young girl – it was fine and hot.'

The trial lasted a mere two days, and after two hours of deliberation the jury returned a verdict of 'guilty' and he was sentenced to death. Baker was executed on Christmas Eve 1867 at the Winchester County Gaol, watched by 5000 people.

Strange circumstances made the Royal Navy perpetuate the name of the unfortunate murder victim, 'sweet Fanny Adams'. By a mere coincidence, it was just around that time that the navy introduced tins of mutton as a regular ration. Sailors, finding the meat far from palatable, in a kind of sick humour suggested that the tins contained the remains of Fanny Adams – 'sweet nothing'. It was a description almost as obnoxious and nauseating as the crime itself.

Pin Money

Why are small sums of money so called?

Pins, although such simple objects, were at one time not cheap. In fact, they were so precious that women needing them for their clothes were given a special allowance from their husbands. This was appropriately called 'pin money'. Once pins became mass produced and obtainable at little cost, the gift was no longer necessary. Nevertheless, the term was retained but given the more general sense of an allowance a husband gives to his wife for the purchase of any minor personal items she fancies.

Pull The Wool Over Someone's Eyes

Why, of all things, wool?

Pulling the wool over someone's eyes obstructs their view and prevents them from seeing what is really going on. The 'wool' actually recalls the woollen wig once worn by English gentlemen and public figures. Some of these wigs were so large that their weight made them slip down over the wearers' eyes, temporarily blinding them. Jokers were said to have teased friends by pulling their wigs over their eyes. More seriously, robbers applied the same method to take their unsuspecting victims by surprise.

Except in the case of certain officers in parliament and in the courts within British-influenced countries, these wigs are no longer worn. Nevertheless, these earlier experiences survive in the phrase used to describe the hoodwinking of a person, 'to pull the wool over someone's eyes'.

Parting Shot

Whoever wants to fire a shot when parting?

All things come to an end, though wits have observed that a sausage has two. Mistakes, however, seem never to cease. Even a 'parting shot' is not what it sounds like to our ears. It is completely foreign indeed and was last heard ages ago.

The ancient Parthians, who lived southeast of the Caspian Sea, had a strange war practice. The moment their mounted archers had shot off their arrows they turned their horses around as if to flee to mislead the enemy. The deceptive manoeuvre became known as 'the Parthian shot'. When the Parthians had disappeared from the historical scene, those ignorant of their former existence and name mistook the 'Parthian shot' as a 'parting shot'.

Home And Hosed

Where was this odd expression born?

Horse riding and racing with their many features have greatly enriched the English vocabulary with a variety of terms. Mostly, their origin is self-explanatory. This, however, does not apply to the phrase 'home and hosed', now generally used for having safely and successfully completed a mission or a trip, or being sure to do so.

'Home and hosed' is an Australianism, derived from the custom of hosing down a horse after it has come 'home' in a race safe and sound. The English slang for it speaks of 'home and dry'. Also born on the racecourse, this originally referred to a victorious runner which had beaten its rivals by such length that it reached 'home' so far ahead of them that it had been hosed down and even dried before the other horses passed the winning post.

'Dives' For Disreputable Nightclubs

What created their name?

Taking a dive, one disappears from view. It is no wonder that the word was also applied, both in New York and London slang, to disreputable establishments, places of illegal gambling or drinking. To keep them away from public view and the eyes of the guardians of the law (particularly during American Prohibition, from 1920 to 1933), they were mostly located inconspicuously in basements or cellars of cheap tenement buildings. Those patronising them, as it were, had to 'dive' into them, like the divers who disappear under the surface of the water.

Even when the dives' illegality became redundant, their name was retained and 'dive' became the common appellation of shady nightclubs or bars of low repute.

Rigmarole

To what kind of 'role' does this term refer?

A rigmarole is a long and complicated procedure. Equally confusing are the claims made as to its origin and even the date of its first appearance which, in different traditions, varies by almost one hundred years.

Most likely, the correct and initial term was not 'rigmarole' but (the) 'Ragman's Roll'. Exceeding twelve metres in length, this medieval document combined numerous oaths of allegiance made by Scottish barons and other noblemen to King Edward I of England during his progress through Scotland in 1296. Reading them out must have become a most monotonous practice which, no doubt, led to the name of the roll being associated with tedium. In addition, with so many seals attached to it, it must have presented a ragged sight. Jointly, these were sufficient reasons to give the Ragman's Roll its name. With its original meaning and purpose forgotten, 'Ragman's Roll' was streamlined (or corrupted) into 'rigmarole'.

Another theory traces the term to much less serious circumstances, to those of a medieval game of French origin. The various people taking part in it drew out scrolls of parchment containing descriptive verses and clues. The players then had to guess their meaning. As the chief character represented in the game was *Ragemon le Bon,* 'Ragman the Good', the entire set of small scrolls was called after him, to become the Ragman's Roll. Playing the game must have been quite confusing – truly a 'rigmarole'.

With its true origin uncertain, the name of the scroll in time acquired its present-day meaning. As confusing as ever, rigmarole metaphorically preserves the original 'scroll', no matter what the items were that rendered it so ponderous, long-winded and incoherent.

Brass Razoo

Which currency possesses a brass razoo?

'Not to have a brass razoo' is an Australianism from the 1920s for having no money at all. The expression is entirely fictitious, as no coin of that name ever existed. Although 'brass' is well-known slang for 'money', there are only hypotheses as to the meaning and origin of the word 'razoo' (also spelt 'rahzoo'). It is interesting to note, though, that perhaps very appropriately the expression is always used in a negative way. Among the often far-fetched etymologies of the word is the claim that it stems from New Zealand, from the Maori word *raho*. However, no real explanation can be traced, just as there never was a brass razoo.

Anchorman

Why is the anchorman so called?

In its modern usage 'anchorman' (or 'anchorwoman') refers to a person with the important central position on radio or television of linking up the diverse sources for a specific broadcast or telecast, particularly appertaining to news items. (Outside the USA he or she is often referred to as a 'presenter'.) By combining, comparing and checking all the data obtained – from reporters, eyewitnesses and camera crews – his is the fullest and most reliable presentation. It is anchored on objective conclusions conscientiously arrived at from all the facts ascertained, and is the very reason for the anchorperson's designation.

Obviously, the name goes back to the use of a ship's anchor. The anchor keeps the vessel in its place and prevents it from drifting and being tossed about by wind, tide and currents.

Previous applications of the anchor, no doubt, were responsible for its final adoption by the media. Not least, the anchorman played an important role early on in sport. In the tug-of-war he was the member placed at the very end of the opposing teams, possibly the heaviest person, chosen for his strength. It was his task to anchor down the rope lest the other side succeeded in pulling his own team across the line. To make sure that this would not happen, he frequently passed the rope over one shoulder and gripped it under one arm. Equally vital was the role of the anchorman in athletics, in which the last runner in a relay race was so called.

Thus, the anchorman, coming from the sea as it were, via the sporting field, has survived in his new, important function on the air(waves).

Alarm Clock

What led to the invention of the alarm clock?

Religion has the distinction of having made a great variety of contributions to civilisation. Few would realise, however, that most likely these include even the alarm clock. It was invented in a monastery – to remind the monks of the time of worship.

The earliest alarm clock might go back to the days of King Alfred the Great (849–899). It then took the form of a wax candle which had tiny bells inserted at fixed intervals. As the candle burnt down, the bells were released from their wax prison to fall into a metal container, doing so with a resounding clang. This could not fail but wake up the monastery's sexton, whose task it was, in turn, to rouse the other residents from their sleep.

The next step in the development of the alarm clock was the adaptation of the Roman *clepsydra*, a water clock. Adopted from ancient Egypt, it was a gadget that measured time using water passing through a small orifice into a basin. Progressively filling up during the night, it ran over at an appointed time in the morning, onto the face of the sleeping person, above which it had been placed. Thus, it simultaneously served two purposes: waking the sleepers and washing their faces!

One of the first mechanical alarm clocks is said to have been constructed by Levi Hutchins of Concord, New Hampshire, USA, in 1787. However, its usefulness was greatly restricted, as its bell rang merely at a pre-set fixed time that could not be changed.

The Roman IV On The Clock Face

What accounts for the diversity of presentation of this figure?

More than 2500 years ago Romans invented a system of numerals. Adopted throughout Europe, it was followed till the sixteenth century. It derived from the counting of the fingers on the human hands. Therefore based on the number ten, it was known as the 'decimal system', from the Latin *decem* for '10', just as each figure came to be called a digit, from the Latin *digitus* for 'finger'. Thus, reproduced in stylised form, using vertical lines, I stood for '1', two lines for '2' and IIII for '4', whilst V for '5' depicted in stylised form the spread-out hand or, more correctly, the open hand with the fingers, except the thumb, held together. Later sophistication around the Augustan age introduced the combination of figures, for instance the representing of '4' by IV, standing for one less than V, and VIII (for '8') showing three fingers joined to the extended hand.

This explains the puzzling depiction of the figure '4' on clocks not by the developed combination of IV but by four parallel vertical lines or four 'Is'. It not only balanced the VIII on the opposite side of the clock face but also retained the four strokes of the original way the Romans presented this figure. Aesthetic reasons, as well as people's innate conservatism, thus were responsible for the mystifying use of the four strokes.

There also exists an apocryphal account of how the peculiar IIII found its place on the clock dial. Claiming it did so by royal decree, it goes back to King Charles V of France, renowned for his wisdom and encyclopaedic knowledge, which made people nickname him 'Charles the Wise'. He himself was not only very much conscious of his own intelligence and wisdom but conceitedly often pretended to know things of which he was totally ignorant as well.

One day around 1370 he ordered a clock from Henri de Vick who, at the time, was one of the outstanding clockmakers of France. When the clock was ready, he presented it to his royal master. Carefully examining it, the latter looked for something in or on it that he could criticise. To his disappointment, he could find no fault. And yet, if you want to beat a dog, you find a stick, and so did Charles the Wise. He pointed out to the expert craftsman that he had made a mistake in the numbers on the dial: the Roman '4' – the sophisticated IV – should have been four Is. De Vick denied having erred and audaciously accused the king of being mistaken. Charles would have none of it. 'I'm never wrong!' he asserted, demanding Vick to take back his clock and to return it only after having corrected the false '4'. All de Vick could do was to replace the modernised 'handsome' IV with the antiquated (Roman standard) four strokes that still appear on some modern specimens.

Pay On The Nail

Why on the nail?

Anyone who discharges a debt at once 'pays on the nail'. This peculiar term goes back to medieval times, when merchants, on completing a deal, paid for the goods by placing the money on top of a squat, flat-topped pillar.

This was known as a 'nail', most likely because of its superficial, though vastly magnified resemblance to one. Four such 'nails' from the eighteenth century are still in existence in England. Made of bronze, they stand outside the Bristol Corn Exchange.

Pay Through The Nose

How can anyone pay through the nose?

The payment of debts has produced a colourful variety of descriptions. People 'cough up' the money. They 'fork' it out, and they are 'bled dry' for it. No doubt, the most puzzling idiom speaks of 'paying through the nose'. The choice of words is not due to a desire to stress the painful experience of having to settle exorbitant debts, comparing it in a far-fetched simile with the forcing of hard cash through the narrow openings of the nostrils, which certainly would be agonising. The phrase is based on specific historic circumstances and English slang.

First of all, it is a relic of the gruesome practice of some governments and countries of enforcing the payment of taxes and other levies. Citizens or subjects defaulting had their noses slit or even cut off. The threatened punishment explains why, for instance, a ninth-century tax imposed by the Danes on the Irish became known as the 'nose tax', and as the fear of such mutilating penalty made people meet the demands of the government, however unfair and unjust, it could truly be said of them that they paid 'through the nose'.

In seventeenth-century England, the slang for money was *rhino*, the Greek for 'nose'. It was not an arbitrary choice of word. Most likely, it was the result of a very expensive and popular sex stimulant. As still today among some primitive societies, many people at that time imagined that powdered *rhino*ceros horn (from the animal's 'nose') was a potent aphrodisiac. Like modern unscrupulous drug dealers, those trading in it took advantage of the demand, selling the powdered 'nose' at outrageous prices. This could well have accounted for people's saying that they were paying 'through the nose' for anything that was overpriced.

Horseradish

How did the equine become part of this pungent condiment?

The pungent condiment known as horseradish, served to add special flavour to some foods, not least a favourite when eaten with beef, has nothing to do with horses. The radish is not so called, as might easily be surmised, because it is eaten by horses. Like not a few other words, it could be the result of mishearing. In reality, it is 'harsh radish', so named because of its piquant, stinging taste. Even its fumes on their own make one's eyes water and nose run when the radish is being grated.

As it were, to explain (and save) the equine presence in the description of the horseradish, some authorities have suggested that it was not due to a linguistic error. Its name recalled the peculiar shape of the thick, contorted, off-white root of the plant from which the condiment was obtained. To the imaginative mind its shape somehow resembled a horse's hoof.

Yet another explanation points out that the mention of the horse is not merely part of this specific condiment, but has been added to a variety of other names, of plants, animals and human expression, which all share some rough and coarse feature. Typical examples are the horse chestnut, horse mint, the horse fly, the horse leech and not least, the 'horse laugh'.

Strikes

Who started strikes?

All strikes began at sea. To 'strike' is the nautical term for the dipping of a flag or the lowering of sails. And that is exactly what sailors did when, for one reason or another, they were determined to make their ship inoperative. They struck the sails. The sea-born word then conquered the land and a 'strike' came to denote all stoppage by industrial action.

All Over But [Bar] The Shouting

Why should people carry on voicing their opinion once something has been concluded?

To speak of something as being 'all over but [bar] the shouting' infers that an action, an election or a contest has been successfully completed and only the voice of acclamation or protest or the shouting of an excited crowd accompanying the event has not yet abated.

Several explanations have been given as to the first usage of the phrase. It has been linked with early polls, when members of a small community, of which possibly many were still illiterate, indicated their view or choice of candidate vociferously, in the literal sense of the word. As in each case the outcome of the poll was known by word of mouth, it could well be said that even before it had been completed and the result had been made public, it was 'all over but the shouting'.

An alternative hypothesis traces the phrase to Charles James Apperley. He used it in 1842 in his capacity as a sports writer. Indeed, some linked it with boxing matches when, at their conclusion and after the announcement of the winner, all that was heard were shouts of approval or of protest. Still in the field of sports, Adam Lindsay

Gordon in his *How We Beat the Favourite* wrote, 'the race is all over, bar shouting'. There has also been an opinion that the saying specifically referred to the shouts of protest at the referee's decision or, on the other hand, in its support.

Possibly the phrase had a much more general application. Even after the decisive conclusion of a sporting fixture or an election, the crowd continue the yelling and screaming with which they have accompanied the contest, either in support and encouragement of the party they backed or in their disapproval of (or attempt to confuse) the opposing side, even though obviously the decision has been made and the shouting will not change the result.

However, the observation might simply have been applied to a task completed, the back of a job broken, with nothing left but 'the shouting'.

Throwing Coins Into A Well

What brought about this superstition?

Throwing coins into a well for good luck is a custom observed all over the world. Coins tossed into the Trevi Fountain in Rome by visitors are thought to ensure their return to the Eternal City. In Shiraz, Iran, Persians use this means to pay honour to Saadi, their world-renowned national poet. A pool for that purpose is part of his magnificent mausoleum.

However lightly such offerings are treated, their origins can be traced to the distant past when people were convinced that a spirit dwelt at the bottom of each fountain. Wells were their sacred abode, and unless one paid them tribute willingly, they would raise it by sending misfortune.

In remote days, to quench the divine thirst of the spirits, people gave what was most precious to them:

their own flesh and blood. Human offerings were the price paid to obtain good luck. Young Mayan girls were drowned in the Well of Sacrifice in Chichen Itza, Mexico. They did not have to be forced to give their lives for their people's good fortune. They regarded the sacrifice as a privilege. They believed that the indwelling spirit or rain god would acknowledge their self-sacrifice and would marry them, and they would live happily ever after in his palace at the bottom of the well.

Eventually, 'civilisation' replaced the deadly sacrifice with money tokens. The throwing of coins into a fountain continues to 'pay' homage to and buy the protection of the spirit 'possessing' it.

The [Last] Straw That Breaks The Camel's Back

What is the background of this well-known metaphor?

The [last] straw that breaks the camel's back (or simply 'the last straw') is something going beyond one's endurance. People can take so much but not more. Even the most resilient of individuals reaches a point of no return, when the slightest incident or untoward remark will produce a breakdown or violent reaction, in the extreme turning a calamity into a catastrophe.

The saying was popularised by Charles Dickens, who used it, in a slightly extended form, in *Dombey and Son,* which he wrote in 1847 to 1848. He did so to illustrate how a piece of 'underground information' crushed the sinking spirits of the central figure in the novel. Dickens himself is said to have adapted it from a proverb he found in an anthology of sayings that spoke of 'the last feather that breaks the horse's back'.

Actually, the phrase can be traced to the seventeenth century and a discussion that then took place on how everybody reached a point of no return. The example chosen was the camel and the amount of weight this ship of the desert could carry. The reason for selecting this animal was its renowned strength and stamina. These made it specially suited to 'carrying' the message of how the endurance of even the most powerful had its limits. In the simile the load of the camel was increased very slowly, adding a single straw at a time. Each straw seemed so little and so insignificant that it really appeared of no consequence, the people imagined. Ultimately, however, the stage was reached when just one more straw (the 'last' one) broke the animal's back.

Turn Down A Proposal

What is it that is 'turned down' when refusing an offer of marriage?

To 'turn down' a suitor is not merely an expressive phrase, but is based on a custom once practised in colonial America. A young man, not bold enough to 'pop the question', proposed to a young lady silently and with the additional aid of magic! He placed a mirror in front of the girl. But prior to doing so, he looked into it, convinced that magically it would retain his reflection, which the girl would see. If she fancied him when gazing into the glass, she would smile. It was her acceptance of his unspoken proposal. If, however, she rejected him, all she would do was to turn the mirror face downward. Without the exchange of a single word, he knew that he had been 'turned down'.

The Heads On A Ship

Why was the term 'the heads' chosen for the lavatory on board ship?

Naval terminology refers to the lavatory as 'the heads'. The choice of name goes back to the old sailing days, when the men used the forward part of the ship as their latrine. Its description was not a mere metaphor for the front of the boat, but a survival from the time when she carried on her prow the figure*head* of a goddess as a divine protection against the vagaries of the sea.

The use of 'heads', always in the plural, is not accidental and has its special meaning as well. It was to remind seamen that the forward part of the ship had two sides: the weathered and the sheltered (lee) side. It was for their own good to use the one not facing the wind, for reasons that should be obvious, as anyone who has ever tried to empty his bladder into the wind will confirm.

The Mantelpiece

Why is the shelf above an open fire so called?

The mantelpiece preserves in its name its original function. Initially a mere wooden ledge with pegs, it was fixed above the fireplace to serve for the drying of wet clothes. Those coming in out of the rain would hang up on the peg their soaking mantles, or cloaks, which explains not only how the mantelpiece came into existence but also why it was so called.

Eavesdrop

Is it not a strange expression for trying to overhear someone else's conversations?

Eaves used to project over the edge of a roof. With guttering still unknown, they made sure that rainwater did not run down and damage the walls, but dripped onto the ground at a safe distance.

Saxon law stipulated that anyone building a house could not do so to the very boundary of the land he owned. He had to leave sufficient room for the eaves. This space became known as *yfes drype.*

People taking shelter, or for no special reason at all, standing under the 'eavesdrip' could easily overhear a conversation taking place inside a house. Architectural style has changed. The introduction of guttering has made the eavesdrip redundant. But people continue to eavesdrop, these days doing so mostly intentionally.

Bogus

What is the source of this intriguing term?

There are so many different versions of the origin of the word 'bogus' that some of them are sure to be bogus themselves.

On the one hand, 'bogus' has been claimed to have been derived from the French *bagasse* for 'rubbish', as it is worth nothing. On the other hand, the gypsy language has been cited as its source, in which a counterfeit coin is known as *boghus.*

All derivations agree, however, that 'bogus' refers to something spurious, used in this sense first in the United States.

Going back to 1827 is the claim that (in May of that year) a gang of forgers was arrested near the city of Painesville, Ohio, who produced such perfect counterfeit coins that even banks and experienced merchants accepted them as real, doing so without the slightest suspicion of their being fakes. They were so good that only a bogey could have made them – resulting in their being ultimately referred to as 'bogus'.

A Boston newspaper of 1857 – thirty years later – linked 'bogus' with the name of a Mr Borghese, a renowned con-man whose dud cheques on non-existing banks deceived many people and institutions. It did not take long to shorten his name to Bogus and, accordingly, to term his forged cheques as 'Bogus money'.

More realistically, it has also been pointed out that the very implement used to turn out the spurious money was called the 'bogus press' and inevitably thus its product became known as 'bogus'. The fact that this description sounded very similar to the name of the bogey presented the counterfeit as something mischievous, unpleasant and objectionable, just as this unwelcome devilish spirit in other dialects is also known as 'bugbear', 'bogie' and 'boogie'.

The first mention of the term 'counterfeit' itself has been traced back to 1290. Etymologically it is derived from the French *countrefaire,* joining *countre* for 'opposite' with the Latin *facere* for 'to make'.

Bidet

How did this French horse get into people's bathrooms?

To start with, a bidet could be found exclusively in France. A low type of basin, it was part of bathrooms, both in private homes and in lodging establishments. It was first introduced in the seventeenth century to serve people's personal hygiene, the washing of their private parts, their anus and genitals. The bidet made it unnecessary to run a full bath and thus saved time and water. The name is borrowed from the French word for a small horse, itself derived from the Old French *bider,* for 'to trot'. The rider, having mounted the animal, had to take good care to pull up his legs, lest they be dragged along the ground. His stance was very much like that of a man or woman squatting on a bidet to perform their intimate ablutions.

Lemon Sole

Why is this fish so called?

The lemon sole is a species of plaice or flounder. The 'lemon' part has been attached to the fish by error. A flat fish, in Old French it was compared with, and actually described as, a 'flat board' (*limande*) which, misheard, was changed into 'lemon'. Others have discovered in the lemon half of the fish the corrupted Latin root *limus,* for 'mud', and assert that the fish was so called because its usual habitat was deep down in the muddy waters.

Cinderella's Glass Slipper

How was she able to dance in glass slippers?

Cinderella's glass slipper has become so much a part of the fairy tale that to change it in any way would spoil its charm. After all, it was by means of the glass slipper dropped by Cinderella on leaving the ball that the prince who had fallen in love with her was able to find her again.

However, with a little thought, it becomes apparent that glass slippers fit neither into the story nor on Cinderella's feet! No one would wear them on a cold winter's night. Moreover, to dance in them would prove very difficult.

In fact, the earliest French version of the tale does not speak of glass slippers but slippers made of fur, much more in character with the story, the season and the occasion. Comfortable to dance in, fur slippers would keep Cinderella's feet warm in the coldest of nights. They would have been of white ermine, fit for a princess!

The French for 'fur' is *vair* and for 'glass', *verre.* Differently spelt, the two words are almost identical in sound. It was quite easy to mistake one for the other. (It must be remembered that, at the time, stories were mostly not read from a book, but related by word of mouth.) Not magic, therefore, but an error changed the fur into glass!

For once the perpetrator of the mistake can be identified. It was the French poet and critic (?) Charles Perrault who in 1697 published the story in a collection of popular fairy tales. He selected it from several versions of 'Cinderella' then in circulation and at his disposal. Each one spoke of a fur slipper which he – erroneously – turned into glass. As all later editions and translations of the fairy tale were based on his text, they copied his mistake, which has never been corrected.

The Foxglove

Is it because foxes favour this flower that it is so called?

Intriguing, indeed, is the name of the foxglove. Its shape does not bear the slightest resemblance to a fox, nor do foxes feed on the flower. Its description is a typical case of confusion of sound.

Botanically known as *digitalis purpurea,* the plant has helped millions of people suffering from heart disease. Appropriately, the drug obtained from it is called after the flower: *digitalis.*

Early on, it was believed that the plant had received its mysterious pharmaceutical power from supernatural beings, the 'little folks'. It was their flower and because of their proprietary rights it was called the (little) 'folks glove'. Obviously the 'glove' part of the name was suggested by the shape of the flower's bell-like blossoms.

Misheard, the folks-glove changed into the foxglove. This was in keeping with a society that had lost its belief in the existence of those little folk of the occult world.

Cough Drops

Who created them?

As applies to not a few contributions to improve the quality of life, the identity of the individual responsible for the medication that was to soothe sore throats and stop, or at least ease, an unpleasant cough is not known. Hard up, he was ready to sell his formula to any bidder. He did so (in 1847) for the paltry sum of $5 to William and Andrew Smith of Poughkeepsie, New York, USA. They were two brothers who themselves had no pharmaceutical interests, but manufactured sweets. Cleverly they combined both fields. Using the unknown inventor's product in combination with one of their sweets, they presented the world with the first cough drops. On early packaging the names beneath their likenesses appeared as 'Trade' and 'Mark' respectively and these were the nicknames by which they were affectionately known to generations of customers. These have remained the tasty remedy, popular everywhere and provided in a great variety of forms.

Pool Of Water On The Road That Is Not There

What causes this strange illusion?

Nearly everyone living in a hot and dry climate at one time or another, whilst driving along a sealed road, has experienced the strange phenomenon of seeing a shimmering pool of water further along which, on approaching, either recedes or disappears altogether. Theirs is an optical illusion caused by a combination of layers of air of different density and temperature with certain refractions and reflections of light. It belongs to the class of mirages which, under identical atmospheric conditions, occur in the desert and even at sea.

The French scientist Gaspard Monge, when accompanying Napoleon's army to Egypt, was among the first to observe and scientifically describe this odd apparition.

Most famous of all mirages is that observed in Sicily across the Strait of Messina. Renowned is its spectre of the city, of fancy castles, palaces and spired cathedrals floating in the air. Known as a Fata Morgana, its designation is based on the myth associated with the fairy (*Fata*) Morgana, a half-sister of King Arthur in the Arthurian legend. She was believed by the Normans to live in Calabria, near the Strait of Messina. An enchantress, she possessed magical powers and this particular illusion was attributed to her.

Put On The Carpet

Why, when speaking of someone being reprimanded, is it said that they are put 'on the carpet'?

The offices of senior British civil servants were carpeted. A conspicuous feature, it became their status symbol. For a minor official to be summoned to such a 'sanctum' for a reprimand literally put him 'on the carpet'.

The Bungalow

From where does this single-storey dwelling get its name?

Bungalow is a Hindustani word. Meaning 'from Bengal', it recalls the region in the Indian sub-continent where this type of building is common.

During the British rule, Europeans living in the interior of India used to reside in such one-storey houses which generally were surrounded by a veranda. On their return to England they introduced the bungalow there, and by retaining its indigenous name acknowledged its original site.

An apocryphal story gives another reason as to why the bungalow was so called. A builder had been commissioned to construct a two-storey house, to be ready at a specified time. Unforeseen circumstances delayed its completion, however, with the result that on the stipulated date only one storey was finished. The client remonstrated with the builder, asking him what he proposed to do. Nonplussed, the latter suggested to *bung a low* roof on to the ground floor which was already finished. That is how, according to this tale, the word 'bungalow' came into existence.

Take Pot Luck

What is the origin of this odd saying?

Nowadays housewives may have their precooked foods stored in the freezer for emergencies. Not so very long ago they were equally ready to serve instant meals – and hot at that! They kept a stew pot on the boil all the time. Thus a warming meal was available constantly to any friend dropping in.

Of course, guests were given no choice. They had to eat whatever was cooking. They had to take 'pot luck'.

Guests today, having nothing specially prepared for them and their taste, have to accept whatever may come out of the freezer.

Chamber Pots

What fascinating facts are known about these useful objects?

The story of chamber pots is indeed intriguing. Going back at least two millennia before the water closet was invented, they were already known in ancient times and made use of by the Egyptians and the Greeks.

Because of their oblong shape then, which reminded them of skiffs, those small elongated boats, the Greeks called them – in their tongue – *skaphe,* their description of that type of seagoing vessel. In fact, chamber pots of that outline were retained in France well into the nineteenth century, whilst elsewhere in Europe, even in medieval days, they were made in circular shape.

For some considerable time 'chamber-potting' was an accepted part of daily life. Without the need of separate closets or outside conveniences, it gave people the opportunity to answer the call of nature in the most diverse surroundings. In some parts of Europe, as late as the seventeenth and eighteenth centuries, such open and undisguised use of the chamber pot was accepted as something inevitable, whilst elsewhere it was disapproved as a most objectionable habit. Anthelme Brillat-Savarin (1755–1826), the famous French gastronomer, recalled how it had been common knowledge that English dining rooms provided gentlemen with the opportunity to relieve themselves without having to leave the room. Equally, travellers in their coaches, judges on the bench and captains on board ship, after having enjoyed plenty of drink, were not loath to make use 'on the spot' of a chamber pot, this 'curious facility', as Brillat-Savarin called it.

In France those potties were known for some time as a *bourdalou,* a fascinating choice of description, as it recalled the name of the Rev Bourdalou and certainly presents the only case in history in which a clergyman was honoured by a chamber pot being called after him!

Bourdalou was a most popular preacher. He attracted such large congregations that, to make sure of a seat in the pews, worshippers had to come to church long before the commencement of the service. Bourdalou was also distinguished by the length of his sermons. This made it doubly difficult, not least for the ladies, to suppress the urge to empty the bladder. To solve the awkward problem, women wisely carried to church, hidden in their large muffs, their individual 'potties'. Of slender shape, they could slip them inconspicuously under their voluminous skirts. One still has to wonder, however, how they could muffle the sound they made when relieving themselves, so as not to drown out the voice of the eloquent preacher or interfere with other congregants' wish to listen to his message.

Apart from fulfilling a very practical purpose, chamber pots also became treasured objects of art. Some of them, made of precious Meissen china, were beautifully decorated. They were ornamented with flowers and plants, often in relief, which added to the aesthetic value of this otherwise so utilitarian object. Potties equally served to express people's opinions and national feeling. They might carry the portrait or initials of admired leaders and public figures, though there was a proviso that these had to be on the outside of the potty. On the other hand, they provided the opportunity of showing contempt for the enemy and, during the Napoleonic campaigns for instance, the hated conqueror's image occupied the very bottom of the receptacle to experience a literal stream of abuse! As it were, its location there was meant to face the posterior of the person, with its unmistakable message. Merely humorous was yet another type of 'decoration', such as an eye with the inscription, 'Oh me, what do I see?' The picture of a frog at the bottom(!) was also expressive.

With such a wealth of features, it is no wonder that entire museums are devoted to exhibiting examples of the great variety of roles this original merely utilitarian vessel came to play.

The Turkish Puzzle Ring

What is the puzzle behind this ring?

The Turkish puzzle ring has been adopted and admired in many countries. This ring is not one solid band, but is made from various parts, combining at least three bands which are cleverly interlocked. Any attempt to put them back together once they are separated presents an exacting and formidable puzzle. A puzzle ring may therefore be a very thoughtful gift, providing a friend with long hours of entertainment, or a group with a lively contest as to who can first achieve the feat of reassembling it.

Traditionally, however, the ring was first introduced for a totally different and not so pleasant reason. It was a gift from a mistrustful husband to his wife! If he was about to go to war or take an extended trip, and was afraid that during his absence she might grow bored and be tempted to yield to other men's advances, he had to find some means to keep her busy. What could better achieve this aim than to give her, on his departure, a disassembled puzzle ring? 'Puzzling out' how its parts fitted together would fully occupy her, theoretically leaving her no time for any other activity. On his safe return, the husband would expect to find the ring in one piece!

An alternate explanation is also based on this idea of a husband's determination to guard his wife's chastity during any absence on his part. However, according to this theory it was not by presenting her with the various parts of the ring, but with the complete item. He placed it on her hand and she was to keep it there till his return. If she removed it to hide her married status, the ingeniously interlocked pieces would come apart and she would have great difficulty rejoining them, thus revealing her unfaithfulness. Aware of this threatened 'give-away', she would hopefully refrain from committing adultery and the puzzle ring would have achieved its purpose as a safeguard against infidelity.

Red Poppies For Sacrifice And Remembrance

Why was this flower selected for this purpose?

The custom of wearing a red poppy in one's buttonhole on Remembrance Day (or Veterans Day in the US) has its moving story and significant background. Symbolically, it remembers and pays tribute to the many who made the supreme sacrifice, shedding their blood and giving their lives for their country during the two World Wars, and other battles fought since.

A variety of explanations has been suggested as to how this flower became the emblem of sacrifice and remembrance. Years earlier, the British historian Lord Macaulay (1800–1859) had drawn attention to the profusion of poppies that grew on many battlefields of the past. It made the flower a most suitable symbol of the sacrifice brought in the clash of arms for the survival of one's country.

Earl Haig who, during World War I, had been the Commander-in-Chief of the British Expeditionary Forces in France and Flanders, subsequently became the Commander-in-Chief of the Armed Forces in Great Britain. In 1921, whilst engaged in establishing the British Legion to serve the needs of all ex-servicemen and women, he was approached by a delegation of French and Belgian war widows, who presented him with artificial poppies they had made. By selling them to the public, the widows suggested, funds could be provided for the support of disabled ex-servicemen and women and destitute war widows and orphans.

Earl Haig immediately welcomed the idea. And thus, on Armistice Day of that same year, the first poppies were sold in the streets of London. Bought by the thousands, to wear them became an annual institution, with the result that the day became alternately known as Poppy Day.

The selection of the poppy by those French women was well founded. The flower grew abundantly in the fields of Flanders, the very site where the decisive battles of the First World War were fought and so many soldiers are buried. Its location and its colour truly symbolised the blood-soaked earth.

To produce the flowers also provided work for the thousands of incapacitated veterans, particularly at a time when they could find no other employment.

Other links with the past, as it were, preselected the poppy for its modern function. Some authorities have associated it with the tradition of medieval artists of using the flower in their paintings to recall the blood which, according to Christian belief, Jesus is said to have shed for the salvation of mankind.

Dating back as far as the thirteenth century, an Eastern legend relates the custom to the savage campaigns of Genghis Khan, the barbarian founder of the Mongol empire. He never took prisoners. Literally, the soil became drenched with the blood of the slain. Originally, poppies growing on those many battlefields used to be white. As a result of the carnage, they turned red, a colour that has distinguished them ever since.

Potholes

Why are these traffic hazards so called?

Potholes in roads, of every size and depth, add to traffic hazards. Nowadays, they are mostly caused by the number and size of heavy vehicles, by bad weather or by lack of maintenance. Their mystifying name, however, possibly points to an origin of a totally different kind.

It has been said that potters, in need of clay for their wares, did not go to faraway places to obtain it. They just dug it up from a road nearby, 'producing' the original potter's hole which, if not in size, in name at least contracted into the modern 'pothole'.

Scrimshaw (Or Schrimshaw)

How did this special art develop on the high seas?

An art all of its own, going back to the time of sailing ships, is that of scrimshaw, also spelt 'schrimshaw'. Its often intricate and ingenious design makes it highly treasured, just as its story is unique.

Scrimshaw is a product of the sea, in more senses than one. It is carved (or scratched) on the tusks, teeth, and (wrongly-named) 'bones' of whales, those huge mammals of the ocean. Hunted and killed by their hundreds, the sale of the animals' oil (from their blubber) and so-called bones promised great wealth. Human greed thus reduced the whales in so great a number that they were threatened with extinction, leading international action to be taken for their conservation. In turn, this near-extinction further enhanced the value of the sailors' scrimshaw.

The sailors who manned the whaling ships were sturdy men. They crossed the seas on voyages that frequently took years. Far from being a romantic pursuit, the whalers' chasing and harpooning of their prey was a squalid and exhausting undertaking. Worse still was the fact that the whaling crews, spending so long a time at sea, were totally cut off from the world. Their prolonged isolation was hard to bear. And it was to overcome their boredom and loneliness that those whaler-sailors started to carve the whale 'bones', and developed their unique art. Each of the objects they produced had its individual character, distinguished either by the men's decorative ingenuity or the article's usefulness, and hence they were highly prized.

The term 'scrimshaw' for the art was first recorded in the 1840s. Most likely of Dutch origin, it is a combination of *schrimpen,* for 'to wrinkle' and *schrong,* for 'to carve'. (The sailor who did the carving was known as a 'scrimsbonger'.) Other, less likely derivations for the word range from English military slang for a 'shirker' and the French *escrime* for 'fencing' (used here particularly for the fencer's making of flourishes with his sword) to the claim that it perpetuates the name of one of the most outstanding sailor craftsmen of the art, supposed to have been an admiral.

Referring to the tools of the art, Herman Melville in his *Moby Dick* (1851) tells how some of the whaling ship's crew had 'little boxes of dentistical looking implements specially intended for the skrimshandering business. But in general they toil with their jack knives alone.'

Snags

Why do Australians call sausages 'snags'?

'Snags' is typical Australian slang. Though widely used, its origin has mystified many. A sophisticated but cynical explanation finds in this Australian sausage a combination that sounds not very tasteful. It is said by some to be an acronym: the abbreviation of *S*omething *N*auseating *A*nd *G*ruesomely *S*uggestive. Taking the initials of each of these words and stringing them together has resulted in SNAGS.

Others see in them the product of mispronunciation. Because of their popularity among Australian people, they became their snacks. In the course of time these 'snacks' deteriorated linguistically into snags.

A third explanation derives from the term used for anything short and not very shapely, such as a tree stump, a jagged tooth, or any sharp protuberance. These were also known as 'snags'. And was not the early sausage just like that?

The most likely origin of 'snags', however, is associated with fishing! It is so easy for a line to become badly tangled. Likewise, the long string of sausages coming out of the machine becomes easily snagged and hard to unravel. Hence they were called 'snags'.

A final claim derives their description from the name of an early Melbourne firm of butchers, said to have been the first to make sausages in Australia. They were Messrs Snags.

V For Victory

Who started the V-sign for victory?

During the life-and-death struggle against the Nazi regime, the V-sign played a powerful role in inspiring the Allies and supporting those oppressed. There is no doubt that Winston Churchill contributed greatly to making the signal famous, not least by making the letter 'V' with two of his fingers whenever he appeared in public. However, Churchill did not create it. Several explanations have been offered as to its origin.

According to one suggestion, Belgian students were the first to introduce it. To join the forces fighting for the liberation of their country during World War II, these students escaped to England, where they formed a freedom movement. They chose *Vrijheid,* their native Flemish word for 'freedom', as their slogan. Imaginatively, they adopted its initial as their symbol. To produce it needed only the raising of the index and middle fingers of a hand.

Victor de Laveleye, a member of the exiled Belgian government in London, then took it up. In a broadcast made to his country on 14 January 1941, he suggested using the V-sign as a salute from one patriot to another. In fact, he further advised, it could serve as a most effective psychological weapon against the invader. Easily and quickly chalked onto walls, buildings or pavements, it would act as a potent message of defiance, unnerving the enemy.

Six months later, on 20 July, Churchill adopted the V-sign. In his forceful and eloquent way, he proclaimed that it was to serve 'as a symbol of the unconquerable will of the occupied territories and as a portent of the fate awaiting Nazi tyranny'.

Strangely, it so happened that the letter 'V' was also the initial of the word for 'victory' in the language of many European nations who were battling for their survival or liberation. *Vryheid* in Dutch and *victoire* in French, it was *Viteztvi* in Czech. Dutch people soon joined two 'Vs' to form the letter 'W', the initial of Wilhelmina, their beloved and undaunted queen.

Going much further back in time – well over five hundred years, in fact – the V-sign might be traced to confrontations between the English and the French, when the English, often greatly outnumbered, nevertheless proved themselves far superior in their fighting power. They had learnt to make use of the long bow, a weapon still unknown to their enemy. Whenever the French succeeded in capturing one of the English archers, the first thing they did was to cut off his fore and middle fingers. The mutilation disarmed him for life, making it impossible for him ever again to draw the long bow.

Tradition tells that, after their decisive victories both at Crécy (in 1346) and at Agincourt (in 1415), the English taunted the defeated foe by holding up their hands with their fore and middle fingers conspicuously pointing upward. Proud and defiant, their gesture indicated that, in spite of the fierceness of battle, they had remained unharmed and, if need be, were ready for further combat. Churchill, being a historian, was possibly well acquainted with the gesture and thus adopted it as the V-sign for the twentieth-century struggle.

Perhaps merely odd is the coincidence that in ancient Egyptian worship the V-shape, made by two fingers of the hand, served as a gesture of petition to one of their gods, asking for his protection.

The V-sign has also been seen as the stylised representation of the crotch. As the seat of the genitals, it was symbolic of the continuation of life and of its victory over death.

The Toby Jug

Who invented this peculiar drinking vessel and when?

A toby jug is a beer mug in the shape of a squat man wearing old-fashioned garb and a three-cornered hat. It was only natural to personify it, calling it by name, and Toby, short for Tobias, was as good as any. However, there is a story behind its choice.

Ralph Wood of Burslem and his son were the owners of one of the famous eighteenth-century English Staffordshire potteries. They specialised in producing this type of jug. They modelled it on the figure of Toby Fillpot, 'a thirsty soul', popularised at the time by a humorous ballad by Francis Fawkes, which had first been published in 1760. Their design was based on an engraving of Toby they had purchased from a London print-seller, Carrington Bowles. It was no wonder, therefore, that in the beginning their jug was also known as a 'fillpot'. It was a name which, apart from playing on words, expressed a thirsty man's wishful thought.

Dow-Jones Index

What is the meaning of this hyphenated name?

The money market, once restricted to business enterprises and a limited number of speculators and investors, has assumed a far more dominant role in modern times. Terms once meaningful solely to merchants and entrepreneurs as well as the few who played the stock market have become part of everyday speech and interest. In fact, nowadays the stock market is a barometer of the economy and political state of a country. Influencing the world's financial scene, it is anxiously followed even by the general public.

Part of every major news bulletin and the daily press is the report of the latest Dow-Jones Index. It lists the price levels quoted on that specific day of representative groups of stocks and shares, as bought and sold on the New York Stock Exchange, popularly known as 'Wall Street' after the street on which it is situated.

'Dow-Jones' combines the names of Charles H. Dow (1851–1902) and Edward D. Jones (1856–1920), two outstanding American financial statisticians, and retains the name of the bulletin first jointly issued by them in 1882. Their subsequent publication, the *Wall Street Journal*, became a most reliable and influential source of information, exerting a worldwide impact.

The Bikini

Who dared to wear the first bikini and when?

The first bikini was shown in Paris on 5 July 1946 by Mecheline Bernardini, a French model. It was called after the small atoll in the North Pacific, part of the Marshall Islands which had been the scene of American atomic tests, detonations carried out shortly before this date with devastating effect.

'Bikini' seemed an apt name for the scanty, two-piece swim suit first known in France as *le minimum*. The emotion it roused in men could be compared to the explosive result of the experiments on the coral reef. And did not the women thus clad look as denuded as the Bikini Atoll after the atomic explosion?

Get The Wind Up

Why does this phrase reflect a state of alarm?

Those very anxious and frightened of something are said to 'get the wind up'.

The saying goes back to the sailing ship days and the belief in sympathetic magic. Whistling on board ship, sailors were convinced, was unlucky, as, imitating the sound of wind, it could conjure up a storm. Hence, to get (too much) wind up was a fearsome and nerve-racking experience.

Bingo

Who started this popular pastime?

A priest of unknown identity has been given the credit for the universal popularity of Bingo, by which name the game is now known.

It happened almost by chance – very appropriate in the circumstances. On a visit to Atlanta in Georgia, USA, in 1929, Edwin S. Lowe, a Polish-born New York toy manufacturer, was watching a game of Beano at a carnival. He was intrigued by its simplicity and its appeal to people's gambling instinct. All that the players had to do was to place beans (accounting for the name of the game) on sheets, each of which carried a different selection of handprinted numbers. The man in charge of the game called out the numbers, which he picked out of a box, and each matching number meant another bean. Whoever completed his card first was the winner and could collect the kitty.

At the end of the game, Lowe purchased some of the cards and a box of numbers and took them home, where he introduced the game to his friends. They came to enjoy it hugely. On one occasion, a young lady who had joined their circle became so excited on hearing the last number on her card being called out, that, as she placed the final bean on it, to announce her 'full house' she shouted at the top of her voice, 'Bingo!', mispronouncing the usual 'Beano'.

Lowe, being an astute businessman, immediately grasped the promotional value of a game called by the erroneously uttered 'Bingo'. Not deliberately or consciously devised, but arising from a mere slip of the tongue, it was a winning proposition. The name was short, crisp in sound and easily pronounced and remembered. It had all the qualifications needed for a best seller. In no time Lowe marketed, at two dollars each, games of Bingo comprising complete sets of twenty-four cards.

Many church functions nowadays run Bingo nights, and so it is not surprising that it was a priest who first realised how the game could help him in raising badly-needed funds. But he also soon learnt that Lowe's set of twenty-four cards was impracticable. There were too many winners to each game. He called to explain the problem to Mr Lowe, who, seeing the point at once, set about producing an improved version of Bingo which, by reducing the number of winners, increased the profit.

Leaving nothing to chance in this game of chance, he engaged a professor of mathematics to provide him with 6000 different combinations. Alas, the professor's success was also his undoing as, in finding the right number of figures, he is said to have lost his mind. But whatever this expert's contribution, the fact remains that it was a minister of religion whose concern led to the final refinement of the game and with it, its universal appeal.

Fragging

What is the meaning and origin of this term?

Of modern American origin, the term 'fragging' can be traced to the 1960s and the Vietnam War.

Horrendous and ghastly, it referred to the wounding or even killing of a superior by his subordinates. They were prompted to do so when ordered by him to take unwarranted risks, mostly to flush out Viet Congs, particularly so when this occurred at a time close to their own repatriation.

In their deep resentment and even hatred, they used to roll fragmentation grenades into the officer's tent, which did not fail to achieve the desired aim. It was this *frag*mentation grenade which – linguistically by the use of its first syllable – added *frag*ging to the modern vocabulary, initially with its gruesome association.

Forty years on, 'fragging' had generally lost its murderous meaning, and was applied more often in the sense of the Australian 'bastardisation'. The latter referred to the – at times – brutal initiation rites performed by bullies on newly-enrolled members of schools, colleges and the army.

Have Someone Over A Barrel

Is this not an odd way to express 'having someone at one's mercy'?

'Having someone over a barrel' means that this person is at one's mercy and in a completely helpless or most embarrassing position.

Completely diverse origins of the expression have been suggested. Those being bent over a barrel – of whichever kind, a cask, a drum or a gun – have their posterior up in the air, a position lending itself best to being given a good hiding.

Another explanation links the phrase with the administration of first aid to half-drowned people by trying to empty their lungs of water. Placing them over a barrel put them in a most promising position for this aim to be achieved.

Knock One Up

How is it possible that this saying has such different meanings in different countries?

George Bernard Shaw's observation that the only thing that divides the British from the Americans is their language is well known. Their different interpretation of a phrase or expression may become a source of embarrassment. A striking illustration is 'to knock one up'.

The American connotation of the idiom (which has spread to other countries as well) is 'to make a woman pregnant'. Oddly, this retains the early English meaning of the words. In Shakespearean times 'knock' described the penis. In modern idiomatic English, as spoken by the British, however, to 'knock one up' usually suggests waking up a person by knocking on the door.

The expression itself is part of English social history. In the early days of the Lancashire textile industry, those employed at the mills had to work from early morning till late at night, returning home totally exhausted, 'knocked up' in a different sense. They could easily oversleep the next morning. To make sure that they turned up at the factory on time led to the introduction of a simple practice. Before sunrise, men walked through the streets of the city, equipped with long staves. These they banged against workers' bedroom windows, mostly situated on the upper floors. 'Knocking them up', they made certain that they were not late for work.

Working hours are now regulated by law. But, as a memento of the sweat labour, to 'knock up' has become an integral part of the English vocabulary, though now used merely metaphorically in an innocuous and harmless sense of being awakened.

Sent To Coventry

Why this city of all places?

Countless visitors now go to Coventry, the famous English cathedral city, which was the site of Lady Godiva's famous ride and also the home of 'Peeping Tom'. At one time, however, 'to be sent to Coventry' was a disgrace and a punishment, responsible for the present-day phrase. Those who are 'sent to Coventry' are ostracised and given the cold shoulder. No one will associate with them.

Two explanations have been proffered for the origin and meaning of the saying. At one time, it is asserted, the citizens of the city were strongly anti-militarist. They would not have any contact with the soldiers of the local garrison. A girl seen to fraternise or merely talk with any of its men was instantly shunned.

Among the worst disciplinary measures meted out to members of the army deserving punishment thus was 'to be sent to Coventry'. The hostile treatment given to soldiers there became known nationwide. It resulted in the phrase 'to be sent to Coventry' eventually being applied generally, to anyone tabooed.

Others have linked the saying with the English Civil War in the seventeenth century. In this historic confrontation between King Charles I and parliament, Coventry was strongly anti-royalist.

Supporters of the king who had been taken prisoner and found troublesome in Birmingham were therefore sent to this Cromwellian stronghold. In Coventry they would find no friends, and be treated with disdain. Totally isolated, it was tantamount to being in solitary confinement.

Butterfly

Butterflies are not particularly fond of butter. Why, then, are they so named?

Who would ever think that the tracing of the origin of a simple name can sometimes give headaches to etymologists. It is known for certain that the butterfly was so called at least 1000 years ago, and many theories and stories have been advanced as to the significance of its name.

Not unlikely is the claim that it was simply a Spoonerism – the transposition of two letters – and that, originally, the butterfly was a 'flutter by'. It would not be so far-fetched a hypothesis, as butterflies do a lot of fluttering. Another feasible though not very attractive explanation associates the insect's name with the colour of its excrement, which – like that of butter – is yellow. In fact, this would tally with its Dutch name, *Boterschijte*, which literally (and crudely) speaks of 'butter shit'.

Already in the days of Chaucer, if not earlier, the Anglo-Saxon *buter-flege* ('butterfly') was applied to any large insect, and the brimstone butterfly, the most common in Britain, was yellow – like butter. It was called 'the yellow flier', which was in Old English *buttorfleoge* – to change into *butterflie* in Middle English. This was sufficient, and probably the real reason for the choice of its name.

Passing from the natural to the supernatural, an occult belief claimed that, to steal butter and milk, witches would shape-change. Assuming the likeness of the winged creature, they became known as – butterflies.

Butterfly Stroke In Swimming

How did the butterfly get into the water?

Swimmers' various methods of progress through the water have been identified by easily explained terms. They may refer to the swimmer who first introduced and popularised them, such as the trudgen (a variation of freestyle with a scissor kick), or to its most conspicuous feature, as is the case with breaststroke, backstroke and the crawl (or freestyle). Not so the butterfly stroke. A variety of explanations has been given as to why it was so called. The most likely reason for the choice of its name is that in this stroke the swimmers' arms are raised simultaneously and brought forward above the water in large circular movements, very much like the wings of a butterfly.

First thought of – and perhaps even 'invented' – by the German E. Rademacher in 1926, it was left to the American Henry Meyer to improve on it and to have it accepted in competition swimming in 1933. It took, however, a prolonged controversy, extending over many years, before at last in 1953 the stroke was recognised as legitimate and finally included in the Olympic Games.

Hoisted By One's Own Petard

What is the meaning of this phrase?

To be 'hoisted by one's own petard' means to become the victim of one's own evil design or 'get a taste of one's own medicine'. People who experience this fate are caught in the trap they have set for others.

The original petard was a device employed in medieval warfare. Loaded with an explosive charge, it was attached to the gate or the wall of a fortified city and detonated. If successful, the explosion would create a breach large enough for the attacking force to enter and capture the town.

It was a hazardous undertaking. Whoever was commissioned with the task of fixing the petard was fully exposed to the enemy. Once spotted, he was an easy target. To detonate the charge was even more perilous.

Not infrequently, the gunpowder exploded prematurely, with the result that the soldier lighting the fuse was lifted into the air by the blast. 'Hoisted by his own petard', he was killed.

Derived from the French for 'breaking wind', the petard was given its name because of the sound it made when it exploded. Petards have long become obsolete in warfare, but they survive in the figure of speech and not least so because Shakespeare used the expression in *Hamlet*.

Pull The Leg

How did this action describe making fun of someone?

There was no fun in the pulling of the leg, when it was first practised. On the contrary, then it occurred on a most gruesome occasion, taking place at the gallows, and that was at a time when these devices still lacked modern 'refinements' – such as the long drop and the knotted rope – to assure the instant death of the condemned.

Thus, for many hours the hanged man could linger on, before he finally expired. That is why friends were given permission to help in hastening his death. They did so by pulling his legs, which tightened the rope around his neck, choking him more quickly.

It was a horrible spectacle, perversely enjoyed by the countless people who came especially to watch the execution and found in the pulling of the legs an extra source of entertainment and even amusement.

With the advance of civilisation, public executions largely ceased. More humane methods of hanging made the pulling of the legs unnecessary. But the phrase was given a new lease of life and meaning in totally different circumstances, in the world of thieves.

A crook out to rob pedestrians often worked with an accomplice whose job it was to trip up a passer-by. This he did by dexterously pulling one of the victim's legs with the curved end of a stick. Before the person had realised what had made him fall, he was deprived of any valuables he carried.

People always laugh at others' misfortune, possibly because they are happy that it has not happened to them. Thus the 'pulling of the leg' with its resultant loss of dignity and property gave the phrase its humour.

Thieves also learnt to improve their methods and their kind of 'leg-pulling' became redundant as well. That is how eventually the phrase took on its present-day, harmless meaning. No longer associated with loss of life or possessions, all the victims might lose now, if they lacked a sense of humour, is their temper.

Jihad

What part does it play in Islam?

The teaching of the Jihad is a major part of the Moslem faith. It has been described as its sixth pillar, supplementing the other five pillars of Islam, obligatory to all believers: the recital of the Creed; Prayer; Relief of Poverty; the Fasting of Ramadan; and the Hajj – the pilgrimage to Mecca. Jihad speaks of the 'Holy War' to be fought to preserve and spread Islam. An Arabic word, literally meaning 'to struggle', it was applied to fighting in self-defence and to overcome evil of any kind, to subdue Allah's enemies and the infidels. More generally, it was meant to call on the faithful 'to strive in the way of God' – both in peace and in war.

Whilst still staying in Medina (according to the second sura of the Koran, 'sura' being the term used for 'chapter'), Mohammed received the first revelation as to the righteousness of such holy warfare. Those engaging in it were promised the divine gift of mercy, and (according to the fourth sura) those laying down their lives in its pursuit would go straight to paradise to receive God's highest reward.

In the spirit of the Jihad, the leadership after Mohammed's death not only reconverted those sections of the population that had abandoned the new faith, but also began the campaigns that were to subjugate vast areas of the world, a pursuit that continued through the centuries. In the name of the prophet, they extended Moslem dominion to the distant east as far as India, to the west to North Africa and Spain, as well as north into large parts of Eastern Europe.

The conquests brought with them multiple problems. These related to the treatment and standing of the subdued nations and the relationship with countries too far away or too strong for the Moslem fighters to conquer.

Obviously, with the passing of time, a variety of interpretations were given as to the official meaning of the Jihad and Moslems' obligations to participate. There was the fanaticism of the zealots, and of those who joined in battle for the sake of booty, out of mere greed and lust for power. On the other hand, it made Moslems excel in spreading a deeply religious spirit, inspired by the conviction that they had been given the sacred task of teaching people everywhere to fulfil the divine will, as they saw it. Joining in the Jihad, too, created in many a new feeling of brotherhood and strengthened their conviction of being called upon to spread Allah's message, wherever they went, finally to embrace the entire world. Naturally, an ever-present danger was the abuse of the command by those who changed the Jihad from a sanctified ideal into a brutal pursuit.

Curry Favour

What is the actual meaning of this saying?

Whoever seeks to gain special advantage by excessively flattering an influential person is said 'to curry favour'. Though the meaning of the phrase is clear, its origin has been misunderstood. It is rarely realised that the expression was born in the stable!

The 'favour' in this case is the corrupted name of Favel (or Fauvel), a legendary chestnut mare and subject of a fourteenth-century French satire. Highly prized, she was well looked after. To 'curry', a term also derived from French and in no way connected with Indian curry, described the grooming and rubbing down of a horse, a meaning still recalled in the curry comb used for this purpose. 'To curry Favel' therefore expressed the special care and concern shown to the horse.

When, eventually, the English adopted the phrase, as on many other occasions they misunderstood and distorted the French, rendering it in their tongue 'to curry favour'. Thus the metaphor became totally divorced from its original equestrian context.

Athletes Running Anti-Clockwise

Why are races run in this direction?

Generally – and in a great variety of circumstances – people favour the clockwise direction. For anything to be anti-clockwise seems somehow out of the ordinary, puzzling and unnatural. Indeed, to the superstitious, 'anti-clockwise' has always carried an ominous note.

Truly confusing are the various suggestions as to why in their foot races athletes run anti-clockwise. Like Stephen Leacock's rider who flung himself upon his horse, riding off in all directions, the explanations proffered lead the questioner nowhere. It is virtually impossible to get a satisfactory answer. Scientists, mathematicians, meteorologists or, for that matter, athletes themselves, each give their own, differing interpretation.

An association with the earth's rotation has been suggested. Equally, natural phenomena, such as water spouts (those starting at cloud level), tornadoes, twisters and cyclones have been held responsible. As all of these turn anti-clockwise in the northern hemisphere and clockwise in the southern, so the runners' direction belongs to a 'natural' category.

Well known is the view held on the flow of water from a basin or bathtub, when the plug is pulled. People have noticed that the water running out swirled in opposite directions, depending on whether it happened north or south of the equator! But this, too, has been disputed and the water's change of direction, if correctly observed, seen as the result of other, minor factors.

In actual fact the running direction does not change according to the athletes' geographical location, so both of the above propositions are unsatisfactory.

Many another hypothesis put forward does not hold water either. In fact, some have led to greater confusion and, mixing metaphors, caused the inquirer merely to run in circles. Typical is the reference to the first modern Olympic Games, held in Athens in 1896, in which, it was said, the athletes ran clockwise. The claim, however, was contradicted by old nineteenth-century lithographs clearly showing their running anti-clockwise! Who then was correct and who mistaken?

Some of the authorities see a link with the ancient chariot races, which were run anti-clockwise. In later years, so they argue, the tradition was adopted by athletes. However, the original reason claimed for the 'odd' direction did not apply to them. The charioteers, it is asserted, found it easier to turn horses to the left.

Turning from the equines to humans, it has also been suggested that the fact that most people are right-handed (and possibly right-footed as well) might have been the deciding factor in their 'right' choice of direction.

Even politics has been drawn into the debate. The choice of direction, it has been said, coincided with political views – being either to the right or to the left!

The very multiplicity of possible reasons and, in many a case, their fatuity and irrationality, show that all of them are mere assumptions. In reality, no one has yet been able to give a convincing answer to the very valid question.

Chequered Black And White Flag In Motor Racing

Why has motor racing adopted this particular flag for 'flagging down' the winner?

Motor racing presents its own thrills and dangers. To avoid fatal accidents and collisions, it necessitates careful supervision and meticulous organisation. For this purpose, the *Fédération Internationale de l'Automobile*, as the controlling body of the sport, introduced a worldwide system of eighteen signals. In the form of flags, these are designed in patterns that can easily be memorised and recognised by the drivers. Proceeding at record speeds, and hence catching only a glimpse of the signal when approaching it, drivers must be able to identify a flag in a split second and against any background. A mistake made in 'reading' the message could cost them the race, if not their life!

Each flag relates to a specific circumstance or emergency. The variety of situations includes the need to stop instantly (conveyed by a red flag), the approach of some dangerous stretch (yellow), information that oil covers the course further along the track (yellow with red stripes) or that an ambulance is ahead (a white flag). But nothing is more significant to those taking part than the end of the race, hopefully the 'winning post'. To make the flag indicating it truly outstanding and distinct from all the others, it is the only one that is chequered, with black and white squares. So different from the rest that no one could ever mistake it. Traditionally, it should only be waved for the winning car, while it is held steady for all the rest.

Being In Clover

What suggested this phrase?

Those who are well off and living in luxury are said to be 'in clover'. This portrayal is borrowed from cattle, fortunate when they graze in fields rich in nourishing clover, which they favour above all other fodder.

The association of clover with such a blissful existence may well have yet another root: not in the soil of the earth but in the supernatural. It has been linked with the four-leafed plant, so rich in minerals and proteins, which, it was said, once grew in the Garden of Eden, and of which Adam and Eve, when expelled from paradise, took a sprig with them as a memento. Ever since, a four-leafed clover has been thought magically to bring good luck to anyone getting hold of it. Though a mere legend, its popularity reinforced the four-leaf clover's association with good fortune and a life of ease. An old tradition links each of the four leaves with a special gift. These are fame, wealth, a faithful lover and constant good health.

The Clue

Who created the clue?

If one 'has no clue', it means that one is totally baffled, devoid of an answer or any knowledge of the subject matter.

For the explanation of the saying it is primarily necessary to ascertain the meaning of 'clue'. Derived from the Old English *cleowen*, used for a 'ball of thread', its etymology is the very clue that almost literally – by a circuitous route – leads to the intriguing origin of the mystifying choice of term, now so common, not least among those fond of solving crossword puzzles.

The earliest clue was not a metaphor but a lifeline. Going back to a famous Greek myth, it relates to the Cretan labyrinth. At the command of Minos, the fabled ruler of Crete, it was built at Knossos by the Athenian craftsman Daedalus. A vast maze, it consisted of a multitude of tangled rooms with endless passages winding their way hither and thither. Once inside that edifice of no equal, it was almost impossible to find one's way out or to be able to escape. To make the conditions of this heinous construction even more horrendous, King Minos had confined within its walls the Minotaur. A dreaded monster of human body and a bull's head, it lived on human flesh. This was provided by the sacrifice of seven young men and seven maidens. These were obtained by King Minos as a compulsory levy, an annual tribute from the Athenians.

When Theseus, the famous hero of royal Athenian descent, heard of this ghastly demand, he volunteered to be one of the victims offered. He was determined not only to prove superior to the Minotaur but to kill the monster as well.

Luck so willed it that Ariadne, Minos' daughter, fell in love with Theseus. Deeply concerned to save his life and have him return to her, she thought out a ruse. Before entering the labyrinth, she provided Theseus with a sword and a ball of thread – a 'clue'. By unwinding it on his way into the maze, it would not be difficult for him, after having killed the Minotaur, to find his way back, to join his beloved. The *clue* thus enabled him to outwit death, and to solve the puzzle of survival.

The ancient Greek myth enthralled Sir Arthur Conan Doyle (1859–1930). It inspired him to create the figure of Sherlock Holmes and with it, to enrich the realm of literature by a new category – that of detective stories.

These, in turn, popularised the 'clue', which now survives in everyday speech in such a variety of associations and applications.

In the early 1900s, Sir Arthur Evans, then in charge of the Ashmolean Museum at Oxford University, actually excavated a palace in Crete. There seemed a strong possibility that it was linked with the story of the labyrinth and there is much evidence to confirm this hypothesis.

Lick Into Shape

What misconception created this odd description?

That people, putting the finishing touches to a job, are said to 'lick (it) into shape' is rather an odd description. No one's tongue is so effective. The metaphor is based on a fallacy, never corrected in speech. At one time it was believed that a bear cub was born formless and that its mother had to lick it into shape. The misconception was possibly due to the mother bear's intense washing and cleaning of the tiny progeny with her tongue.

Box Office

Why is this tiny cubicle so called?

It is a common practice now to buy tickets for a show at the box office. It is wrong to imagine that this is so named because the ticket seller is ensconced in an office as small as a box.

At one time, spectators did not share seats in rows, but had their individual boxes, which nowadays are merely reserved for special visitors and the wealthy. It was only logical thus to call the office at which one obtained tickets for the performance, a 'box' office.

Another theory advanced for the peculiar choice of the name goes back to the early days, when admission tickets were still non-existent. Those wanting to see a show took their seats in the pit (or the orchestra stall, as Americans came to call it). A member of the company then came around to collect contributions and did so not on a plate, as is done in church, but in a box. When the theatre had become more organised, the procedure was changed. The collection 'box' was left outside the auditorium in an office and people paid prior to taking their seats. This avoided unnecessary distribution and lent dignity to the show.

The Hoi Polloi

What's wrong with the hoi polloi?

Those speaking rather condescendingly of the masses refer to them as 'the hoi polloi'. They imagine that their use of the learned term reflects their own superiority in standing and education. In reality, however, it reveals their own lack of knowledge. *Hoi polloi*, though now spelt in Latin letters, comes from the Greek. In that classical tongue of great culture, *polloi* means 'many'. (Still part of numerous terms in the English vocabulary, it is responsible for the description of the practice of having *many* wives as *poly*gamy and of the belief in *many* gods as *poly*theism.) *Hoi*, on the other hand, as anyone with the most elementary knowledge of the Greek tongue is well aware, is its definite article, 'the'. 'Hoi polloi' on its own therefore already speaks of 'the many', and using 'the hoi polloi', doubles up the article, saying 'the the many'. In their ignorance those doing so might try to belittle the masses, 'the great unwashed' but, in reality, show their own limitation in learning and how true it is that a little knowledge is a dangerous thing.

And yet, the great paradox is that the usage of the faulty phrase has become accepted and is so general that it is regarded to be the correct wording, so that anyone adhering to the proper application and not speaking of 'the' hoi polloi is thought to be wrong and their wording unacceptable. In this context it is interesting to know that even John Dryden, that great poet and critic, committed the error. Maybe it was his faulty example and that of other renowned figures that contributed to the ultimate acceptance of this misrepresentation of the great mass of humanity.

In The Limelight

What actually is the limelight?

To be 'in the limelight' is an expression now used only figuratively. In the beginning, however, its meaning was very real. Prior to the invention of electricity, the lighting up of a stage presented many problems. After all, actors wanted not only to be heard, but to be seen as well.

The theatrical world was therefore delighted when, in 1816, Thomas Drummond invented a spotlight with a brilliance that exceeded anything known before. It was produced by burning lime. Its focus on an actor was so bright that, divorced from the stage, 'in the limelight' was adopted as a fitting description for anyone occupying a prominent position.

It is also believed that a lime-green coloured light used to be thrown only on the 'star' performer. The rest of the cast was picked out by white lights.

Gazumping

Who introduced this rather strange word and practice?

Gazumping is an unethical practice. Although not illegal, it is certainly frowned upon. When about to buy a house or property, both parties concerned agree on the purchase price. With nothing yet put down in writing, in the proverbial phrase, theirs is a 'gentleman's agreement'. In other words, it is not legally binding. It often happens, however, that the vendor makes use of the offer as a bargaining tool to get more money from another interested party, or to force the original buyer to raise his bid.

The word 'gazumping' is of Yiddish origin, in which tongue it means to 'swindle'. The term is an even more appropriate choice if it is realised that gazumping is derived from the German *Sumpf,* for a 'bog' or 'swamp'. Is not the falling through of the deal like being 'bogged down'?

Rickshaw

Who invented this vehicle?

In some Asian countries and even in southern Africa, not so long ago, rickshaws used to be a common feature. Fortunately, they have almost disappeared. At best, tourist attractions, in the main they have become mere exhibits in museums. Nevertheless, they are part of social history and their 'passage' through time, the way they came and then left, is a record of human ingenuity, improvisation and discrimination.

The rickshaw might be described as one of the early international products. Its name is Japanese. An American is said to have first conceived the idea. A Frenchman promoted it in China where, for some considerable time, it came to serve as a general means of transportation.

The rickshaw owes its existence to an American Baptist missionary. Stationed in Yokohama, he was greatly helped in his work by his wife. In 1874, her health deteriorated and, on consulting a doctor, she was advised daily to take to the fresh air but to avoid any exertion in moving about.

Concerned to fulfil both conditions, the reverend conceived the idea of providing his wife with a simple carriage. Cheaply and easily constructed, it was to be light enough for one man to pull along.

In no time, a local carpenter was able to make such a carriage, a two-wheeled wooden cart with a canopy held up by bamboo sticks. In search of a name, very appropriately, they called it *Jinrickisha*, the Japanese for a 'man-power vehicle', exactly what it was. *Jin* is the Japanese for 'man', *riki* means 'power' and *sha* a 'vehicle'.

Having obeyed doctor's orders, it did not take long for the patient to regain her strength. Most unexpectedly, her unique cure had a side effect that was to make history. A Frenchman who had watched the minister's wife take her daily outings in the only man-powered vehicle in existence immediately became interested, not in the lady, but in her coach. What an opportunity, he thought, to commercialise the idea and introduce it into China with its teaming millions. That is how eventually in 1887 the rickshaw took to the road. For practical reasons it had been shortened, at least in name.

The rickshaw proved so much more practical than the traditional litter or sedan chair. No wonder that soon it was to ply its trade by the thousands across the vast expanses of China. It explains why foreigners came to regard it as indigenously Chinese, though the Chinese themselves called it – correctly – *yang ch'e,* 'the foreign cart'.

Its almost explosive proliferation came to a sudden end. Modern China felt that it was most undignified for a man to pull along another person. It meant 'loss of face' for both the human horse and the passenger.

Meanwhile in Japan which, after all, was its native country, the rickshaw had caught on, to be mass produced there and exported to other Southeast Asian countries, the South Sea Islands and even further afield. And yet, like all things, the rickshaw as well was to have its day. Slowly but inevitably, it came to a stop. Consideration of human dignity and most of all technological progress acted as the brake.

Get The Sack

Why should one get a sack when being dismissed?

To speak of a person as 'getting the sack' may have several explanations. Originally, a workman taking on a job had to provide his own tools. He brought them along in a sack, which he then left at his place of work. When his employer wanted to dismiss him, there was no need on his part to say even a single word. All he had to do was to give the worker the sack, so he could put in his tools and go home.

Another suggestion recalls the practice of doing overtime. Men took their work home with them in a sack. But when they were no longer needed, all they were given was their (empty) sack.

A rather gruesome interpretation of the phrase links it with a certain Turkish sultan. He was said to have used a sack to get rid of an unwanted wife or concubine. When fed up with her, he ordered his servants to put the woman into a sack which they were to drop into the waters of the Bosphorus.

Down And Out

How did prizefighting contribute to the Salvation Army?

Anyone who is 'down and out' is in great trouble. The expression comes from the boxing ring. It relates to the fighter who has been knocked down to the ground and is unable to get back on his feet within the specified period of time.

No one would have expected that one day this sporting term, well-known from prizefighting and expressing defeat without hope of a come-back, would be adopted in a totally different sense, by adapting it to give hope and optimism in a desperate situation.

In its new context, 'down and out' was changed into 'a man may be down, but he is never out'. The observation goes back to the Boer War and the ingenuity of Elmore Cornell Leffingwell (1878–1942), an American news-paperman. At the time, he served as the Publicity Officer of the Salvation Army. He himself got the idea from an episode that occurred during that war in South Africa.

When, in pursuit of their mission, members of the 'Army' were distributing food and clothing to those who had been rendered homeless by the conflict, someone referred to those unfortunates as 'down-and-outers'. On hearing it, one of the Salvos' reaction was instantaneous. 'A man may be down, but he is never out,' he retorted. His encouraging words expressed so much hope for the future that in no time, at Leffingwell's suggestion, the Salvation Army adopted them as one of its slogans.

Spend A Penny

What made people 'spend a penny'?

Among the many euphemisms used in everyday life, some obviously relate to people's natural functions. Having to go to the toilet whilst in company gives rise to one of these. Only the vulgar will excuse themselves by (im)properly, though truthfully, spelling out the reason: having to urinate or to empty their bowels. Still popular and acceptable for those finding themselves in the unwanted situation of having to answer the call of nature is to say, 'I have to spend a penny'.

To start with, the expression was no mere case of circumlocution. It was based on the actual necessity for those wanting to take advantage of a public convenience to pay a fee. This practice is still followed in many parts of the world, particularly where there are plentiful supplies of free-spending tourists. The use of the toilets cost one penny (one cent) per person and only after the coin had been inserted in the lock of the door would the cubicle open. The first lavatories of this kind were introduced in London in 1855. Although part of the pre-decimal era, the expression has survived. It continues to be employed as a most acceptable metaphor in public and polite society that has not lost its 'currency'.

Knock Off Work

What does one knock off when leaving work?

No one can be expected to keep on working all the time. Even Roman galley slaves deserved a rest, if only to renew their strength for further exertions. But it was their masters who determined when and gave the signal. The way they did so has caused people to 'knock off work' to this very day.

To ensure that the slaves manning the oars pulled them in unison, the rhythm was beaten out on a block of wood. When those in charge of a boat realised that the men were tiring and needed a break, they announced it by a distinctive 'knock'. Thus they (were) 'knocked off work'. The retention of the phrase makes one wonder whether perhaps even the freest of people have become slaves to their jobs.

Set The Thames On Fire

How does one set a river on fire?

To set a river on fire – prior to oil slicks – seemed an almost impossible undertaking. Nothing could describe vigorous pursuit of a task more vividly than to compare it with such an achievement. Romans, Frenchmen and Germans a long time back thus spoke of indolent people as being so slow in their work that they would not set the Tiber, the Seine or the Rhine, respectively, on fire. It therefore appears that the English phrase of the identical kind, speaking of not setting the Thames on fire, was only a later version of the almost universally-used metaphor.

And yet, in this case 'the Thames' did not refer to the famous river at all. It must be realised that originally its name was Temze or Temse, which accounts for the odd pronunciation of the word today. (The 'h' in the Thames did not occur until 1377.)

Temse was an Old English word for a 'corn sieve'. If used at great speed, the friction would heat it up so much that sparks would fly, setting the sieve with its contents on fire. Masters who felt that their workers were slack and dragged their feet in doing their job urged them on to hurry up, telling them that in the way they were carrying on, they would never 'set the temse on fire'. It was the confusion of the sieve with the river (of identical spelling then) that made the paradoxically-sounding phrase so attractive that it was widely applied as an idiom.

Mardi Gras

What is the background of the Mardi Gras?

One of the most famous present-day celebrations of Mardi Gras is held annually in Sydney. Arranged by Australia's gay and lesbian communities, thousands of visitors from all parts of the world flock to it.

Few of the people participating in or watching the festivities and procession would realise the very paradox of the origin of the Mardi Gras and how it received its name. A secular occasion now, it started in the realm of religion, and was part of one of the most solemn seasons of the Christian calendar.

Mardi Gras goes back to the observation of Lent, the forty days preceding Easter and distinguished by a period of abstinence. During that time, the faithful would not eat meat, eggs or anything that contained milk, butter or fat. Equally severe was the prohibition of any sexual relations.

With the imminent extended period of total withdrawal from the joys and delights of life, the very day before the commencement of the 'Fast' (which started on Ash Wednesday) gained its own particular meaning and associated practices. People went to church to confess their sins and do penance. Their act of 'confession and absolution' used to be referred to in archaic English as 'being shriven'. Accordingly, the day became known generally as Shrove Tuesday.

This, however, did not remain its exclusive designation. Diverse features linked with it led to its being called by other names as well. As no eggs would be eaten for the ensuing forty days, housewives used up any they still had in their pantry. They did so, not least, by baking pancakes, with the result that Shrove Tuesday also became known as Pancake Tuesday.

Bereft of any joys for so long a time, communities went out of their way to compensate for the loss, as it were, in advance. On the very day on which they bade 'farewell to (all) meat', they joined in exuberant merrymaking. Highlighting the occasion, the day assumed the further designation of Carnival. From the Latin, it referred (literally) to this strange celebration of a 'farewell' (*vale*) to all 'meat' (*carnis*). Or it may derive instead from *carnem levare* and *carnelevarium*, referring to taking meat away.

Just as there was a variety of names for the day, so its observations differed from place to place. In France it became known as Mardi Gras, the French for 'Fat Tuesday'. It was so called because of the form of local merrymaking, not least so in Paris. Accompanied by an exuberant crowd, a fat ox, decorated for the event, was paraded through the city's streets. The well-fed animal was meant to serve as a live reminder of the lean days about to commence. Simultaneously, once again to make up for the imminent deprivation, people indulged in frivolity and revelry. But still, it was all linked with the calendar of the Church and religious ritual.

At the time, the American region of Louisiana was a French possession, with a French garrison stationed at Fort Louis de la Louisiana. It is not surprising therefore, that French colonists introduced there, from their homeland, the Mardi Gras. It was the first of its kind to be held in that part of the world. To begin with, early in the eighteenth century, it took place on the site of the future Mobile, Alabama. In 1827, young men returning from Paris to New Orleans started the Mardi Gras in that city. Its parades and festivities took fantastic forms, with the most colourful and imaginative floats and the holding of exuberant masked balls. It is no wonder that the celebrations eventually gained world renown.

New Orleans' example of the festivities ultimately reached the Antipodes. With their marching units, fancy dress costumes and numerous bands, the crowds throng the Sydney streets. Totally unaware of the true origin of the Mardi Gras, it has become a completely secular event, frowned upon by the majority of ecclesiastical authorities. None of the participants or the spectators would ever guess its deeply religious roots, nor why it carries the French designation of a 'Fat Tuesday'.

Alabaster

What role has this stone played in the history of civilisation?

Not without reason was the cat worshipped in ancient Egypt. Its population was deeply indebted to the feline, as it helped to keep their vast grain silos free from rats and mice. The goddess linked with the cat was Bast or Bastet, and she was therefore always represented as cat-headed.

No wonder that sacred cats were kept in Bastet's temple, there to be ritually fed and cared for. When a cat died, as the goddess's incarnation, it was given a special burial. Its often mummified body was solemnly placed in a coffin. Made of the finest type of grained gypsum, the casket became known as *a-la-Baste,* 'the vessel of Bastet'. This was the divine (and funereal) origin of 'alabaster' in which, as it were, the cat goddess still hides.

Pens And Pencils

What was nature's gift to the art of writing?

The modern pen belies its name, which – from the Latin *penna* – means a 'feather'. It is a relic from days long past, recalling the obsolete practice of scribes of using a quill for writing. Equally outdated and wrongly applied is the description of the pencil. This goes back to the use of a miniature brush which imaginatively became known as a 'little tail', *penicillum* in Latin.

The modern graphite pencil owes its existence to an accidental discovery made in the mid 1500s near Keswick in the Lake District of northern England, during a destructive thunderstorm. Blowing over a large tree, shepherds discovered among its exposed roots a black, soft material, entirely new to them.

People soon came to realise that this black matter, a sort of carbon, later identified as graphite, could be used to leave some imprint on paper. Prominent among the various names chosen for it was *plumbago* – the Latin for 'lead ore' and 'wad', synonymous with the German *Watte,* for 'wadding'. Aware of its great potential and usefulness, people took up mining it, subsequently to develop a new and important industry. Craftsmen learnt to put narrow strips of the substance into styluses. This eventually led to a significant improvement: its insertion into small tubes of wood – the creation of the modern pencil.

Appropriately, etymologically the very description of graphite itself refers to the act of 'writing'. Its name is derived from the Greek *graphein.*

The Penny Has Dropped

What figure of speech makes use of money to describe one's comprehension of a matter?

When people who are slow in comprehension finally get the gist of things, it is said that at long last 'the penny has dropped'.

The expression originated with the mechanisation of early vending machines. These would supply any of the goods they contained – such as sweets or small bars of chocolate – after a charge of a penny had been deposited in a slot. However, like modern vending machines it would only do so when the coin had actually dropped. The same applied to door locks (like that securing entry to a public toilet), which would open up only when the penny inserted had 'dropped'.

Between The Devil And The Deep Blue Sea

How did devils become associated with ships?

The devil might well sail under false colours. On occasions, however, his presence may be suspected at places where he is not. This applies to the mention of his name in the phrase 'between the devil and the deep blue sea'.

A sailor's duty was not only to man the ship, but also to keep it seaworthy. This necessitated constant overhauling and repairs, at times in very awkward, hard-to-reach places. The garboard, which was the first plank on the outer hull of a wooden vessel, was one such spot. To caulk (or stop up) this seam, the boat had to be careened, i.e., keeled over to one side. But even then it was difficult to keep the seam above water. It was such a 'devil' of a job for the caulker that he 'christened' the garboard seam 'the devil'. Positioned so hazardously when undertaking this task, he found himself 'between the devil and the deep blue sea'. His precarious situation became a popular metaphor to describe anyone's experience when awkwardly placed between two equally undesirable alternatives.

To Eat Crow

Why would anyone want to eat this type of bird?

To make someone 'eat crow' is one way to describe the humiliation experienced by people forced to admit their errors. Certainly, a crow is not an attractive bird and to have to eat of its flesh might well be as distasteful as to have to eat one's words.

However, originally, the phrase spoke more fully of 'eating boiled crow'. Its earliest known use goes back to the United States and the 1870s. Nevertheless, generally it is linked with an incident on Canadian territory during the War of 1812.

Soon after a truce had been declared between the American and British forces, an English officer watched an American soldier shoot a crow. Since the act was committed on Canadian soil, he arrested the man, made him hand over his gun and then forced him to eat a piece of the crow he had just killed. But being a gentleman, so the story continues, having taught the American a lesson, he not only released him but even returned to him his weapon. Swiftly, the American reversed the situation. Pointing the gun at his former captor, he now forced him to eat all that was left of the crow!

Dead Reckoning

When did death become part of calculations?

Death – so ubiquitous – has even intruded into spheres where it does not belong. Its presence in naval terminology is merely fictitious. There is nothing fatal in 'dead reckoning'.

A system of measuring at sea, its deadly association has been totally misunderstood. For many centuries, when still lacking modern navigational aids, boats far away from land charted their course by purely theoretical calculations. They established their position by taking into account the distance and direction they had travelled, making due allowance for currents and tidal streams. For at least 400 years, this system was described as '*ded*uced reckoning'. As this was a rather lengthy and learned term sailors shortened it. Both in speech and in their logbook entries, they referred to it as 'ded. reckoning', a description which to ordinary people made no sense. Not realising that 'ded' was an abbreviation, they wrongly took it to stand for 'dead'.

Others believe that 'dead' reckoning went back much further, to the very days when large parts of the ocean were still uncharted. Not knowing how far the waters reached, sailors then referred to the 'unknown sea' as 'dead'.

Drop A Line

Why are people asked to 'drop a line'?

Someone going on a holiday or extended trip might well be asked by their friends not to forget to 'drop (them) a line'. If taken literally, it sounds an odd request. To ask for (merely) 'a line' instead of at least a short note or a postcard seems to show a lack of real interest.

However, the very wording, though now with E-mail and other modern ways of communication it has become mostly obsolete, might suggest a totally different background. A colloquialism, it may well apply to the use of the postal service and the practice when sending a letter (of whatever length) of *drop*ping it into a postbox. The reference to the line, on the other hand, is a typical case of using a part for the whole, or as the Latin phrase has it, *pars pro toto*.

In The Nick Of Time

What is the odd origin of this phrase?

Scoring plays a significant part in all sports, though its methods vary. In early ball games it was done by means of a tally stick. Each goal was recorded on the stick by the making of a notch. When, as sometimes was the case, a team won the game by a goal it scored at the very last moment, this was described – very appropriately – as 'a nick in time'.

Scores are now kept mostly electronically. However, the antiquated tally survives, totally divorced from sport, whenever one refers to something as having happened just 'in the nick of time'.

Ten-Gallon Hat

Can a large hat really hold that much liquid?

Almost proverbial is the ten-gallon hat worn by Americans in the 'Old West', particularly so in Texas. Its description is taken to refer to its enormous size, which would conform with all the other Texan superlatives. The implication, of course, is that the hat was so large that it could be filled with ten gallons (45.46 litres) of liquid. This is an error due to a linguistic 'mix-up'. In this case the gallon is not the unit of capacity, but the Spanish *galon* for 'braid'.

The hat is not Texan at all but stems from Mexico. When Spaniards occupied the country, they wore sombreros (as Mexicans still do today) because the wide brims protected their faces from the burning sun. Spaniards' love of beauty made them embellish this utilitarian brim with braid. The more of it they used the happier they were. Some men thus wore a hat with ten different braids. Very accurately and without exaggeration, it was a ten *galon* hat.

When the Americans adopted the Spanish head-covering, they acquired its Spanish name as well. Continuing to call it a ten gal(l)on hat, the Spanish braid was soon misunderstood and mistaken for the liquid measure. This created the ten-gallon hat.

Start From Scratch

How did a sporting term come to denote a new beginning?

People who have suffered a great loss, of their business perhaps, or even their home, determined not to be beaten, will say that they will just have to start (again) from scratch.

A variety of sports has made use of a scratch in the ground. In athletics, it serves as the starting line for runners, and it has its specific place in prize fighting. In its application to the rebuilding of a destroyed career or property, the saying comes from horse racing. In England a scratch race denotes a type in which the horses start not from gates but from a scratch, responsible for the name. Any horse can be entered, irrespective of its age or whether it has been handicapped by weight when having won previous races. To win, the horse and jockey have to rely completely on their own ability. And does not this equally apply to the race of life, particularly when having to start all over again – from scratch?

Bitter End

Is the end not always bitter?

Everyone agrees that to stick to something 'to the bitter end' shows character. However, not so unanimous are the opinions as to the beginning of the phrase. It may well be a combination of strands. Undoubtedly, it brings to mind the end of Socrates, the Greek philosopher. Determined to abide by the laws of his country, though strongly disagreeing with them, he emptied a cup of hemlock to its bitter end.

Those acquainted with the Bible may recall the passage in the Book of Proverbs (5,4) that cites a father's warning to his son, 'Beware of the honeyed words of a seductive woman', whose own end was 'as bitter as wormwood'. Knowing the Scriptures' influence on western tongues, the simile must have greatly contributed to the popularisation of the phrase, which, however, like much of life itself, goes back to the sea.

'Bitt' is the nautical name of a post (one of a pair) on the deck of a ship to which a cable is attached. When the cable is played out completely, it certainly is at the *bitt*er's end. It has reached the point beyond which it cannot go. Except in language. Sailors brought the bitter end home from the sea, where it became the telling phrase of finality it is now.

Madame Tussaud's Waxworks Museum In London

What is the background of this unique museum?

'Madame Tussaud' is a name of world renown. It perpetuates the work of a Swiss modeller in wax and the exhibition she created, now a landmark in the heart of London. It also shows how strange circumstances can 'mould' people's lives.

Born as Marie Grosholtz in 1760, in 1795 she married a wine grower by the name of François Tussaud, only remembered through his wife's work.

Marie's uncle was a Dr Curtius. Practising in the Swiss city of Bern, he specialised in making wax models of his patients' organs and limbs. He did so to help him in diagnosing their illnesses and in studying the human body generally. In the process, he developed a special skill and his medical research became an artistic hobby. Away from sickbeds, he started to produce miniature replicas of his friends.

Prince di Conti, a cousin of Louis XVI, the French king, became his patron and invited him to come to Paris. There Curtius gave up medicine altogether, devoting himself entirely to his art of making wax figures, not least lifelike replicas of people of renown. Indeed, among his models were the truly famous, including Voltaire and Benjamin Franklin.

Dr Curtius's sister, together with Marie, her little daughter, had accompanied her brother to Paris. It did not take long for Marie to reveal a remarkable aptitude for her uncle's work. This did not go unnoticed, with the result that she was asked by Elisabeth, the king's sister, to teach her the art. In no time the two young women became close friends, and for the ensuing nine years Marie stayed at the palace as a royal guest.

At the outbreak of the French Revolution her royal connection immediately put Marie under suspicion, resulting in her imprisonment (she even shared a cell with the future Empress Joséphine). However, it was her gift of modelling that led to her release. As a trade-off, so to speak, for gaining her freedom, she was to make wax masks of the heads of both the leaders and especially of the unfortunate victims of the revolution (including her former employers, King Louis XVI and Queen Marie Antoinette). She was later to recall her horrendous task when being forced to use the severed heads of the latter – fresh from the guillotine.

Her uncle had died in 1795 and few of her former friends had survived. Perhaps out of loneliness she then married Tussaud, who at the time was a soldier. However, their marriage did not last long. In 1802, abandoning François, she moved to London, taking with her her two sons. (According to other reports it was actually her husband who left her.) From Paris she also transferred her exhibits, losing no time in displaying her wax effigies all over Britain. Attracting vast crowds, she went from success to success. The addition of a 'Chamber of Horrors', thanks to people's love of the macabre, made her show all the more popular.

'Madame Tussaud's' had its ups and downs. Some of its outstanding models, for instance, got lost during a storm whilst being shipped for an exhibition to Ireland. In 1925 the collection, by then permanently housed in Marylebone Road, London, and containing more than 400 figures, burnt down. But the descendants of its creator rebuilt the museum, which became a unique place to visit. It has remained so ever since, perpetuating the name of Madame Tussaud, who herself had died in 1850, at ninety years of age.

Face The Music

Why does one have to face music when having done something wrong?

Whoever has done something wrong must be prepared to be reprimanded and to accept the consequences of their misdemeanour. In short, they have 'to face the music'.

This strange figure of speech may be the result of various circumstances. It may well be associated with a military practice in connection with the cashiering of a soldier. His dishonourable dismissal took the form of a public spectacle, possibly as a warning to others. He had to face the military band which drummed him out. To the very last, even in his disgrace, he had to show military bearing.

There was nothing discreditable in the facing of the music in the way it started, according to another claim. It was part of the training of army horses. They had to learn to stay calm under all conditions. No noise – whether it was the booming of guns, battle cries or the striking up of the band – must upset them. To teach them resistance, they had to 'face the music'.

Completely divorced from the army is a third theory. This places the origin of the phrase not on the battlefield or the parade ground, but on the stage. No matter how nervous actors are, they must not show it to the audience. They must play their part without the slightest sign of stage fright. In their performance they have to 'face the music' of the orchestra (situated in front of them, just below the stage), intrepidly.

Saved By The Bell

Who owes his escape to a bell and why?

That anyone escaping defeat or misfortune by the narrowest margin or at the very last moment is said to be 'saved by the bell' is generally traced to the boxing ring. It originally referred to a situation when one of the contestants, on the verge of being beaten, is spared this fate because at that very moment the ringing of the bell announces the end of the round. However, the phrase has also been linked with a much earlier occasion, the striking of a famous church bell in an incident of the seventeenth century.

A sentry on night duty at Windsor Castle was accused of having been asleep, a capital offence at the time. He was court-martialled, but at the trial firmly denied the charge. In defence, he recalled that he had, in fact, heard St Paul's bell ring the hour at midnight, but oddly (he distinctly remembered) doing so by striking thirteen times!

His claim was dismissed as a fiction of his mind, a dream or a clever ruse to save his life. Apart from the fact that the considerable distance of Windsor from London made it most unlikely that he had heard the chimes, the bizarre allegation that there were thirteen chimes seemed incredible. Consequently, the court condemned the soldier to death. But when news of the sentence reached London, and with it the sentry's assertion, Londoners confirmed his testimony. On that very night St Paul's had chimed not twelve but thirteen hours! Thus, 'saved by the bell', he was set free.

Not Worth His Salt

What role does salt play in daily speech?

Already in antiquity in many parts of the world people realised the value of salt. It was one of the necessities of life, for which reason Roman soldiers did not receive money for their services but were paid in salt. A precious substance, it was essential for their nourishment and helped in maintaining their strength and good health. The practice explains the very meaning of the word 'salary'. It is derived from *sal*, the Latin for 'salt'!

The realisation of the value of salt was responsible for many well-known figures of speech. People had to 'earn their salt'. Those renowned for their outstanding character and qualities were referred to as 'the salt of the earth'. It was no wonder therefore that the spilling of salt was regarded as unlucky. Irrespective of its superstitious roots in the occult, it constituted the loss of a valuable substance, treasured everywhere and, as it were, serving as international currency. It also explains why people not doing their job properly are said to be 'not worth their salt'.

Bread And Salt For A New Home

Why does one give bread and salt as a gift?

It is a well-known tradition to bring to those who have moved into a new home a gift of bread and salt. A strange custom which has puzzled many, it has a deep and significant meaning. Salt, apart from being one of the indispensable needs of life (even instinctively realised in the animal world) also adds flavour to food. Equally significant, it fulfils yet another important role in serving as a preservative. Bread, on the other hand, figuratively and literally has been called 'the staff of life', with all that this description implies.

As a moving-in gift the message of bread and salt is more valuable than any expensive present to the occupiers of a new home. Symbolically, it expresses the wish that the home may never be short of the essentials of life nor lack the qualities that give genuine and lasting enjoyment. Quite possibly, it all started in an ancient belief that those gifts would magically ensure that these very qualities would be a permanent feature in the recipients' new abode.

Bribery

What does the word actually stand for?

Originally, a bribe had nothing to do with an offer, particularly of money, in expectation of a special favour. It referred simply to a lump of bread given to a beggar, with no strings attached. But the practice, and the word, degenerated, and 'bribe' is now understood to mean a corrupt inducement.

During the Middle Ages, wandering friars depended on alms for their sustenance. They would call on homes to ask for food. Acknowledging the gift, the mendicants (by which name they became known) promised, in return, to say a special prayer for the provider.

Many times, no doubt, the donors acceded to the request not out of compassion and charity but for selfish reasons. They hoped to gain God's blessings through the friar's supplication, so that he ended up paying for the gift after all. This is how the modern bribe came into being.

At Sixes And Sevens

What is the meaning of this odd saying?

Those experiencing a state of confusion or unable to come to an agreement are said to be 'at sixes and sevens'. The odd figure of speech has been traced to pilgrims on their way to Canterbury. Chaucer tells how they whiled away their long journey with games of dice. These were said to have included higher numbers than those used nowadays. To roll for a six or a seven was most hazardous. Only someone who lacked self-discipline and was of an irresponsible disposition would venture 'at sixes and sevens'.

To confuse the issue further another claim suggests that it all started in the City of London, at one of its auspicious events. In the annual procession of Guilds, an unpleasant dispute arose between the Skinners and Master Tailors. Each claimed the right to precede the other and, as the sixth in line (and in status), immediately to follow the Goldsmiths. They were truly 'at sixes and sevens'. In 1484, a typical British compromise finally resolved the acrimonious rivalry. The then Lord Mayor decreed that the two Guilds were to take precedence in alternate years.

Ice Cream

Who first produced it?

To the Chinese belongs the credit of having been the first to make ice cream, at least 3000 years ago. Different from the present day, it then consisted of flavoured snow or what could be likened to the 'shaved ice' of modern times. They learnt to conserve ice collected in winter for the summer season when nature did not provide them with the substance, ingeniously storing it in so-called 'ice houses'.

Roman emperors were said to have enjoyed their own kind of 'iced treat': flavoured ice with fruit. A luxury then, and regarded as exotic, it belonged exclusively to the royal table. The ice itself was obtained from the Alps, with slaves being ordered to fetch it from there. Certainly apocryphal is the story that Nero had not only a penchant for arson and fiddles (of which the latter, of course, in reality did not exist at his time), but also for eating snow with honey.

It was Marco Polo, the explorer, who in circa 1290 brought with him back from the East a recipe for making ice cream, introducing the latter to Italy. Her people have never been surpassed in the art. From Italy, the frozen delicacy then found its way to France, to gain popularity there, initially as water ice, but eventually (in the eighteenth century) as dairy ice cream. When first produced by the owner of a famous Parisian coffee house, it was served there on silver dishes as 'iced butter'.

Ice cream remained unknown in England till the seventeenth century. A first mention of it (as 'iced cream') appeared in the *London Gazette* in 1688. As the name indicated, to start with, the dish was (heated up) cream that, enriched with some sweetening, was placed on a bed of ice. Cooled down, it was enjoyed as – literally – ice*d* cream.

The first American record of ice cream goes back to 1744. A report in the *Pennsylvania Magazine of History* of that year recorded the existence of 'fine ice cream which, with strawberries and milk' provided a delicious dish.

For many years ice cream was exclusively made in homes. It was only in 1851 that a milk merchant in Baltimore, USA, conceived the idea of mass producing, and with it, commercialising it. He could thus be regarded as the first in the world to have established an ice cream factory. However, it was only the advent of mechanical refrigeration in the late nineteenth century that led to the major industrial production of the sweet that, ever since, has never lost its appeal.

Spuds

Who was responsible for bringing the tuber to Europe and from where?

Humans are creatures of habit. They frown upon and suspect anything that is new. When in 1585 Sir Francis Drake brought the potato from America, the English shunned the strange tuber. For a long time, in fact, they decried it as a dangerously unhealthy vegetable.

Food fanatics, the story goes, went so far as to establish special associations to warn and discourage the population from eating it. They called themselves the *S*ociety for the *P*revention of *U*nwholesome *D*iets. Too much of a mouthful to be remembered, they soon were referred to colloquially by their initials alone, as the SPUDs. It did not take long for their name to be identified with the potato itself.

This is a mere story, an apocryphal anecdote. The real, linguistic root of the spud is the instrument used to dig it up! A short knife, generally employed as a weeding tool, was known as a spudde. And out of it, slightly shortened, grew the (potato) spud!

Have The Willies

Who is this scary Willie?

The reason why something that gives one the 'willies' means one gets the creeps is a puzzling problem. Numerous attempts have been made to explain the odd description of a state of alarm, jitters or supreme agitation. What or who is it that fills us with such dread? Most suggestions link the idiom with some individual called Willie, the mere mention of whose name causes this fearful state of mind. And yet, who was the mysterious Willie originally referred to remains a puzzle. According to one source it relates to Canadian humorist Stephen Leacock's line 'Willie is no good, I'll sell him'. Whoever it was, the Willie in question and responsible for all the consternation must have been a frightful character and perhaps it is all for the best that his real identity is still a mystery and left to pure guesswork.

Bankrupt

Anyone going broke is bankrupt. How and where did the saying originate?

In modern parlance, money merchants who had no cash left to repay creditors would have to close their bank. In the days when they transacted their business on a counter in the open, the original 'bank', this 'bench' was broken up. That is how they became 'bank-rupt', which created the now merely figurative expression of 'going bankrupt'. At the time their broken bench indicated their insolvency. The practice also survives in people's colloquial description of those without money as 'broke'.

Seventeenth-century Britain required bankrupts to walk about in special clothing. It was easy thus to recognise persons who were not credit-worthy. This had a dual purpose: it made them pay off their debt as quickly as possible and saved tradespeople from suffering a loss by doing business with them.

Public outcry against the custom made authorities discontinue it generally in 1688. For some time, however, it continued to be enforced on those convicted of fraudulent bankruptcy.

Traffic Lights

What is the story of this mechanical traffic control?

There is a reason for everything, even for the red, amber and green traffic lights. The choice of their colours, later internationally adopted, was not arbitrary. It was the result of traditions, careful considerations and experience.

Traffic lights were first introduced on railways – the American railroads. Their application and adaptation to the road came only later.

Today the colours on traffic lights are taken for granted. Few people realise the amount of deliberation and the various factors that led to their selection. To begin with, fundamental conditions had to be met.

- The colours had to be recognised easily, quickly and unmistakably.
- This had to be possible from a considerable distance and while in motion.
- The quality, intensity and contrast of the colours had to be such that they served their purpose in all weather, day and night.

As for the choice of the individual colours best-suited to convey the essential information, some seemed to be 'preselected'. Certain colours were traditionally linked with the very purpose they were now meant to serve. Almost from antiquity their association had prepared them to express to the modern age of speed the command to stop, to pay heed, or to go 'full steam' ahead.

Red for 'Stop'

Red was an obvious choice for 'stop'. It had always represented danger. Fire was red; people had learnt early on to keep a safe distance from it lest they be burnt. Blood was red; to shed it brought death. It is no wonder therefore that red became associated with emergency and with danger. Native tribes in many parts of the world made use of red to give warning and strike terror. The Incas in ancient Peru, for instance, made their messengers carry red beads when they wished to give warning of war.

Hence red was best qualified because of the constant battle for life. In addition, in the prism of hues it was vivid and distinct.

White for 'Go'

Although 'to give the green light' has become the proverbial permissive signal in many a situation, green was not the original choice for 'go'. White had been the first colour to indicate that the railroad was safe and that the train could proceed without danger. After all, white had always been regarded, though unscientifically so, as a pure and clear colour. Consequently, in the language of symbolism it came to express purity. Therefore it was not surprising either that initially it was decided to make it the signal that the line was 'clear'.

Other factors favoured the choice as well. A white light was the most easily produced. It was a 'natural', without the need of paint or other colouring aids. Like red for danger, it seemed the obvious selection.

'Caution'

At first two lights were to control the running of trains: white for 'go' and red for 'stop'. It was then realised that safety would be served better still by introducing a 'cautionary' light to warn the driver of an imminent change. Its colour once again was to be determined by considerations of contrast, distinctiveness and visibility. The eventual choice was green.

At a meeting of railway officials in Birmingham, England, in 1841, it was finally agreed to make red, green and white the standard signals for 'danger', 'caution' and 'go ahead'.

Green for 'Go'

It did not take long for 'white' to prove the wrong colour for 'go'. Bitter experience taught that it was far from ideal. In fact, it could prove fatal. And for a very pertinent reason. At that early stage, kerosene lamps served as the source of light. Any colour other than white was produced by fixing a coloured glass plate in front of the lamp.

It sometimes happened that the glass plate was smashed or just fell off. In either case the red warning light instantaneously changed into the white 'go ahead'. An approaching train then had no apparent reason to stop. Full steam ahead it would rush on, with possible disastrous consequences.

White had proved unsuitable also for another reason that could cause confusion, if not a collision. After all, the white lamps were not the exclusive property of railways or used as traffic signals alone. They served generally, and in an ever greater number, as a source of illumination during night. Therefore how easily could it happen that those in charge of a train could mistake a kerosene lamp put up to shed light as their signal telling them that the 'road' was clear? As 'green' had already proved its value in clarity and noticeability, it was now appropriated to replace the faulty white.

Indeed, people must have wondered why no one had thought of it previously. Green, after all, was a 'natural' colour. It was the hue of all foliage and growing things. Environmentally, it spelt out life, safety and normality. Like the green sap in a plant, it was symbolic of motion, drive and vitality. Therefore, from the very beginning it should have been the obvious colour for signalling permission to proceed. Thus green found its rightful place in the scheme of traffic lights. All that was needed now was to find a replacement colour to caution drivers. The second and final choice fell on yellow or amber.

That is how green, yellow and red became the standard combination of colours for railroad signals. The New York, New Haven and Hartford Railroad, USA, was the first to introduce them in 1899.

The increase of road traffic in cities necessitated its regulation. Policemen on point duty did a good job, but soon were outnumbered by intersections demanding attention. It became clear that only mechanical aids could solve the problem. The traffic authorities did not have to go far in their search. They simply adopted and adapted – though very gradually and even before their final standardisation – the ready-made and well-tried system of railroad signals. The way this was done has many an intriguing feature, at times not lacking in drama.

In England, primary consideration was given to members of parliament! To help them safely across the street to reach the Houses of Parliament, the Metropolitan Commissioner of Police in London had the first lights installed at a 'danger spot' nearby. It was a revolving gas-lit lantern mounted on a pole almost seven metres high that indicated the red and the green (the latter then still being used for 'caution'). A policeman stationed at its base controlled it by turning a lever. These 'lights' were inaugurated on 10 December 1868. No one then guessed the hazard they presented. On 2 January 1869, the gas container supplying the lights with fuel exploded, badly injuring the policeman.

One of the world's first electric traffic lights was developed in 1912 in Salt Lake City, Utah, USA, by Lester Wire, a detective on the city police force. A wooden box with a slanted roof, the lights were coloured with red and green dye and shone through circular openings. The box was mounted on a pole and the wires were attached to the overhead trolley and light wires. It was manually operated. Cleveland, Ohio, adopted a more elaborate electric signal in 1914, which became the prototype of all modern systems. Its two colours (red and green) could be controlled both by hand or by an automatic timer. They were supplemented by warning buzzers. These could still easily be heard, as traffic then was not as deafening as it is nowadays. The number of buzzes – one or two – indicated the direction.

In 1918, New York City put up the first automatic, three-coloured lights. Britain followed suit as late as 1926 with a still manually-operated set in the West End of London. The first English automatic lights were installed – as a one-day experiment – in the following year at a busy intersection in Wolverhampton, a town in Staffordshire, northwest of Birmingham. The test proved so successful that within a month the new lights were adopted in Leeds, and subsequently in Edinburgh, to become eventually and inevitably a common and essential feature of traffic control everywhere.

Bark Up The Wrong Tree

Why is it said of those on the wrong track that they 'bark up the wrong tree'?

Dogs used in the chasing of raccoons, chiefly undertaken at night, were trained to indicate the tree in which the animal, running for its life, had taken refuge, by barking at it. But, of course, even dogs can err and at times they 'barked up the wrong tree'.

Well-Heeled And Down At Heel

What is the reason for anyone well off to be referred to as 'well-heeled' and anyone badly off as 'down at heel'?

Although so small in size, the heel – the back of the human foot – has played a not insignificant role in diverse ways by its contribution to everyday speech and life. As part of footwear, the heel has been used to give greater stature to people of little significance and lacking height. Going in the opposite direction, linguistically it served as a term of abuse by calling a cad a 'heel'.

Through the well-known Greek myth the 'Achilles heel' became a metaphor for a vulnerable spot, the weakest part in any situation. People running off are said to 'take to their heels', whilst those determined not to budge, but to stand their ground, 'dig in their heels'.

Most shoes have heels, to give more comfort when walking. Naturally, in the course of time, by a process of attrition, these become worn down, eventually needing repair or even replacement. Easily done for the ordinary person, those out of luck and lacking the necessary means, however, are unable to replace their damaged footwear or at least have it mended, obliging them, literally, to walk about 'down at heel'. Not surprisingly, this description of the poor state of shoes or boots became synonymous with impoverishment. Thus used, the phrase became current early in the 1700s.

It could easily be surmised that, conversely, speaking of anybody as being 'well-heeled' applied to those well off and prosperous. They never had the need to walk about shabby.

The origin of the 'well-heeled', however, goes far beyond the observation of a person's being prosperous and well off generally. The expression may have its roots in either of two totally different aspects in the history of civilisation. It might go back to the sorry state of the public roads, when these were muddy and filthy. To protect their feet and shoes from being soiled, members of the upper classes – both men and women – then wore high heels or their equivalent in the form of platform shoes, fashionable in the 1500s. The high heels raised them, both symbolically and conspicuously, above citizens of inferior social status.

Completely different again, the alternate theory traces the term to cockfighting, a sport popular both in the United States and Britain in the eighteenth century. With cocks pitted against each other in the original 'cockpit', the spectators made bets as to which of the contestants would be the winner. Prior to the fight, the owners of the individual roosters had sharp spurs fixed to their rooster's heels to make the bird more formidable and deadly in its attack. A well-heeled bird, no doubt, would prove superior indeed and, by defeating its opponent, earn its backers a considerable sum of money – a twofold reason to give 'well-heeled' its present-day meaning, far removed from the dirty roads hypothesis.

Swan Song

Do swans really sing when about to die?

Poetically, the last performance of great artists is known as their 'swan song'. This romantic figure of speech goes back to ancient legend, according to which a dying swan bursts forth in glorious song.

Greek myth featured the swan as Apollo's bird. It is no wonder therefore that the god endowed it with a magnificent voice. It is equally not surprising that the bird joyfully used it at its very best at the moment of death, when about to join its master who, after all, had so blessed it.

Swans, of course, never sing. Although, almost 2000 years ago, in his *Natural History* the Roman writer Pliny had pointed out the fallacy, his words went unheeded. Poets and dramatists, once again among them Shakespeare, continued to give credence to the myth and to perpetuate it in their works. Because of their authority, its authenticity was seldom doubted.

There might be a rational explanation for the fanciful swan song. People were mystified by the weird, prolonged death rattle the dying bird produced, when its expiring breath slowly passed through its elongated windpipe. People have always given much thought to death and dying. Piously, if not wishfully, they felt that it need not be destructive or tragic. In fact nothing had to be feared. They therefore beautified those last moments of passing away – whether from the public eye or from the stage of life. They imagined they could hear a jubilant note in the generally terrifying sound of death, thus creating the swan song. It made Byron express the wish of most people, 'Swanlike, let me sing and die.'

Blow Hot And Cold

How is it possible to do both simultaneously?

People who vacillate in their opinions and quickly change from being enthusiastic to showing disinterest are said to 'blow hot and cold'.

The saying can be traced to one of Aesop's *Fables*. This tells of an encounter between a wayfarer and a satyr, the Greek woodland deity portrayed as a human with animal features.

It was a cold winter's day, and the freezing traveller was blowing on his stiff fingers. Mystified, the satyr wanted to know what he was doing. The man explained to him that with his breath he was warming his chilled fingers.

Taking pity on him, the satyr invited the man to his home for a hot meal. This time, he watched him blowing on the food, which intrigued him all the more. Inquiring why he did so, his guest explained that he was blowing on the stew to cool it down.

The satyr told the traveller to leave at once. He was not prepared to entertain or ever mix with anyone who could 'blow hot and cold from the same mouth'.

Bunyip

What is really known about this mysterious creature?

A multitude of grotesque features is attributed to the bunyip, that legendary Australian creature. Called by other names by different Aboriginal tribes, these include those of a 'spirit' and a 'devil-devil'. The subject of numerous folk tales and traditions, it was said to haunt water holes (the Australian billabong), the bottom of deep rivers, creeks and swamps.

Of fantastic appearance, it has been variously described to be enormous in size, long-necked with the head of a dog, a horse or an emu, and with a bovine tail. Its body was alleged to be covered with fur, feathers or long, shining, jet black hair. Its eyes were said to glow like live coals, and it had tusks, resembling those of a walrus, protruding from its jaws. Its voice sounded like a penetrating bark or a small explosion.

Although at times compared with the mysterious Loch Ness monster, the bunyip differed from it in significant ways. Whilst the Scottish creature seemed to be shy and benign in nature, the Australian amphibian had the reputation of being a man-eater, out to catch young children to devour them, but particularly fancying indigenous women.

The bunyip did not remain exclusively the subject of Aboriginal myth. European colonists and even scientists also claimed to have caught sight of the mysterious being. They did so in various parts of Australia, especially (as early as in 1801) in the Bathurst area.

A notable claim, made by Hamilton Hume, the famous explorer (after whom the highway between Sydney and Melbourne is named), is recorded in the minutes of a meeting by the Philosophical Society of Australasia, held in Sydney on 19 December 1921. It states that at the gathering, Hume had asserted the existence of such an odd creature, resembling a hippopotamus and residing in Lake Bathurst. At the time, the Society promised to recompense Hume for all expenses he would incur in obtaining a specimen of this weird animal, naturally presumed to be a bunyip.

One of the many other incidents and stories linked with the bunyip relates to the 'Three Sisters', the famous rock formation in the Blue Mountains at Katoomba in New South Wales. Originally, these had been three beautiful young girls. To save them from a fearsome and ferocious bunyip that was roaming in the valley below, their father had magically turned them into stone!

After 1850, the bunyip entered the Australian vocabulary. Sydneysiders thus used it to dub an imposter, a fake and a humbug. In 1853 the bunyip even became part of politics as the nickname given to William Charles Wentworth's proposal to create a colonial peerage as part of a new Constitution for New South Wales, a nobility equalling the British class of hereditary titled Lords and Ladies. His project was strongly opposed by the public, who ridiculed it as an absurd attempt at establishing a 'bunyip aristocracy', with the result that it proved abortive.

Trying to ascertain the true identity of the bunyip, it was thought most likely that it was actually a seal (fur seal and bear seal have been suggested) which, one way or another, found its way inland from the sea to become the subject of the bunyip legend. Alternatively, it has been surmised that the animals were stray and bogged cattle which by their bellowing cries had frightened the natives.

Real or imaginary, if nothing else, the bunyip came to serve also the role of a bogeyman. So strange a creature, it was truly fit to frighten naughty children, and make them conform and obey their elders.

Russian Wedding Ring

Is this ring indigenously Russian?

Several explanations have been given for the so-called Russian wedding ring, a combination of three intertwined rings, each of a different coloured gold.

It has been seen as symbolising the Holy trinity, the central dogma of Christian theology which occupies a prominent place in Russian Orthodox Church rituals. The sacrament of holy matrimony was solemnised in the name of the Holy Trinity, thus the triple ring would constantly remind the couple of the sanctity of their union.

According to a second explanation, two of the rings represented the bride and groom being joined in marriage, while the third one stood for the witness whose presence legalised their bond in perpetuity. Various methods were used for joining the three bands. One way was to interweave the rings. Alternatively, they were held together by a pair of clasped hands. This was reminiscent of the 'handfasting' custom that once was part of a betrothal, the confirmation of the marriage agreement with a handshake.

There is also the claim that, in its present form, the Russian wedding ring was designed as late as 1923 by Cartier, the internationally renowned jewellers. It was to be yet another of their distinctive creations, in which they adopted and made use of an ancient tradition, rendering it in their own exquisite style.

Bring Home The Bacon

Why just the bacon and no other food?

The state of matrimony has always had its ups and downs. To encourage couples to care for each other and not to quarrel, a strange custom developed in Great Dunmow, one of the many attractive towns in East Anglia, England.

For years this became the scene of a mock trial, at which a flitch of bacon was presented to any couple 'who have not had a brawl in their home nor wished to be unmarried for the last twelve months and a day'. Whoever received the award was privileged to 'bring home the bacon'. This is the origin of the phrase. In the fourteenth century Chaucer referred to the tradition as firmly established. Over a period of more than five centuries (between 1244 and 1772), the flitch was won, it is said, only eight times.

In later years, the phrase was applied as well to the winner in a contest at country fairs. The competitors vied with each other to catch a greased pig – then to take it home as the prize.

Mae West

How did an actress take to the air and sea?

Fame is short-lived and often even those who once made the headlines ultimately are forgotten. Not so Mae West, the one-time idol of film-goers, attracting vast crowds. Although she passed away (at the age of eighty-eight) in 1980, her name has remained one of renown. However, not necessarily as the name of the popular American actress did 'Mae West' gain perpetuity, but as that of an appliance called after her and responsible for the survival of numerous airmen, forced to bale out over water.

Her name was immortalised by a gift with which nature had endowed her: a buxom figure, distinguished by an eye-catching and most generous bust. It is not surprising therefore that when, in World War II, the British air force adopted the inflatable life jacket, blown up, it reminded the airmen of Miss West's bulging breasts! It was no wonder that they came to call this life-saving pneumatic contraption, after her, a Mae West. The acknowledgment was well merited.

When Miss West first heard of the peculiar use of her name she wondered, having been so far merely included in the transient Who's Whos of the time, how now (in 1943) on becoming part of the dictionary, permanently enriching the language, *the* Mae West would be defined. Was it as 'a warm, clinging life-saving garment worn by aviators' or as 'an aviator's jacket that supplied a woman's touch while the boys were flying around at night'?

French Leave

Why is unauthorised leave described as 'French leave'?

The military practice of taking French leave is a telling example of how language reflects prejudice and how national antagonism can linger, even when former foes have become close friends. The British and the French, renowned allies in World Wars I and II, used to fight each other previously, on and off, throughout a period of more than 800 years, ever since 1066. Englishmen thus (just as in the case of the Dutch) chose to describe as 'French' practices and phenomena they wanted to denigrate. Syphilis was known in England as 'the French pox' and a condom was called a 'French letter'. For the same reason, Englishmen came to refer to soldiers' unauthorised absence from the army as 'taking French leave'. Certainly, this was not typical of the French, and most unfair. Frenchmen, to retaliate, did so in kind and called such conduct 'to leave like an Englishman'.

However, it is generally believed that 'French leave' did not originate in the army and therefore, initially, was not a military colloquialism. It was a reflection by the English on seventeenth-century French 'etiquette'. Guests on leaving a party were then not expected to say good-bye formally to their host. They just made their exit. Englishmen, aware of the custom, regarded it as utterly rude and unbecoming to a gentleman. Contemptuously they decried it as 'taking French leave'.

Bugbear

What actually is this creature with a name combining two animals?

A bugbear is something that causes alarm and frightens people beyond reason. No wonder that at one time the mere mention of it scared disobedient children.

A potent factor in rendering the term so effective, no doubt, is its background, which combines several traditions. Etymologically, it joined the ominous 'bug' that flies at night (mentioned in the Psalms) with a bear, the animal dreaded for its ferocity. The bugbear became a figure of English folklore, a goblin, a terrifying monster that haunted people.

Whilst a bear was known to all, the bug itself presented a mysterious being. Its name might well be derived from the Welsh *bwg* (so unpronounceable to the non-Welsh) for a 'spectre', a 'phantom', a 'ghost'. Like the bogeyman, it came to play the role of a 'bugaboo', the description of both a dreaded creature and, supposedly, an old Irish war-cry, so appropriately ending with the frightening 'boo'!

Skid Row

Why is a place where derelicts hang out so called?

Logging was hard work and did not end with the actual felling of trees. Often, from the heights, the giant logs had to be transported down to the waterfront to be floated or to be loaded onto boats. To facilitate their movement, small logs were laid transversely along the route. These 'skids', as they were called, were greased with oil, to make the logs slide all the more easily down the track.

The loggers referred to the route along which the timber was thus pulled (whether by manpower, bullock team or, eventually, mechanically) as the 'skid road'.

All along the way, but particularly so at its terminus, the skid road attracted all sorts of people. Some came just to watch and to idle away their time, others, to sell wares of many kinds to the timbermen who, especially at the end of the day, were only too ready to relax and have some fun.

In no time, bars and brothels had opened up. It was this final development that made the skid road synonymous with sordidness and vice. Soon it became the description of the most dilapidated section of a town, the meeting place of the 'down and outs'. As if to descend to its low level, even the name of the skid road slipped, to deteriorate into the present-day 'skid row'. Seattle, Washington, USA, is credited with having had the first of all skid rows, Yesler Way, along which, in the old logging days, the logs slithered down to Puget Sound. And it was the lumberjacks living along this route, it is claimed, who first called their settlement Skid Row.

Something Old, Something New, Something Borrowed, Something Blue

What is the background of this superstition, still followed by many brides?

Many a bride makes sure to wear on her wedding day:

Something old, something new,
Something borrowed, something blue.

She does so without realising the original magic and psychological significance of the practice. It was aimed at overcoming and resolving deeply-buried feelings, fears and superstitions at this so crucial moment in her life.

Primitive people believed that, just like every living being, every object had a soul. An item brought into close contact with the body, particularly so during the highly-charged occasion of a wedding, could exert strong occult power, with significant and lasting effect. Anything a bride wore, therefore, had to be thoughtfully chosen. She had to remember that her manner of dress might influence her entire future and with it, not least, her happiness. This accounts for the selection of something old, new, borrowed and blue. Each in its own way has a fascinating background and purpose.

However progressive, people have always been afraid of change. The old familiar way creates a feeling of security. Getting married inevitably breaks with the past. Starting a completely new phase of life thus is fraught with an awareness of uncertainty and its accompanying anxiety. To ensure her future, the bride, therefore, holds fast to 'something old'. It has proved its value and, reducing the element of novelty and insecurity, it will sustain her and make her start the marriage with confidence and happy anticipation, instead of with suppressed feelings of foreboding.

Paradoxically, in spite of their innate conservatism, humans also believe in the potency of novelty. 'Something new' is regarded as a bringer of luck. This explains why, for instance, people carefully retain, and even carry with them, a new coin that has come into their possession. They might not know it, but the original reason for it was the belief that its newness would make it a source of good fortune. Therefore, for a bride to wear 'something new' on her wedding day was not merely in keeping with the festive occasion or symbolic of her new status as a wife. Much more significantly, it was designed to act as a powerful bringer of happiness.

It was thought that an object that had been worn by a person during a deeply emotional experience would absorb, as it were, its radiation. Becoming saturated with the emotion, it would preserve and then magically transfer it to another wearer. This was responsible for the choice of 'something borrowed'. It had to be borrowed not just from anyone, but specifically from a woman who had once worn the very object at a moment of great joy. The bride expected, supernaturally, to secure for herself the blessing associated with it.

That is why frequently the veil once worn by her mother on her wedding day was among the most coveted items for 'something borrowed', while a bride would shun borrowing anything from a widowed friend. A contributing reason for merely loaning the item is rather obvious. No woman would part with something linked with her happiest day. She would not give such an article to the new bride 'for keeps', but merely loan it to her.

Protective magic and expressive symbolism account for the wearing of 'something blue'. This colour acquired its special meaning by a chain of associations. God was believed to dwell in heaven. Heaven was 'located' up in the sky. (Do not, to this day, people praying to him, look up?) The sky, when cloudless, is blue. Hence, the blue colour was identified with the divine and became symbolic of purity. Evil forces therefore would shun the colour. The bride was most vulnerable to them on her wedding day, as a focus of their evil intentions and jealousy. Thus she donned 'something blue'. Magically, it acted as a powerful shield that made the evil entities ready for attack turn around and flee.

The four 'somethings' of a simple rhyme and wedding custom, in their odd combination, thus perpetuate age-old concepts, scares and superstitions. No doubt, they are rooted in people's constant concern with and search for lasting happiness.

Pizza (Pie)

What is the story of this culinary speciality?

Coming in all varieties, the pizza (pie) is a filling and nourishing food, inexpensive to prepare and particularly loved by youngsters, possibly because of its piquant and spicy taste. Bread dough forms the base, which is topped with a colourful and flavourful mixture of tomatoes, onions, anchovies, sliced pieces of sausage, ham, green and red peppers, all covered with melted cheese. Today the ingredients are often far more exotic, blending cuisines from around the world.

Generally believed to have originated in Italy, how it was first produced there – in the city of Naples – and how it received its name is told in several versions.

Most popular is the (apocryphal) story that tells how necessity was the mother of its invention. A Neapolitan baker had run short of dough to make the traditional pie. There was not enough of it left for the upper crust. Ingeniously, he lined the tin with dough which, before baking it, he topped with chopped meat, cheese, anchovies, olives and such like. Unexpectedly, the end result proved so delicious that soon people clamoured for the novel pie, with its popularity spreading far and wide.

Some experts have denied the Italian source. They assert that the pizza goes back to much earlier times and different countries. The latter include Armenia, where traditionally people used to top a bread-like crust with minced lamb, and Morocco, where it was baked from seasoned yeast dough. Even the Holy Land and ancient Israel have been quoted as the birthplace of the pizza. Its forerunner there was the *Matzah,* the local unleavened flat bread eaten by the Jewish people, particularly as a religious symbol during their Feast of Passover. Roman soldiers who had been stationed in occupied Judea had found the unleavened Matzah too bland for their taste. To enhance it they added olive oil and spices and by doing so, according to this claim, created the earliest kind of pizza!

As for its name, this has been given a number of explanations. Some have related it to the medieval Greek *pitta*, for a 'cake'. Others have derived it from a simple tool, which was known as such and used by Italian bakers to decorate the edge of the pie by pressing it into the soft dough. This, the original pizza, etymologically was derived from *pizzicare* for 'to prick'. And what better choice of name was there by which to call the delicious pie than that of the very gadget employed to decorate its edge?

Alternatively, as *pizzicare* was also used to describe the act of 'extracting' or 'plucking', it was suggested (though not very convincingly) that in the case of the pizza pie, its name referred to the 'removal' of the piping hot bread from the baking oven.

Pizza Hut

How did the pizza get into a hut?

Pizza Huts – a proprietary name – can be found in almost every township, even in the smallest of hamlets. Their name is taken for granted and few would guess how – by mere chance (or oversight) – it came to be chosen. It happened in Wichita in the State of Kansas, USA, in 1958. Two enterprising local university students, the brothers Frank and Dan Carney, were eager to start a pizza parlour. Aware of the popularity of the food, it promised to be most profitable. Lacking the necessary funds, they obtained a loan from their mother, sufficient to embark on the venture. With the money they rented a property, located on a busy corner of their city and purchased (second-hand) the essential equipment for their new business.

Once ready for its opening, all that was still needed was a conspicuous signboard to draw the public's attention to the parlour. In large lettering it was to display PIZZA, the name of their goods. Somehow, whoever painted it did not centre it properly, with the result that it looked lopsided and the empty space left on one side needed filling in. There was room for a three-lettered word. In search for one, fitting the purpose, HUT came into their minds. And this is how the modern Pizza Hut was born.

Life Is Not All Beer And Skittles

Who coined this saying?

The pub has always been an integral part of British life. A meeting place for the people, they gather there to relax and enjoy themselves.

Innkeepers realised that the longer their guests stayed on the premises, the more they would drink. At the time, bowling, in the form of ninepins and known as skittles, was a favourite pastime. Thus, the proprietors of public houses wisely had bowling alleys and greens built adjacent to their establishments.

As an additional attraction, it greatly contributed to the happiness of the patrons and no less to the coffers of their host. 'Beer and skittles' came to express a lifestyle of delight and pleasure.

Sooner or later, however, people were to realise that life was 'not all beer and skittles'. The figure of speech was popularised by well-known poets and writers, and became so much a part of everyday language that it has outlived the game of ninepins that had played such a significant role in giving birth to it.

Eat Humble Pie

What is a humble pie?

No one likes to 'eat humble pie'. The phrase goes back to the early days of a very class-conscious society, though it actually does not mean what it appears to say.

There was no humility in that pie. Usually, the uneducated are said to drop their 'h's'. But the case of the humble pie is a telling example in which an 'h' was added – out of ignorance.

'Umbles' was once a common description of offal: the heart, the liver and the stomach of an animal. As umbles were not credited with much culinary merit, they were reserved to feed servants and the poor and made into a pie for them. Very appropriately and logically, this was known as an umbles pie.

When 'umbles' became an obsolete term and people no longer knew what it meant, they began to speak of 'eating humble pie', which has now become an expression relating to humility. Yet, in the way of speaking, it still contains 'leftovers' from those early offal days.

Pee'd Off

Why does one use this vulgar term for being frustrated?

This rather vulgar verbalisation of one's frustration is not as obscene an expression as at first it seems. It has nothing to do with the process of urinating, being 'pissed off'. 'Pee'd off' is merely a shortened form of 'peeved off'.

Earmark

What gave this term its distinctive meaning?

Strangely, the doorpost of a home became the source of an ordinary, everyday word of the English language: the verb 'to earmark'. Now totally detached from religion and completely secular in its connotation, its origin is biblical. The circumstance of its creation was the Jews' passion for freedom.

Ancient cultures regarded slavery as a natural institution. Those sold as slaves belonged to their master for the rest of their lives. Even to the civilised Greeks they were not human beings, but animated tools. But this was not the Jewish way of life. Jewish teaching saw in everyone a child of God. To enslave anyone was against its very principles. Yet to abolish slavery at once and altogether was practically an impossibility. The nature of human society necessitated a process of gradual weaning. Accordingly, Judaism decreed that no one should serve any other person as slave for more than six years, after which time, in the seventh year, their master had to release them unconditionally.

Jews never considered their slaves as chattel. They respected their human dignity and treated them with kindness and consideration. The position of Abraham's trusted slave, Eliezer, is an obvious example. No wonder, then, that frequently slaves felt a deep affection for their Jewish masters and, in the year of release, refused to go. It may be also that they had become used to their subordinate place and no longer wished to live independent and free lives. Judaism condemned such an attitude. For anyone to despise their hallowed right to be free was to deny their divine heritage. To emphasise this point the Bible introduced a special ceremony. The master of a slave who had lost the desire to be free had to lead the slave to the entrance of his home and there, against the doorpost, to pierce the slave's ear with an awl. This 'earmark' was to serve as the irremovable and perpetual sign of shame of someone who had refused their freedom.

The rabbis later explained that the choice of the ear was based on the fact that the slave had been deaf to the eternal command once heard by the Israelites on Mount

Sinai to be servants only to God. But the literal 'earmarking', losing completely its shameful content, became the origin of the figurative expression, which speaks of the assignment of anything to a definite purpose.

Birds' Song

Why do birds sing?

The song of birds is one of the most lovely sounds of nature. Nothing could be more beautiful than to wake up in the morning to birds' song. It has inspired people through the ages and made them wonder why birds sing.

Explanations have changed over the years and ranged from the realm of legend to the sphere of religion. Some have been highly imaginative and others strictly scientific. They have produced many a fallacy and it has been only in modern times that unexpected findings have been made.

Medieval society believed that birds joined in song first thing in the morning to praise God for the grandeur of nature with which He has blessed the world. More prosaically, in later generations it was suggested that their early song was meant as a welcome to the rising sun, with its implicit promise of a day of brightness, warmth and renewed life.

It is now assumed, however, that birds sing to fulfil two major functions. First of all, it is to stake out and protect their territory. Since it is their exclusive hunting ground, the song warns other birds not to trespass.

The second purpose is the perpetuation of the species. A bird sings when it is ready to mate. Broadcasting this fact by its song will attract a partner in the same physiological condition.

Contrary to popularly held belief, in the majority of cases it is not the female but the male who is the songster, sending out his message to the opposite sex.

Birds' songs offer a multiplicity of interesting observations and have been the source of not a few misconceptions. It is not correct that nightingales sing only at night. They do so during daytime as well, but other birds then also singing drown them out. Their song might therefore go unnoticed.

Surprisingly, birds have dialects and the song of the individual bird may differ in various regions of the world. On the other hand, each kind of bird has its own type of song which seems innate. Young cuckoos, for instance, even when hatched in the nests of other birds, will not acquire their song, but keep that of their own kind.

A bird's song must be differentiated from birds' calls. They have their individual sounds and specific messages. Among the variety of functions are the mother bird's call to 'round up' her stray brood, to help lost birds to find their way home, to express fear or to sound an alarm.

Dry Wine

What does the word 'dry' denote?

To speak of 'dry wine' at first seems a contradiction in terms. How could a drink ever be dry? Apart from its use in describing a lack of wetness, however, 'dry' has other meanings as well, all of which relate to some deficiency or absence. Dry bread is not buttered. A dry greeting is without warmth, and dry wine is light in flavour, without sweetness.

Line One's Pockets

To what sort of lining does this saying refer?

The giving of bribes may take many forms and so does the description of the (mal)practice. An actual incident, it is said, explains the phrase 'to line one's pockets'.

London-born dandy Beau Brummel led Britain in elegance for almost twenty years. An intimate friend of the then Prince of Wales, the later King George IV, another dandy, he set the fashion. Obviously, his patronage and recommendation carried much weight. To obtain them, and with it countless new customers, a certain tailor used devious means. He presented Brummel with a coat, having cleverly lined its pockets with money. In acknowledgment of the 'gift' Brummel sent the message that he very much approved of the coat, but particularly of the lining.

Go [or Get Off] Scot-Free

What part does Scotland play in this phrase?

Similarity of sound or, even more so, the use of the identical word for two completely different matters have been the cause of not a few misunderstandings or perplexing situations. 'To go [or get off] scot-free' is a telling example. To many it has seemed almost a paradox, a contradiction in terms. Undeservedly, the Scottish people have been calumniated as being mean or 'tight-fisted'. To speak of someone going scot-free therefore appears incomprehensible and unlikely.

Indeed, such (mis)interpretation is based on two striking fallacies. The Scots have never been mean. They have always excelled through their strength of character, industry and intelligence. A persecuted race, they have learnt to make the most of the least which, not unlikely, was responsible for their respect for education and their excelling in many fields, leading to their considerable contributions to civilisation.

Secondly, the 'scot' in 'scot-free' has no link with Scotland or anything Scotch or Scottish. Its linguistic root is the Old Norse *skot* for 'a contribution', the equivalent of the Old English *sceot*. Persons going scot-free thus were exempted from payment, whether in the form of a contribution such as a tax or a levy, or retribution in the way of a penalty or punishment. They got away for free, avoiding or being spared paying their debt to the authorities or society.

Escape

What is the root of this word?

Some of the simplest of words have an unexpected explanation which, if known, makes them all the more striking and meaningful. This applies to 'escape'.

Combining the Latin *es* or *ex* for 'out of' and *cappa* for 'cape', it recalls ancient Roman days and the Roman pursuit of justice. Many a culprit, having been arrested for an offence, succeeded in getting away by 'slipping out of his cape' – he 'escaped'.

Give Short Shrift

What is the origin of this saying?

To give short shrift to anyone does not let them have much time. It cuts very short whatever there is left for them to do or, originally, even the time left for them to live.

'Shriving' was the archaic term for the Church rite of confession and absolution. It is still recalled in the name of Shrove Tuesday. Being the last day before the long fast of Lent, the faithful went to confession; they were 'shriven'.

'To give short shrift' refers to this very religious act, but in the most morbid of circumstances. Prior to their execution, criminals condemned to death were given the opportunity of confessing their sins to a priest. Since in medieval times even minor offences carried a capital punishment, the axe and the gallows were kept busy and with it the executioner. More concerned with himself than the felons' fate and last moments, he was anxious to get through his work fast. Resenting the slightest delay, he did not leave much time for someone's last confession. Hurried on his way to eternity, the condemned was urged to make haste in telling the priest of his evil ways and asking God for his forgiveness. Indeed, he was given (a) 'short shrift'.

A Thorn In One's Side

Should this saying not really be self-explanatory?

To have 'a thorn in one's side' is a painful experience. To trace the phrase to its original source may lead in completely different directions.

Most likely, it goes back to St Paul. A well-travelled man, he had seen much. To appeal to the masses, he had learnt to use common metaphors, often chosen from daily life. An experience not rare at the time among those travelling on foot along narrow paths was to brush against bushes. A thorn might thus easily get stuck in their flesh and, starting to fester, cause much pain.

That is how people came to speak of 'a thorn in one's side'. In his Letters to the Corinthians (II,12,7) St Paul relates how, possibly to save him from becoming unduly elated, he experienced severe physical pain. Adapting the popular phrase, he described it as 'a thorn in the flesh'. And as the Apostle's words were greatly heeded and became part of the Christian Bible, his figure of speech became proverbial.

Nevertheless, the 'thorn' may have grown in different soil and be associated not with the early history of the Church, but with pagan superstition.

Husbands have called their wives all sorts of names. The reasons for their choice may range from feelings of deep affection to extreme dislike. The men of some native tribes, the Tuyangs, for instance, never referred to their spouses by their individual names. They feared that in so doing, they would bring misfortune to their family. Instead, they used a general and most unkind term, 'the thorn in my ribs'. Taken literally, this certainly did not reflect favourably on their marriage, and yet to draw such a conclusion would be to misinterpret the circumstances.

The motivation for their choice was the exact opposite. They loved their wives so much that they feared that any expression of their true feelings would rouse the jealousy of evil spirits, at all times ready to destroy happiness. Their pretence of a painful relationship – like a thorn in their ribs – would not attract the attention of those malevolent forces. Thus, married bliss could continue.

As descriptive a phrase as 'a thorn in my ribs' could not go unnoticed. With the slight change from 'rib' to 'side', it caught on everywhere, though the thorn no longer stuck (in)to a spouse but to any kind of torment or anguish.

Crap

How long has 'crap' been in existence?

To 'crap' is to defecate and 'crap' as a noun refers to excrement. A vulgarism, often attributed to the Americans, it used to be shunned in polite society and should not be confused with 'shooting craps', a game of chance played by rolling dice, again particularly favoured by Americans.

The often tabooed 'crap' is of British origin, though its source there has been subject to controversy and a false claim. Wrongly, it was assumed to have been called after Thomas Crapper (1837–1910). An outstanding English sanitary engineer, in the 1870s he developed the first flushing water closet of its kind, the Crapper Valveless Water Waste Preventer. His biography (written by Wallace Reybury) was published in London in 1969 under the telling title *Flushed with Pride*. According to a reviewer, it gave ample evidence of a lasting contribution to human comfort. He could have added, if the hypothesis of this origin of 'crap' had been correct, 'and to vile speech'.

Flushing toilets themselves had been in existence since early Roman days. But once activated, the water went on flowing freely, until stopped by the user. Crapper's significant innovation was the invention of a mechanism that automatically stopped the water from running after it had fulfilled its purpose of flushing down the wastage. It was a tremendous advance in sanitation and it also prevented an expensive waste of water. No wonder that Crapper's name (or rather, part of it) thus was said to have been chosen to 'enrich' everyday speech as well.

American servicemen first made use of the new type of toilet when stationed in Europe during World War I. They were so taken by it that, on their return, they introduced it to America.

Actually, 'crap' had belonged to the vocabulary for centuries before Crapper's history-making invention. The term was derived from the Middle English *crappe* for 'rubbish' and has also been traced to the Dutch *Krappe* for 'scraps' and 'rubbish'. Through the years it became a common expression for 'offal' and 'excreta'. Some people lost no time in making use of the word metaphorically, adding it to the vocabulary of vulgarisms, not least so by some memorable phrase. Typical was the rejection of something as utter rubbish by saying, 'that's a lot of crap'.

Till The Cows Come Home

Why was this phrase chosen to express waiting for a very long time, if not for ever?

In most European countries during the cold of winter, cows are kept in sheds. With the coming of spring, they are turned out to graze in the fields. They relish the fresh young grass, particularly after having been fed on hay and straw through the long winter months. If left to their own devices, it takes a long, long time 'till the cows come home'. They go on gorging themselves till an over-full and therefore painful udder makes them return to be milked.

Spick And Span

What is responsible for this description for anything that is neat and tidy?

Anything trim and spruce is 'spick and span' or, as it was initially called, 'spick and span new'.

A 'span' was a chip of wood, freshly cut from a tree. Often serving as a spoon, never having been used before for any other purpose, it was thoroughly clean and completely new.

A 'spick' was a spike or nail. Just as the wooden chip was entirely new, so the spike came straight from the blacksmith's anvil. (Germans still speak of something as *Nagelneu*, 'nail-new'.) It has even been suggested that, next to the wooden spoon (span), the spike might have once served as a complementary eating implement, a primitive kind of fork.

Another derivation links anything span-new (from the Anglo-Saxon *spanna*) with the weaving of cloth. It had been 'spun new' and came straight from the loom!

Going back to the sea, 'spick and span' has also been claimed as relating to the beauty of a new ship which, with all its timber and its nails totally new, looked sparkling and stately.

'Spick' and 'span' thus said the same thing, only in different ways, a common phenomenon in English. Reinforcing each other, no doubt they were specially joined because of their attractive alliteration.

Instant Coffee

To whom does the world owe this beverage?

Nowadays millions of people all over the world drink instant coffee, a practice that is taken for granted. Prior to its introduction by the Nestlé Company in 1938, to prepare a cup of coffee took some time. After grinding the roasted beans – first by a hand-operated grinder and then by a faster and less cumbersome electric one – the pulverised coffee had to be percolated or filter-dripped, an equally protracted chore.

Nestlé's spent eight years of research in their factory at Vevey in Switzerland to perfect their product and start marketing it. Its brand name, Nescafé, combined the surname of Henri Nestlé (1814–1890), the firm's founder, and the French for 'coffee', *café*. English-speaking countries, ignoring the accent, pronounced it 'Nestle's'. It was a mispronunciation welcomed by the promoters of the product, as its sound associated it immediately with a cozy atmosphere, people's *nestling* down to a relaxed lifestyle, whilst enjoying the new kind of beverage, which simultaneously stimulated their nervous system.

No doubt, to Nestlé must go the credit for having made instant coffee the popular drink it has become. There have been claims of earlier attempts to produce it, though none apparently with lasting effect or leaving any definite data. The only exception is a record that at the Pan American World Fair held in 1899, a Japanese by the name of Satori Kato had exhibited some form of instant coffee of his making.

Lock, Stock And Barrel

Why is completeness paraphrased by parts of a weapon?

Anyone acquainted with the component parts of a gun can appreciate the phrase that describes the completeness of anything as 'lock, stock and barrel'. The lock is the mechanism that explodes the charge; the stock, the handle to which all parts are attached; and the barrel, of course, the tube through which the bullet is propelled.

Sir Walter Scott (1771–1832), the Scottish poet and novelist, is said to have popularised the phrase. He might well have picked it up from a joke current at the time that poked fun at the Highlanders. It said that a Highlander's gun to be effective required only 'a lock, a stock and a barrel'. Possibly taking a fancy to the metaphor, Scott used it and, according to John Gibson Lockhart, his son-in-law, was thus responsible for its adoption into everyday speech.

Noah's Ark

Which animals were in the Ark?

The biblical story of Noah's Ark (Genesis 6–8), very similar to and yet showing notable divergencies from that related in the Babylonian Gilgamesh epic, and also resembling myths in other cultures, has several distinctive features. Apart from contributing to present-day symbolism, they relate to Noah himself, to the circumstances of the Flood and a detailed account of the building of the Ark, including the measurements of its length, width and height, of what could have been considered an enormous houseboat. The account relates the way this was constructed. Made of cypress wood, it was coated with pitch both inside and outside to make it watertight and had three storeys, each containing separate compartments, like cabins. There was one skylight, a door in the Ark's side and a window, extending, with slight interruption, right around the boat.

It is rather odd that though the Bible recounts the story of Noah and the Ark in great detail and precision, when it concerns the actual inhabitants of the vessel, it identifies only two animals by name: the raven and the dove.

As for the rest of the animals, all that is told is that they represented every living species to ensure their survival after the Flood and that there were seven pairs of all 'clean' animals and one pair – male and female – of those that were 'unclean'. As the Bible gives no explanation as to the meaning of the term, a variety of interpretations has been suggested. The most likely is that it was a ritual and religious differentiation. 'Clean' were the animals which were regarded as a fit sacrifice to God, whilst those labelled 'unclean' were creatures worshipped by pagans and it was in protest that they were minimal in number.

As for the choice of the raven and dove as the only creatures identified, when Noah expected the Flood to have sufficiently subsided, to make sure that it was safe for all those on board to disembark, he sent out, as it were as scouts – first a raven and then a dove. Their mission accounted for their special mention out of all the animals in the Ark. The dove's return with an olive branch in its beak, indicating the end of the Flood, resulted in its becoming a permanent symbol of peace.

God is said to have sent the Flood because human depravity, lawlessness and violence had reached proportions that were beyond any hope of change. Noah alone was regarded as worthy to survive because of his being – though only relatively speaking and compared with his contemporaries – 'blameless'.

Taxiing

Why does one speak of planes 'taxiing'?

Taxis take fares to the airport, but they are strictly banned from the tarmac. How then did it happen that nevertheless they operate there, verbally, in the description of the movement of an aircraft on the ground prior to takeoff or after landing that is known as 'taxiing'.

The taxi landed on the airstrip, so to speak, quite by chance. It is a relic from the early days of aviation and goes back to young airmen's fancy whilst being trained around 1911 at Brooklands, one of the pioneer airfields, situated in the county of Surrey, England.

Just as a baby has to crawl before learning to walk, so the trainees received their first 'flying' instructions on the ground in a monoplane that was no longer airworthy. As taxis stay safely on the ground, it was perhaps not surprising that the cadets soon fondly referred to this craft as 'the taxi'.

It was a well-chosen name. The distance a taxi travels is metered. The kilometres (then miles) the would-be pilots covered were also counted, to entitle them eventually to take off.

The English novelist George Eliot wrote that 'words have wings'. It seems all the more appropriate if applied to a word used by flying men. And so the novel description of a training craft as 'the taxi' soon spread to other airfields.

It did not stay with crews of fledgling airmen. Transformed into a verb, as 'taxiing', it became the general description of the movement of all planes that are not yet or no longer airborne, but advancing along the tarmac under their own power.

Toothbrush

What is its story in the pursuit of dental care?

Hygiene is not a modern pursuit. It already belonged to life in antiquity. Part of it was to look after one's teeth, a practice highly recommended by both Greek and Roman medical authorities.

For the cleaning of one's teeth a variety of methods was employed. Among the simplest and most primitive was rubbing them with a rag. To increase its effectiveness, people learnt to cover or soak the latter with some substance chosen for its cleansing properties. This was imagined simultaneously to remove any bad smell from the mouth and to improve the taste of one's food.

Surprisingly, as well, human ingenuity had learnt to use in its dental care what came to be known ever since – and very much to the point – as 'toothpicks'. Still not abandoned and a feature of many households, they were the forerunner of the modern toothbrush. In his history-making excavations at Ur in Chaldea in the 1920s, Sir Leonard Woolley, the British archaeologist, unearthed, among other toiletry utensils attached to a ring, a golden toothpick, going back to circa 3500 BC!

Other specimens and records preserved testify that the use of the toothpick was widespread and, in fact, never went out of fashion. In its simplest form it was a mere splinter of wood. On the other hand, materials employed also included bronze, silver and ivory as well as quills. Desire to make the useful also beautiful resulted in the creation of toothpicks that were both effective and ornamental, frequently shaped like a human figure or that of an animal, with one of their limbs serving as the actual pick.

Whether wood, quill or metal, much care was taken in the selection of their source, the kind of tree or the species of bird. Each was known to vary in its effect on the teeth. Pliny thus claimed, for instance, that porcupine quills gave firmness to the teeth, whilst those obtained from vultures were believed to make one's breath sour.

Eventually, the advent of the toothbrush, though never totally replacing the toothpick, greatly reduced its importance. China is alleged to have been the first to develop it, according to a record in a seventeenth-century encyclopaedia, in 1498. A simple gadget, it consisted of hard bristles – mostly from pigs – stuck at right angles into a handle. It took more than a century to reach Europe, to be adopted there as late as the eighteenth century.

A story which might well be apocryphal asserts that the modern toothbrush in the western world was not imported from the East, but conceived in gaol, some time during the 1770s. Its inventor was William Addis, a London tanner who, having been found guilty of provoking a riot, was serving a prison sentence at historic Newgate Prison. Whilst doing so, he gave much thought to his future after his release. It so happened almost by chance that one morning, whilst washing his face and in the process cleaning his teeth in the customary method with a piece of cloth, he somehow realised that this practice could vastly be improved. He also felt that he could be the person to do so and that this would give him a new aim in life. At the first opportunity, when being served a meat dish, he saved one of its many bones and, boring holes into it, glued into them tiny bundles of bristles, having obtained the latter from a friendly guard with whom he had shared his idea. The result was the creation of the modern toothbrush. Once freed, the ex-tanner and now ex-convict lost no time in taking up the manufacture of toothbrushes and establishing an ever-growing, worldwide industry.

Marmalade

Why is this conserve not called 'jam' as with other fruits?

In the genealogy of foods, 'Sir Loin' has a close relation in Mary, Queen of Scots. What the fictitious knight did for the dinner table, the Scottish queen matched for breakfast.

It all happened, so it is told, when Mary had taken ill. On her sickbed she refused all food and those in charge of the royal invalid were worried. To regain strength, Mary had to eat.

How could they coax her to do so, as she lacked all appetite? How delighted therefore were they, when they discovered that the queen relished a certain jam, then a rarity and a delicacy. In their joy, they named it (after) 'sick Mary' and did so in the French tongue they then used, speaking of *Marie malade* which gave the world its marmalade.

Of course, all this, though charming in itself, is fiction. Actually, there is no trace of 'sickness' in the breakfast spread. What it really contains is another wrong notion. Marmalade now is made of oranges, as every recipe book tells. But to begin with, marmalade was far removed from the orange tree. Its origin goes back to classical times and an unknown Greek gardener. Fond of experimentation, he grafted scions from an apple tree on the quince. The result was a fruit so deliciously sweet, that he called it 'honey-apple', *meli-melon* in his Greek tongue.

Marmalade thus is truly a preserve. It continues to keep in its name this original Greek honey-apple out of which it used to be made. The name, if not the jam, then travelled a long way from Greece to reach England via Portugal (*marmelada*) and France (*marmelade*). It is no wonder that along the way, by its use on the various tongues, *meli,* the Greek 'honey' with its mellifluous 'i' developed the rasping 'r' of marmalade. All this belongs to the forgotten past, though it still sticks to the jam.

Pyjamas

Who created these?

To call the two-piece sleepwear 'pyjamas' does not do justice to their name. If they were truly pyjamas, they would be topless! Of Persian origin, the word literally speaks of leg-clothing, *pae-jamah*. In fact, to start with, it described loose-fitting trousers, held up by a cord around the waist. Worn as a unisex garment by Moslems in the East throughout the day, the English adopted them from the Portuguese. In the transfer the original day-apparel had become night attire and a jacket was added to the trousers.

In early days, pyjamas even had 'foot-ends' sewn on to them. Asked by a customer what their purpose was, a London West End outfitter is said to have replied, 'I believe, sir, it is because of white ants.'

Mall

What contribution did a once-favourite game make to modern civilisation?

Shopping malls, now a worldwide popular feature of daily urban life, are the result of the genius of American commercial enterprise, joined with memories of a now-obsolete game.

The first of their kind were established in the United States, early in the twentieth century. Whether located in the open or enclosed, they were reserved for pedestrians, with no vehicular traffic admitted. Their very description of 'mall' recalls their link with the once popular game of pall mall.

A favourite pursuit – similar to croquet and golf – it started in Italy, to reach Britain via France during the reign of King Charles II in the seventeenth century. The players struck a ball (*palla* in Italian) with a *mall*et (a sort of hammer, *maglio* in Italian) through iron hoops along an alley or fairway, aiming to reach the goal with a minimum of strokes.

Its earliest playing area in Britain was a course constructed in St James Park, London, soon called after the hammer used, 'the Mall'.

Even when the game had ceased to be popular, its former fairway was not destroyed. Changed into a shady avenue, a broad public walkway, in typical British conservatism, it nevertheless retained its by then obsolete designation – 'the Mall'. Perhaps most famous of all is Pall Mall, also in London's West End, which experienced the identical fate, to develop into the centre of the most distinguished London clubs.

Other thoroughfares opened up, also becoming known as 'malls'. Everything was done for the comfort of the ever-increasing crowds spending much of their time there. The area was either still out of doors or enclosed, as a shelter from inclement weather. Stalls and shops opened up, eating places catered for all tastes and entertainment was offered to both young and old.

Americans then realised that an enclosed mall would provide an all-weather space for every type of business and activity. Providing an outlet for small traders as much as for the largest department stores, this was the birth of the shopping mall, which soon reached the dimensions of huge shopping complexes.

It is interesting to note that, etymologically, the term 'mall' is related to 'maul', most likely so called after the damage done by some players striking the ball (hammering it) with the mallet. They truly were 'mauling' the fairway.

Lamington

Who created this delicious Australian cake?

The lamington is a 'dinkum' Australian cake. A square piece of sponge, coated with a soft chocolate icing and rolled in desiccated coconut, once it belonged to every garden party and church fête. In spite of such claim, its name has no connection with the English town of Leamington Spa. Even the spelling is different. Like peach Melba and Melba toast, it honours a person.

Lamington was the titled name of the Scottish-born eighth Governor of Queensland. Appointed to the office in 1895, he assumed his duties the following year. He so endeared himself to the people that on his departure, they called their most favoured cake after him.

No one really knows whether the choice had any specific reason. Was the lamington first served at the governor's garden parties? Did he himself relish it so much that eventually it became identified with him? Or was the name chosen merely because people felt that he should be remembered by something that was really sweet?

Baron Lamington's popularity was due not least to his youth. He was a mere thirty-six years old when he took up his position. An avid sportsman, he freely mixed with the people and felt at home 'down under'.

Bobby-Calf

Where does it get its name from?

To call a calf that is a few days old a 'bobby-calf' is not in the way of endearment, using the diminutive of the name Robert. The custom goes back to Britain and money. A few days after its birth, English dairy farmers would sell a bull calf, generally being paid one shilling (ten cents) for it, and it was the slang for one shilling – a 'bob' – that created the term bobby-calf.

Passing On Stairs

Why is this considered unlucky?

The belief that it is unlucky to pass anyone on the stairs going in the opposite direction has a biblical foundation. It goes back to Jacob's dream of the ladder (related in the book of Genesis, chapter 28), on which he saw angels ascending and descending.

No one ever knows whether the apparent human passing on a stairway is not in reality a divine being 'going up' or 'coming down'. To obstruct a messenger from God in any way would be sacrilegious. One's presence on the stairs might make it swerve and thereby delay its progress. To avoid any such possibility with its dire consequences, it was best never to pass anyone on the stairs.

Carat

What is the origin and twofold application of this measurement used in the jewellery trade?

People have always been concerned to know the value of things. This applies particularly to highly-prized objects, to diamonds and other gemstones. Merely to call them precious would be too relative an observation and very much subject to individual circumstances.

Like in the case of other measurements, such as those of time, distance, volume or speed, it needed a generally accepted code, easily ascertained and understood. Gemstones thus are weighed by units known as 'carats', now standardised internationally. This type of carat must not be confused with the measure applied to gold, also called carat (often spelt 'karat' in the United States). Too soft a substance for practicable use, gold is alloyed with other metals, such as silver, copper and bronze, the choice determined by the gold's intended purpose and desired colour and hardness. In such case the value of the item is expressed by the proportion of gold in its content. Pure or fine gold is 24 carats.

The term 'carat', though used in this double and easily confusing sense, shares the identical source. It referred to the seeds of the carob or locust tree which grew abundantly in many regions of the Middle East, and whose seeds lent themselves ideally to serve as the desired units. Dried, the seed pods looked very much like a small, curved horn, which made people call the unit 'carat'. Derived from the Greek *keration,* the diminutive of *keras,* it denoted a small horn! Alternatively the Arab *qirat* (meaning 'horn' as well) has also been quoted as the source of the name.

Born With A Silver Spoon

Why does one speak of those rich and pampered in those terms?

A spoon was once commonly a godparent's gift to a child on the occasion of its christening. Customarily, the spoon was dedicated to a patron saint with his image embossed on it. The spoon therefore not only served a practical purpose but, by its sacred association, was also believed to invoke the saint's protection for the child.

At a time when everything was still hand-carved and the spoons of ordinary people were made of wood or horn, to be given a silver spoon was especially appreciated. It was not only a useful gift, but a precious one as well.

Wealthy people really had no need for the present. Metaphorically speaking, their offspring was born 'with a silver spoon in its mouth' already.

The silver spoon got stuck in everyday phraseology. It continues to serve, though in a secular way, to point to those lucky enough to have been born of rich parents and without a care in the world.

Pay A Visit

Why should one have to pay for it?

Although everything these days seems to be charged for, a social call still costs nothing – unless one brings a gift.

However, there is even a reason why, rather formally, one speaks of 'paying a visit'. It stems from a visit to a doctor, a lawyer or any other professional, for which most certainly one has to pay.

When applied to a private visit, it might in certain cases reflect its obligatory nature. Not done for pleasure or out of friendship, it amounts to a duty call, to 'pay one's respects'.

All these are possible, though not totally convincing reasons for speaking of 'paying' a visit. Much more likely, the phrase might go back to the days when people did not live in close proximity and could not easily be reached by public transport, so to visit them implied incurring travelling expenses of – at times – not an inconsiderable amount of money. Truly, people paid (for) a visit.

Devil's Advocate

Who is he?

The official decision by the Church to exalt an individual to sainthood carried tremendous responsibility. Enthusiasm, human error or misinformation could mistakenly ascribe to the candidate the necessary qualities of extraordinary worthiness. Everything possible therefore was done to avoid the slightest chance of such error. The nominee had his (or her) merits and character examined in the most minute detail. To make doubly sure, the papal court appointed a special officer whose duty it was to contest the candidates' claim. He was to raise every conceivable objection and scrupulously examine all evidence put forward by those recommending them, and the case was allowed to proceed only after every one of his objections had been answered.

Called 'the promoter of the faith', popularly he became known by the telling title of 'the devil's advocate', *advocatus diaboli* in Latin. It was a name well chosen as, after all, no one could resent sainthood more than the devil, and presumably he would do everything in his power to prevent yet another saint from being added to their already considerable number.

The original purpose of his office was then forgotten and with it his title's original religious context. To 'act as the devil's advocate' took on a totally different meaning and function: to argue for the unpopular side of an issue, a cause or a controversy.

On The Nose

How did the nose get stuck on the loom of language?

One and the same expression may have a completely changed meaning in different parts of the world. This applies to the use of the saying 'on the nose'.

In the United States, where it originated in the broadcasting studio, it came to signify that something was right on time and exact. It was part of the sign language used by producers, silently to convey a message to those live 'on air'. To indicate that the program was running right on schedule, he or she would place a finger alongside or on the tip of their nose. Their choice of body language was essential in the circumstances, as spoken instructions or information would be heard by the listeners.

Australian slang, totally differently, uses the words for anything that is obnoxious and offensive. It is 'smelly' and no good at all.

Kodak

How did this name come into existence?

A special category in the study of the origin of names deals with that of trade names. Obviously, their main purpose is to promote the product. To do so, it is essential to fulfil some fundamental conditions. The name must be easily remembered, attractive, euphonic and, if possible, it must refer to some significant features associated with the article. These might be summarised by some pleasant-sounding acronym or an appropriate abbreviation. Equally effective is a name which by its very quaintness or mystifying nature makes it memorable.

Some of the origins are well documented and not difficult to ascertain, whilst others have created a diversity of claims, hard to verify or even totally fictitious.

'Kodak' was patented as a trade name in 1888. Ever since, its use has instantly 'pictured-up' its photographic association. In itself it is meaningless, neither a derivation from nor an abbreviation of any word. It is pure invention, the brainchild of George Eastman of Rochester, New York (1854–1932). An American inventor, industrialist and philanthropist, he became renowned as a pioneer and manufacturer in the field of photography. In this capacity, he looked for a most suitable trade name, one that was succinct, dynamic and could not be misspelt or mispronounced to become unidentifiable.

Of all the letters of the alphabet, Eastman had always favoured the letter 'K'. It had attracted him, as he himself explained, because 'it seemed a strong, incisive sort of letter'. Not surprisingly, therefore, he determined that 'K' should be conspicuous in the name to be coined, in fact appear in it not once but twice, best of all, as its first and last letter. All that was needed was to select the most suitable letters to be inserted in between. By a method of trial and error, Kodak appeared to be the ideal combination of such letters, just the right word.

It has been suggested that its final adoption was not merely the result of Eastman's experimental choice and placing of letters, but that some additional factors contributed to its coinage. Kodak shared its initial with that of the family name of his mother and thereby added a personal note to his commercial endeavour. Even more significant perhaps was the fact that to the imaginative ear the name Kodak sounded somehow like the click of a camera's shutter – so appropriate in the circumstances.

A totally different explanation of the name is also attributed to Eastman. This relates that, on being asked why he had called his product 'Kodak', he is alleged to have replied that he had not done so arbitrarily but thanks to a stroke of pure luck. One day, when the question of finding a suitable name was still uppermost in his mind, he was having a plate of alphabet soup. It then so happened that when he had almost emptied it, five letters were still left at its bottom. They spelt out K O D A K and seemed to be the answer to his quest.

Sirloin

Who so named this cut of beef?

King Henry VIII not only loved pretty women but was equally enamoured of good meat. One day at a banquet at Hampton Court Palace he particularly enjoyed a choice cut of beef. He was determined publicly to proclaim his pleasure, and he did so in truly royal fashion. He conferred a knighthood by drawing his sword and dubbing the beef 'Sir Loin'!

Obviously this is a legend which has been told for many years in many versions and also has been ascribed to other monarchs. Actually the sirloin owes its name to its very position prior to removal from a side of beef, but as described in French. Cut from 'above' (*sur*) the 'loin' (*longe*), adapted to English speech, it became the 'sirloin'.

On The Water Waggon

Why are those abstaining from alcoholic drinks said to be 'on the water waggon'?

That those who abstain from alcoholic drinks are said to be 'on the water waggon' has a simple historical explanation. It goes back to a practice of the Salvation Army in New York. Its members would pick up drunks in the city streets, to drive them to a safe shelter, for which purpose they used a water waggon, the then traditional means of transporting water to the general population. Their compassionate practice and rescuing mission has been perpetuated in the simple phrase, though its original literal significance as a means of transport is no longer remembered.

Gavel

Why is a chairperson's hammer so called?

The gavel with which a chairperson calls a meeting to order was originally a small hammer. One of the working tools of a stonemason, its cutting edge was used to smooth rough stones.

The gavel owes its title to its shape which, viewed from the front, reminded people of the gable of a house. Gable, in turn, is derived from the German *Gipfel*, meaning a 'top' or 'summit'.

Bigwig

Why are 'stuffed shirts' also nicknamed 'bigwigs'?

Some now discarded practices have left their trace in everyday speech. This applies to the bigwig. Colloquially, it is the nickname given to individuals who fill an important position, or act like such. It recalls the days – particularly in the seventeenth and eighteenth centuries – when members of the nobility, judges and bishops were distinguished by wearing a full-length wig, one so large that it covered not only their head, but their shoulders and back as well. The tradition is still maintained in some parts of the world, though restricted to a few individuals, occupying some high office, such as members of the judiciary and parliamentary dignatories.

It is only natural to identify people by some conspicuous trait of theirs or some feature that sets them apart, as it were. Certainly, the donning of a wig could not fail to do so and the more important the person, the bigger was the wig!

To refer to people as 'bigwigs' no doubt recognised their superior status. Somehow, however, it carried with it a note of contempt for the often pompous and conceited attitude on the part of those so called. Well aware of their prominence, they were not reticent in letting others know about it.

The wearing of wigs goes back to the very early days of civilisation. They have been discovered on excavated Egyptian mummies and can be seen on figures depicted on the friezes of Knossos, dating back to the days of ancient Crete. Etymologically, the word 'wig' is a shortened form of 'periwig', derived from the French *perruque*.

Have A Bone To Pick

How did a bone find a place in an argument?

A 'bone of contention' no doubt stems from the canine world, where dogs fight over a bone. From the same kennel, as it were, also comes anyone who has 'a bone to pick'.

English Tommy

Why was a British soldier so called?

That a British soldier was popularly called a 'Tommy' is based on an official form of 1815. In that year the British War Office introduced a new service Record Book, which every soldier had to carry. This was to contain all his personal data, including any wounds he had sustained or decorations received. To make it easier for the men to fill in the details, a specimen form was attached, fully completed for an imaginary soldier. Leaving no blank, he was even given a fictitious name: Thomas Atkins. This was retained for several further editions. The alias became so proverbial that when eventually it was omitted, it was not forgotten. 'Tommy' had become so well known that the nickname survived his existence in the specimen form.

Almost eighty years later, in 1892, Rudyard Kipling made 'Tommy' the subject and title of a ballad which, widely read, further popularised this description of an English soldier.

The question remains why of all names the War Office chose that of Tommy Atkins. Most probably it was quite arbitrary, a name as good as any. An apocryphal story, however, claims that it was personally selected by the Duke of Wellington. He wanted to perpetuate the memory of a soldier of that name who, while delivering a dispatch during the battle of Waterloo, had dropped dead in front of him, from wounds received.

Bonsai

What is the story and symbolism of bonsai?

Nowadays bonsai – the art of raising uniquely shaped ornamental miniature trees and shrubs – is regarded as the Japanese people's gift to the world and their finest contribution to horticulture.

The growing of these dwarfed masterpieces is a delicate and painstaking task. It demands meticulous care and thoughtfulness. In its pursuit, numerous conditions have to be observed. The plants have to be selected for their suitability and they have to be carefully potted in shallow bowls. To prevent their too rapid growth necessitates frequent transplanting and regular pruning. They need the right kind of soil, different for each type of plant, controlled watering and appropriately timed fertilisation.

The bonsai is not merely an inimitable creation in the world of nature, 'nature in concentration', as it has been called. Significantly, it also expresses some traditional features of the Japanese lifestyle and philosophy.

The art of bonsai shuns the haste and restlessness of everyday life and teaches patience, deliberation, and not least, it fosters the spirit of discipline, self-control and attention to the smallest detail. Those practising the art are rewarded with an overwhelming sense of the grandeur of nature. In an age that only too often worships the gigantic in size, they learn and are fascinated by the monumental quality of the most minute.

The name of the bonsai combines the Japanese words for a 'bowl' (bon) and 'plant' (sai). Its earliest authentic Japanese reference has been traced to picture scrolls from the beginning of the fourteenth century. One of them even depicts such a dwarfed plant in its now traditional shallow receptacle.

Not surprisingly, like so many facets of Japanese culture, the idea behind the bonsai originated not in Japan but in China, where, already some 2000 years ago during the Han dynasty, it was known as penjing, the equivalent term for the Japanese 'dwarfed tree'. To the Chinese people gardening, going far beyond a natural pursuit, was of profound spiritual and philosophical significance. It was thought to enrich the quality of one's life. They referred to the stunted trees as 'silent poems' and said that the aim of the art was to 'shorten thousands of miles to a single foot'.

It was in the twelfth century that Buddhist monks introduced the first of these unique plants to Japan. They attributed to them deep religious meaning and saw them as representing 'verdant stairways to heaven', and acting as a link between the human and the divine.

To begin with, the Japanese aristocracy, the Samurais, made the bonsai their own. Only gradually was it adopted subsequently by the rest of the population to become a generally accepted art as late as the 1800s.

The western world first encountered bonsais at a Paris exhibition towards the end of the nineteenth century. It took another thirty years before these beautiful little creations, so thought-provoking and aesthetically enriching, were introduced to Britain, from there to capture the imagination and admiration of people internationally.

Fuzz

Why, when speaking derogatorily of the police, does one refer to them as 'fuzz'?

'Fuzz' is one of the many and not always complimentary names given to the police. It was early cockney slang for anyone who was resented or disliked. How Londoners came to use it first in this sense has been given a variety of explanations.

Some believe that generally it reflected their contempt for those who were 'fussing' (or 'fuzzing') around in matters that were really not their concern. Surely, no one did so more than a 'copper'. Over-particular in his demands and hard to please, he well deserved to be called a 'fuzz'.

On the other hand, 'fuzz' might be all that remained from a hostile encounter of the British with Sudanese tribesmen. In Kipling's words, those 'pore benighted 'eathen' fighting men were given the nickname of 'fuzzy-wuzzies' because of their curly hair. Shortened to 'fuzzy', it became the description of anyone to be avoided, as a policeman was by criminals.

Others have claimed that 'fuzz' was an American term, though of doubtful origin. It has been seen as a corrupted version of 'feds', the nickname given to the *fed*eral narcotic agents by those engaged in early drug trafficking. For reasons unknown, they transferred the description to policemen. Also American is yet another derivation, related to the first one given above. Over-zealous policemen who were hard to please were referred to as 'fussytails'. And it did not take long to change the 'fussytails' into a 'fuzz'.

Pneumatic Tyres

By whom and when were they invented?

It would not have been surprising if, of all names for their machines, the early cyclists considered that of 'boneshaker' most appropriate. A ride certainly shook them up. Even the solid-rubber tyre was not a sufficient cushion on the rough, ill-made roads. It was his own experience of such bone-shakings, as well as his ten-year-old son's complaints at the discomfort, that led John Boyd Dunlop to develop the pneumatic tyre. He himself was the first to apply the word 'pneumatic', in this new sense, adding it to the world's vocabulary. The word is derived from *pneuma,* the Greek for 'wind' and 'air'.

Dunlop was a Scot. He practised as a veterinary surgeon in Belfast, Ireland. His son, Johnnie, loved riding his bike, although it was not always a pleasure on the cobbled streets of the city. The boy told his father that he had set his heart on outdistancing his friends, all of whom were cycling enthusiasts. To help his son get both a smoother ride and greater speed, Dunlop set to work in his back yard. He was convinced that a hollow tube, filled with air under pressure and attached to the rim of the wheel, would act as a cushion and achieve both his aims at the same time. There are two versions of the story of how he did so.

One tells how he went straight to a chemist to purchase a rubber tube. He filled this with air and then, with strips of canvas, fixed it round a wooden wheel. Trained in exact methods of research, he now felt compelled to test his idea by comparing the two types of tyre. He did so in a simple experiment. He sent a wheel with the inflated tyre and another with a solid tyre spinning across the yard of his home. The result confirmed all he had thought. The solid-tyred one toppled over halfway across. The newly 'attired' wheel went not only all the way but also bounced wonderfully on striking the wall!

More anecdotal is the second report. This relates how Dunlop, deep in thought, was pacing his garden. While doing so, he suddenly caught sight of a length of water hose. At once he grasped its importance to the problem he wished to solve. Picking it up, he inflated and fixed it to Johnnie's cycle, with remarkable results. He patented his invention in 1881. So it was that an inventive father's love for his son and desire to please him gave the world of locomotion one of its great advances, still recalled by the trademark of 'Dunlop'. One of the original wheels with the Dunlop tyre is in the Royal Science Museum in Edinburgh. It is said that it had covered 4800 kilometres (3000 miles) before being 'retired'.

See Red

Why, when angry, is one said to see this colour?

That people whose anger is roused are said to 'see red' has been given several explanations. Oddly enough, the most popular and accepted is based on a misconception. It links the description with the sport of bullfighting, equally responsible for the proverbial (though totally incorrect) simile that speaks of something being 'like a red rag to a bull'. In fact, this very phrase might well be the forerunner, if not the actual source of the saying.

For a long time, it was assumed that in the mortal combat of the *corrida*, or bullfight, the matador enraged the animal with his red cloak. It has been established, however, that the bull, like most animals, is actually colour-blind and not affected in any way by the red (or any) colour. What provokes and infuriates him is the matador's waving of his cloak, irrespective of its colour!

There might well have been other factors that contributed to the creation of the colourful phrase. Blood and fire are red, and both have been associated with passion, with those who are hot-blooded and those whose wrath is kindled.

Not least, some people's faces become flushed when angry and, looking red, it was easy to link their colour with their state of mind.

Stumped

Why, when baffled or lost for a reply, is one 'stumped'?

Anyone lost for an answer to a question is said to be 'stumped'.

The term, like not a few other figures of speech now part of the English language, owes its existence to cricket. In the game the wicket is also called a 'stump'. This alternate name goes back to the original wicket which was a convenient stump in a field, the part of a tree trunk left standing after the tree had been felled or decayed naturally.

A bowler who has hit the wicket or stump has outwitted the batsman – he has *stumped* him.

Leave No Stone Unturned

Why, when determined to solve a most difficult task, does one use this simile?

To 'leave no stone unturned' is a piece of advice going back well nigh two and a half millennia, to one of the early great battles fought in world history. The counsel was given by the oracle at Delphi to Pausanias, the Spartan general in command of the allied Greek army in its decisive victory over the Persian forces at Plataea in 479 BC.

After defeating the Persians, Pausanias was determined to take possession of a treasure of gold, which, he had been informed, Mardonius, the enemy leader, had hidden somewhere on the battlefield prior to the encounter. However, his efforts to locate what promised to be the most highly-prized booty failed. Not giving up the quest, he consulted the Delphic oracle. This directed him to 'leave no stone unturned'.

Thus, renewing his search, assiduously he explored every possible site, finally to discover the hoard of gold under the stones that covered the floor of the luxurious headquarters of the defeated Persian general.

Mostly historians study the events of the battle. But the counsel given at Delphi has lived on as a valuable admonition to everyone in pursuit of a worthwhile goal.

Index Finger

Why is this finger so called?

The use of a specific finger of one's hand for a particular task or its resemblance to some real or imagined object has been responsible for the choice of the names of all the fingers. An obvious and self-explanatory example is the ring finger. That the Romans called the middle finger the 'impudent digit' (*digitus impudens*) had its basis in their seeing in it a phallic symbol.

The finger next to the thumb has become known as the index finger for an equally valid reason. Derived from the Latin *indicare,* for to 'point' or to 'indicate', it is used to point out things, to show the way. Children, learning to read, often use this finger as well to run along the line of a piece of text to point to the word they are about to decipher and so as not to lose their place.

The index at the end of a book shares the identical source. It is so called because it 'indicates' and 'points' to the page on which to find a specific item.

Start [And Keep] The Ball Rolling

What kind of ball is referred to here?

To speak of to 'start the ball rolling' obviously nowadays refers to any sort of beginning, to take the first step, to get anything under way. It is equally clear that the choice of the simile comes from sport and certainly a sport in which the movement of a ball plays a central role.

In the context of the phrase, croquet can be assumed as the most likely source. At one time a very popular game, particularly among the English aristocracy, it became a vogue around the middle of the 1800s. Played by houseguests at country estates, it was also part of the entertainment offered at garden parties.

One significant feature of the game, however, gave it its special slant. Not everyone participating in it (not even the most proficient player) had a fair chance. Whoever had the first shot, 'started the ball rolling', was very likely also to finish the game first – in one go – and thus become the winner.

Aware of the benefit of being the starter, it became traditional to choose the so fortunate player by tossing a coin, a practice that at least eliminated the impression of any favouritism. Nevertheless, this did not do away with this so objectively selected player's likelihood of coming first, and to 'start the ball rolling' came to reflect not only the act of initiating anything, but also the added advantage it brought with it.

To make sure that some project embarked upon is not abandoned midway or anything of whatever kind, having been started, is not allowed to peter out, it is essential for those involved – again borrowing the metaphor from the popular stick and ball game and doing so as its logical sequence – to 'keep the ball rolling'. Unless it was kept in motion ('rolling'), the game became dull, with both players and spectators losing interest.

It is generally believed that actually the saying was first applied – away from the sporting field – to English dinner parties of the sixteenth century, when in fact, so tradition has it, this phrase was first coined. It referred to the duty of the hostess to see to it that the spirits of her guests never flagged, and that they kept on enjoying themselves to the very end without their conversation ever drying up. Indeed, it was her responsibility to 'keep the ball rolling'.

Hawker

Did the name denote that a person so called sold hawks?

The hawker's name describes a feature of the early way of trade. Going from place to place, hawkers often carried wares on their backs, and would become bent by the load. Or the trader might squat down to sell his goods.

Derived from the German *hocken,* the hawker portrays either practice. In German the word was used both for 'bending down' (*niederhocken*) and the description of old people who walked with a stoop.

There is no truth, however, in the suggestion also made that originally a hawker was an itinerant dealer in foreign hawks, making his way from castle to castle.

Once In A Blue Moon

What accounts for this metaphor for a rare occurrence?

Speaking of 'once in a blue moon' suggests 'very rarely indeed'. Obviously, a blue moon is not an everyday occurrence.

The moon has been blamed – rightly or wrongly – for many things. She is responsible for the tides and lunatics. One speaks of the moon as being yellow as cheese, though in reality its proper colour is probably a dark brownish-black. The 'blue moon' is an optical illusion. It has never existed in reality.

All the light of the moon is reflected sunshine, and the colour that it appears to the eye changes according to the atmosphere surrounding the earth through which the rays have to pass. That is why the moon may look bright yellow, whitish, orange or, very rarely, blue.

Any change in the atmosphere, caused by particles of dust or other matter being absorbed in it, immediately influences the colour of the rays of light reflected by the moon from the sun.

That is why in 1883, for example, the world saw a blue moon. The moon had done nothing. But on earth, the Indonesian island of Krakatoa had been blown almost into halves, and enormous clouds of volcanic dust and water vapour had been thrown into the atmosphere and were circling the earth for many weeks.

This dust and other matter changed the light rays reaching the earth from the moon, and made people believe that the moon was blue. Things are not always what they seem to be!

Chop Chop

What explains this exhortation to hurry someone along?

People urged not to linger but to get on with the given task quickly are sent on their way with the words 'chop chop'.

Pidgin English 'chop' is akin to the Cantonese *cap* for 'quick'. The word's duplication (already occurring in its Cantonese parallel) gives additional emphasis to the urgency of the job and is a reminder not to waste a single moment. By its almost explosive sound and brevity, the exhortation gives all the more weight to the request.

A completely different suggestion links the wording of the request with nineteenth-century traders who, whilst visiting China, were struck by the way the Chinese ate, the speed with which they partook of their food – by the use of chopsticks. It prompted the merchants to 'pick up' – linguistically – the first part of the utensil's description – the *chop* – as a word with which to hurry people along. It must be realised that the choice of the name of the chopsticks so aptly and in simple terms described the slender 'sticks' that enabled diners to eat 'quickly' (*chop*): 'quicksticks'. Almost literally it translates the Chinese, in which tongue chopsticks are known as 'the quick (and nimble) ones', reminiscent of nimble fingers. In this context it is good to learn the paradoxical Chinese saying about 'admiring flowers at full gallop'.

Fight Like Kilkenny Cats

Are these more ferocious fighters than other felines?

The Irish town of Kilkenny has a colourful past and a rich history. It has become world-famous through its cats. To 'fight like Kilkenny cats' means to battle ferociously to the bitter end.

Until 1844, the city was divided into two parts, segregating the native Irish from the Anglo-Normans. Constantly at loggerheads, they often came to blows. They fought like cats, people said. The observation survived the struggle but, losing its merely metaphorical sense, it was misinterpreted. Imagining that it referred particularly to the town's felines, these were misrepresented as being exceptionally belligerent.

Gruesome are two other traditions. Each of them traces the phrase to a specific incident in the city's history.

Hessian soldiers who had served as mercenaries in the British army against the Americans were billeted for some time on their way home in County Kilkenny. After all the excitement of battle, they soon were bored. To pass away the time and amuse themselves, they caught stray cats. After tying their tails together, they threw them across a clothesline, and watched the unfortunate creatures struggle to get down.

Hearing their yowling, the commanding officer rushed from his quarters to investigate the cause of the rumpus. Afraid of disciplinary action for their cruel pastime, the men quickly tried to cover it up. They freed the cats by cutting off their tails with a sword. The poor animals ran away as fast as they could. There was no time left, however, for the soldiers to remove the knotted tails from the line. On being questioned about them, they explained that the Kilkenny cats, renowned fighters, had engaged once again in so fierce a battle that all that was left of them were their tails! (A slightly different version relates the occurrence to the occupation of the town by Cromwell and his rampaging troops.)

Another derivation of the saying links it with sportsmen. They had heard a rumour that Kilkenny cats excelled all others in fighting prowess. To verify the story, they caught a thousand 'ordinary' cats from all the other counties, to pit them against a thousand Kilkenny felines. The latter lived up to their reputation. In no time they confronted the intruders, attacking them viciously. The battle raged all night. At sunrise, all that remained of the thousand intruders were their badly-mauled bodies. The thousand Kilkenny cats had survived the fight. Although looking the worse for it, their fighting spirit was undiminished. To 'fight like Kilkenny cats' is thus the remnant of the unsportsmanlike sporting event.

Without reducing their fighting quality, a popular Irish limerick limits it to two cats:

There once were two cats in Kilkenny,
Each thought there was one cat too many,
So they fought and they fit
And they scratched and they bit
Until instead of two cats there weren't any.

Chutzpah

What does this word denote?

Jews who had migrated from eastern Europe to the United States continued to converse there in Yiddish, the language they had used back in their old homeland. Their vernacular, it was not to be confused with Hebrew, though it used Hebrew letters and, like Hebrew, was written from right to left.

More than a thousand years old, Yiddish is basically Middle High German, mixed with Slav, French, Hebrew and even English words. Its very existence mirrored the

Jewish fate of wandering. When fleeing from persecution or expelled from the country that had been their home, they did not abandon its culture. They preserved much of it, not least its language, as it was spoken at the time of their migration. Through the years then they further enriched it with words borrowed from the tongue used in their new environment.

Some of the telling Yiddish expressions were untranslatable to Americans. Rich in meaning, the Jews' new countrymen adopted them literally. Subsequently, from America, they spread to other English-speaking countries, to become part and parcel of the vocabulary there.

One of the most outstanding examples is *chutzpah*. It reflects an attitude that combines and condenses in the one word brazenness, impudence and impertinence. To 'have chutzpah' means to have cheek and be arrogant.

At times, an anecdote can convey meanings more eloquently than any definition given by a dictionary. This certainly applies to the explanation of chutzpah. It gives the example of a man who had murdered both his parents and then, at court, pleaded with the judge to show mercy, as he was now orphaned.

To pronounce the word properly, it must be realised that the letter 'ch' (called *chet*), the initial of *ch*utzpah, is guttural and must be sounded like the 'ch' in the Scottish 'loch'.

Give Someone The Brushoff

How did this metaphor come into existence?

Not wanting to have anything to do with a person and see the back of them, one gives them the 'brushoff' – one rebuffs them. It is like ridding oneself of unwanted floss, specks of dirt or dust that have got stuck to one's clothes and need brushing off.

Some have derived the expression from a practice claimed not to have been uncommon on the American railroads and their luxurious Pullman coaches.

Porters assigned to look after the passengers' comfort and keep their clothes neat and tidy spent the shortest time possible with travellers whom they thought to be poor tippers. They gave them just a quick (and very superficial) 'brush off', then 'brushing them off' – in the metaphorical sense of the words – by quickly moving on to other commuters whom they expected generously to reward their services in looking after them and their clothes.

Red And White Flowers In Hospitals

Why are they considered unlucky?

A widespread English superstition, also adopted elsewhere, regards it as unlucky to bring a bunch of mixed red and white flowers to a patient in hospital.

The superstition is based on an ancient belief in floral magic. Red and white flowers, it was assumed, by their very colours would trigger off supernatural forces, causing the recipient to bleed to death (the result of the red), ultimately thus taking on the (white) pallor of a corpse.

One tradition links the superstition specifically with the Crimean War. Wounded soldiers then believed in the harmful magic potency of flowers of those hues. They would make them bleed profusely and, consequently, necessitate lots of white bandages.

Pull Up The Stakes

What accounts for this odd phrase to say that one is about to move on?

Leaving their place of residence, people are said to 'pull up the stakes'. The words recall the early days of settlement in the United States, when whoever was allotted a certain area, to leave no doubt as to its exact extent and position, had its boundaries 'staked out'. If, subsequently, they decided to move on to some more promising tract of land, they literally pulled up the old boundary stakes, to use them to mark out their new choice of plot.

An alternative theory traces the expression specifically to the once-popular itinerant circus. Travelling the countryside, those making up the company put up their tent the moment they arrived at their next scheduled place of performance. Once having given the show, they lost no time in pulling up the stakes that had anchored down the tent, to move on to the next town.

Hairbrained

Not very bright people are described so – why?

Anyone hairbrained has little or no brains, just as a hairbrained scheme is a badly conceived one. In either case, their description makes no sense. Properly presented and spelt, however, it does. To be *harebrained* or to act in such a fashion is more fitting to the brain of a hare than that of humans.

Paterson's Curse

What is the story behind the puzzling variety of names given to this plant?

An interesting study is how one and the same object is named differently, not only in diverse parts of the world but also within various regions of the same country. This applies not least to the field of botany. The circumstances behind such variations reveal much about local culture, folklore and environmental conditions.

Australians are familiar with a purplish-blue weed that grows abundantly in widely dispersed rural areas. Even more so, they are bewildered by the multiplicity of both ordinary and abstruse names given to it. Generally identified as viper's bugloss, it is classified as a boraginaceous weed (from the *Boraginacea* Family). The stories linked with the colourful and exotic-sounding names applied to it are themselves revealing. Its general description as a boraginaceous plant suggests that it causes perspiration to those partaking of it. The term is believed to be derived from the Arab *abu-'araq*, 'father of sweat', because Arabian physicians used to prescribe it as a diaphoretic (a medicine inducing perspiration).

Its being specifically called viper's bugloss refers to another of its real or imagined features and qualities. Bugloss, bearing no relation to bugs, joins the Greek words *bous* for 'ox' and *glossa* for 'tongue' and literally means 'ox-tongued'. An odd description, it is due to the plant's thorny, hairy-leafed flowers and scratchy stem which reminded people of the roughness of the tongue of an ox! Stranger still is its further association with a viper. It is said to be based on the imagined resemblance of its seeds to the head of a viper and their supposed effectiveness as an antidote against the venomous bite of that snake – a case of sympathetic magic and a medical myth. The plant indeed has produced a most colourful and complex combination of bizarre claims. How much more simple is the American way of just calling it a 'blue weed'.

Puzzling are the popular names of 'Paterson's curse' and 'Salvation Jane' given to the plant in the Australian vernacular. Theirs is not only an interesting background, but they almost contradict each other.

It is claimed that in the 1880s a gardener by the name of Richard Eyre Paterson, living on a property near Albury, New South Wales, grew the weed in his garden. From there it had spread far and wide, very much at the expense of rural areas, by crowding out cereal crops and pasture plants, as well as making harvesting more arduous.

Becoming a real pest, not undeservedly, recalling its very source, it was referred to as 'Paterson's curse'.

On the other hand, during periods of drought it proved good fodder and thereby saved much stock. No better name could then be given to it than 'Salvation Jane'. It is said that this name was suggested because the flower resembled the bonnets of the Salvation Army women. It was a well-merited distinction.

Butter Would Not Melt In Their Mouth

Butter easily melts. Why would it not do so in the mouth?

Nothing is easier than for butter to dissolve in the warmth of the mouth. Therefore, to say of anyone that 'even butter would not melt in their mouth' suggests a person who is cold, haughty and offish. But traditionally it is taken to speak of someone who seems so prim and proper that they could never do anything wrong.

Significantly, the phrase is exclusively used in a negative sense. It is applied to someone suspiciously mild and meek. Their appearance of being so innocent is misleading. The original context of the words justifies this interpretation.

The phrase, as now used, is incomplete and almost reverses the meaning it carried in its early, fuller wording. This referred to a man who, though he looked as though even butter would not melt in his mouth, was so tough that 'not even cheese would choke him'. Not soft at all, he was as hard as nails. His apparent harmlessness was a fake, a mere front.

A Hair Of The Dog That Bit You

Where does this superstition come from?

To 'fight fire with fire' is an age-old practice. The ancient Romans already believed that 'like cures like'. Applying this rule, people imagined that the best treatment for a hangover was to have another drink.

In his diary, Samuel Pepys relates how he himself, though disbelieving it, tried out this cure and found it effective. On 3 August 1661 his head had been aching all morning as the result of the previous night's debauchery. When at noon, he dined with friends, they made him drink from the same wine that had caused the condition, promising him that it would help him, 'which I thought strange, but I think find true'.

To call this treatment 'a hair of the dog that bit you' is an apposite metaphor. It recalls an imagined cure once applied to people bitten by a dog that had rabies. To avoid hydrophobia, they ate a burnt hair of the mad dog.

The Gideon Bible

What is the story behind its name?

Copies of the Gideon Bible can be found worldwide in the rooms of almost every hotel, motel or guesthouse. In the year 2000 more than 900 million copies in seventy-nine languages had been distributed throughout 159 countries! How this came about shows what the accidental meeting of two like-minded people can achieve – by their power of faith, sheer determination and infectious enthusiasm.

It all started a mere century ago in the small township of Boscobel in the state of Wisconsin, USA. When arriving there on 14 September 1898, John H. Nicholson, a commercial traveller from Janesville in the same state, having not booked any accommodation in advance, was at a loss as to where to stay for the night. The Central Hotel, where he usually stopped over, was full. Its owner, who over the years had become a good friend, then recalled that a certain Samuel Hill, also a commercial traveller, was occupying a twin room. The two men seemed congenial company and, if it was agreeable to them, they could share the room for the night. That is how a mere emergency and pure chance brought the two men together, with a result that neither host nor guests could have anticipated.

Before retiring that night, John invited his newly-made companion to join him in a short act of worship, a prayer and a reading from the Scriptures. It was a practice he had followed ever since having promised his mother to do so just prior to her death. Sam had no objection and so both men, after a short supplication, read together a passage from the Bible.

As it were, it sowed the seeds of what was to come. Once having turned towards the subject of religion, they continued to discuss it. They agreed how beneficial it would be for people of their age and occupation to join together to foster a Christian fellowship. At the time, they thought of calling it the 'Christian Commercial Young Men's Association of America'.

That was, however, as far as they went, taking no further action. A few months later, once more by pure accident, they again met, this time at Beaver Dam. They had not forgotten their previous conversation. Feeling that they should now pursue the idea, they arranged a meeting for July 1899 in Janesville. Although they had sent out numerous invitations, only one other person, William J. Knights, attended. Undaunted, the three men decided to proceed and there and then founded the Association. In search of a telling name, at the suggestion of the third man, whom they elected president, they agreed to call themselves 'Gideons'.

Knights had been deeply impressed by the scriptural account (in the Book of Judges, chapters 6 and 7) of how Gideon's selfless devotion and ingenious guidance of the Israelites made faith conquer adversity and brought the country peace for many years to come. That is how the

Gideons came into existence. Spreading all over the world, by their own generosity they and their followers supply millions of Bibles called by their name and meant to be a source of inspiration to their readers.

Ham Actor

Why is a bad actor so called?

Traditionally, actors in minstrel shows blackened their faces. They used to do so by putting on ham fat, which they then darkened with burnt cork. It made people refer to them as 'ham-fatters'. A popular song thus spoke of 'The Ham-fat Man'. A minstrel had a very low rating among other actors and that is how the 'ham', his shortened nickname, was eventually applied to poor, amateurish performers of any kind.

Others, however, believe that the ham is all that is left of *Hamlet.* It was a role any aspiring actor wished to play, but not being up to it, he often did so very poorly.

Reindeer

As other animals are also guided by reins why then should this one be singled out?

Not only children might imagine that reindeer were so called because of the reins held by Father Christmas to direct the animals drawing his legendary sledge. In fact, the second part of the animals' name merely echoes the first, which is the Old Norse word for 'deer'.

Unlucky Green

Why is the colour green thought to bring misfortune?

The superstition that green is an unlucky colour which might bring misfortune to one who wears it is based on the ancient belief that green, the colour of nature, was the fairies' colour. They treasured it and would resent anyone else using it. This would amount to a misappropriation of their monopoly rights. Their hostility roused, they would be determined to punish the offender.

Actors are known to be superstitious. The very uncertainty of their profession makes them so. Does not the success or failure of a performance depend only too often on irrational imponderables? It is no wonder therefore that they shun the colour green, though paradoxically they relax in a 'green room'. Using green, they, too, would become the target of the possessive little gnomes.

In the case of the theatre there was an additional, practical reason to avoid green. To begin with, plays were enacted on lawns in the open. An actor wearing anything green would not stand out. Even when eventually performances were held on an indoor stage, the force of tradition made producers adopt for its floor covering the green lawn colour.

Another development rendered the wearing of green even less suitable. The original limelight was of a greenish colour. If focused on an actor who wore green, it would make him look insipid. Thus green, the luscious colour of the fertile earth, became shunned, if not feared, both in daily life and in the theatre.

Iron Bars

Why are these thought to be a magic devil repellent?

In the world of magic, iron is the most effective guard against the devil. It is this belief that contributed to the good-luck connotation of the horseshoe. It must be realised, however, that the horseshoe does not attract good luck but rather repels the devil.

The ability of iron to ward off the devil has its roots in remote history and people's early powers of observation. First there were the meteors that struck the earth and were seen as heavenly missiles. Everything connected with their 'supernatural' appearance combined to make the meteors carriers of divine and occult power: their fiery streak on their passage downward from the heavens, their mysterious arrival and the discovery of these ancient meteors embedded in the ground.

People soon learnt to make good use of the salvaged meteoric iron. With the aid of the sacred fire, they forged their tools and weapons from it. They saw in the iron a divine and magically mysterious gift especially sent to them from above. Most of all, the fact that it had come from outer space and was thus identified with heaven or the seat of God made the devil loathe it. Always ready to attribute the still-inexplicable to supernatural causes, people soon credited iron with being the divine element against which those serving the devil were powerless.

The stone-wielding natives of many a country had no chance against the superior power of iron weapons which, in their primitive way of thinking, they ascribed not to the metal itself but to its magic. On the other hand, the victorious foe seemed invulnerable by protecting themselves with shields and armour made of iron. This also was thought to be due not to the hardness of the metal but to its mystic force. Early warriors cleverly used it to increase the terror of their enemy, and their own reputation of being unassailable and immune from attack, by spreading the notion of the magic power of iron.

Numerous customs can be traced to this belief in the magic potency of iron. The first-century Roman author Pliny recorded how the idea had taken root in his time. People removed nails from coffins to stick them into the lintel of their bedrooms, to 'lay' spirits who might haunt them at night. Scots and Irishmen used iron to ward off attacks by fairies. Christian families believed that by putting an iron poker across the cradle of an unbaptised child, they would protect the infant against the power of the devil.

Anzac Biscuits

Why are they so called?

To Australians and New Zealanders 'Anzac' is a term that symbolises courage, mateship and unfailing loyalty. Equally, it brings to mind indomitable valour that even military defeat and horrendous carnage cannot subdue. An acronym, it was first coined – for telegraphic use – to identify the joined forces of the Australian and New Zealand Army Corps, dispatched to Europe and the Middle East in World War I.

Anzac is a proud and almost sacred name which to commercialise would amount to sacrilege. The existence of an Anzac biscuit is therefore all the more surprising.

A popular biscuit indeed, through the years a great number of recipes for it have been given, each said to be the original one. They differ slightly in the ingredients to be used, their specific amount and the particular instructions to be followed in their preparation. The basic components, however, are more or less the same. They are rolled oats, golden syrup or treacle, butter and sugar.

There is even the suggestion that the biscuit now known by the Australian name in reality is an adaptation of an earlier popular non-Australian cookie. This was particularly favoured in Yorkshire and other parts of northern England, but mostly in Scotland. Migrants from that part of the British isles had then introduced it to the Antipodes. A typical example is a sort of gingerbread, made of oatmeal and treacle and known as 'parkin' (or 'perkins'). Its name was believed to perpetuate that of the very family who were the first to produce it. Its earliest mention has been traced to an entry in the *Journal* kept by Dorothy Wordsworth, the poet's sister. On 6 November 1800 she recorded that on that day she had been 'baking bread ... and parkins'.

The story goes that the parkin, so tasty and sweet, was particularly favoured by youngsters. Their liking did not go unnoticed by bakers who took due advantage of it to promote their sales. As a special treat, they gave the children who were usually sent by their mothers to pick up bread one such parkin. This, no doubt, was sure to make them all the more eager to return to the bakehouse as soon and as frequently as possible, certain to be rewarded each time with one of these most welcome gifts.

A further quite plausible claim has it that, prior to being linked specifically to Anzac, the wafer was known generally as the 'soldiers' biscuit'.

Even more puzzling and significant than its original recipe is the question as to what prompted the creation of the Anzac biscuit. Here as well, a variety of reasons has been advanced. Though all give much food for thought, and all are convincing, none of them has been authenticated.

Like in the case of the possibly preceding 'soldiers' biscuit', the avoidance of spoilage may have been the primary consideration. To reach the troops, the biscuits had to be transported over a large distance. To remain palatable, they had to be durable and stay crisp in all weather conditions.

Sent as a special greeting from home, they were meant to nourish not only the body but also the spirit of those serving so far away and exposed to countless dangers. The biscuits were to assure them that they were not forgotten and that their wellbeing was of great concern to their dear ones left behind and whose prayers and thoughts were with them constantly.

Not so far-fetched is the further suggestion that the biscuits were intended to supplement the soldiers' monotonous ration and give them a most enjoyable treat. Not least, with supplies limited at the home front and funds restricted, the making of the Anzac biscuit was economical. It could be afforded by both poor and rich alike, to be included in the food parcels to either the troops generally or to the individual beloved, away from home but so near to their hearts. An additional factor was that they could be mass-produced.

The Red Cross and other welfare organisations, concerned to provide ever more needed comforts for the troops, were short of funds. Thus they baked those 'cookies' not to be sent overseas to the soldiers, but to be sold at home to raise money to purchase the goods best suited to give the men some extra pleasure and comfort.

How strange that a simple biscuit can give so much food for both body and mind and play a notable part not only in the world's gastronomy but also in a country's history.

Anzac biscuits are an inspiring Australian and New Zealand tradition, whatever the authentic story of their origin.

Make A Beeline

Do bees always fly in straight lines?

Not a few generally accepted and frequently quoted expressions and phrases are fallacious. A typical example is the proverbial beeline.

'Making a beeline' to anywhere, one takes the shortest possible route – the direct way. It is, however, erroneous to think that bees, after having collected pollen or nectar, return from their successful sortie in a straight line to their hive. In fact, frequently they interrupt their flight to perform a remarkable variety of dances in the air, with each pattern intended to convey a specific message to other bees from their hive. It may relate significant information as to the exact location of rich sources of food supply, whether of nectar or pollen, or even as to the colour of the flowers containing them. Thus, far from straight, theirs is a roundabout 'beeline' and they are not concerned to return quickest but in the manner most beneficial to other members of their hive.

Call A Spade A Spade

Who first used this expression and why?

To 'call a spade a spade' shows forthrightness and trustworthiness. Speaking plainly and to the point avoids ambiguity and misunderstanding and no one will doubt one's words. People will know where one stands. To say what one means and mean what one says, leaves no room for conventional lies and hypocrisy.

Confusing and misleading is the practice of some people of modifying truthful observations and exact data for the sole reason that these might be upsetting and offensive. It is worse still if they do so to achieve a desired objective, even if only to gain others' good will. And yet, such attitudes have not been rare. They were common in certain societies and epochs. Examples abound and show how standards and lifestyles have changed through the generations.

Typical are the euphemisms used for anything related to death. People do not die, but 'pass away'. Whoever professionally looked after the burial of a deceased became an 'undertaker', a name totally divorced from death and chosen solely because he 'undertakes' funerals. The description of the burial place was changed from the gruesome-sounding 'graveyard' to a 'resting place', which is the literal meaning of the Greek-derived present-day 'cemetery'.

There have been times when the use of the proper term, however correct, has been regarded as 'improper' – a sign of depravity. This applies particularly to matters connected with human and animal bodies and bodily functions, but most of all to sex. People thus excuse themselves to 'go to the bathroom' or 'restroom' (particularly in America). They 'open their bowels'. They 'make love' and a pregnant woman is 'expecting'. To mention a chicken's leg was so offensive that it was replaced by the 'drumstick', just as its breast is still referred to not as such, but as 'the white meat'. A universal phenomenon, Chinese culture at one time thus branded 'calling a spade a spade' as an almost unpardonable offence.

No doubt, the use of euphemisms was most prevalent during the Victorian age. Anything then regarded as crude language was frowned upon. This applied even to people's apparel. No one would dare to mention trousers. They were called the 'unmentionables'. The legs of a chair, table or piano had to be covered up, as seen 'bare' they would shock the delicate mind!

Well-known in British parliamentary etiquette is the prohibition ever to decry a fellow member's statement as 'a lie'. This made a clever statesman introduce as an acceptable substitute the euphemism 'a terminological inexactitude'. George Orwell went to the very extreme when he alleged that political language generally was designed to make lies sound truthful.

The principle of calling things by their real name, and in the simplest terms, even if this may be regarded as blunt, if not rude, goes back to antiquity. One of the earliest examples is the Latin proverb *ficus ficus, ligonem ligonem vocat* – 'He calls figs figs, and a hoe a hoe', a translation of words attributed to the Athenian comic playwright Menander (342–291 BC) whose works abounded in maxims. The earliest English versions of the saying go back to the sixteenth century. Among the best-known examples of the time are words by John Knox (1513–1572), the Scottish religious reformer, who wrote, 'I have learnt to call wickedness by its own term: a fig a fig, and a spade a spade'. Advice given in the following century counselled that 'God's people shall not spare to call a spade a spade, a niggard a niggard'.

An experience encountered in many cultures is that whenever people try to replace expressions that are unseemly and obnoxious to them by euphemisms, in due time the latter becomes equally tainted and, in turn, needs substitution.

Modern society, having become most outspoken, has dispensed with a great number of euphemisms common in the past and certainly has no longer any qualms about 'calling a spade a spade'. Australians, in fact, in their free and easy manner, are said to go even further by calling a spade 'a bloody shovel'.

With A Grain Of Salt

Why does this saying suggest that one should take things with caution?

It is hard to understand why the phrase, 'to take things with a grain of salt' should caution one to accept a statement with certain reservations. Its origin goes back to ancient Roman days and to a fallacy.

First-century historian Pliny the Elder relates that Pompey (106–48 BC), the famous general and statesman, lived in constant fear of being poisoned. Consequently he took all his food 'with a grain of salt' (*cum grano salis*), believing that by adding it any lethal substance contained in the food would be counteracted. Pompey certainly was not poisoned. But he did not die a natural death either. When, on his flight from Rome after his defeat by Julius Caesar at Pharsalus he reached Egyptian soil, he was stabbed to death.

In relating the story, Pliny adds that after the general's death, a note was found among the royal papers listing the ingredients of the antidote for poison. However, he does not divulge the prescription. He merely quotes its last line, saying that it had to be 'taken with a grain of salt'. It is this grain of salt, taken out of its context, that has survived as a warning never to take highly exaggerated statements too literally.

The Bull And Bear Market

When the stockmarket goes up or down these strange terms are used. Why is that so?

A 'bull' market is one in which people purchase stocks and shares in anticipation that they will rise in price. Optimistically such speculators recall the bull's practice of tossing things up into the air. They ought to remember that what goes up must come down.

In a 'bear' market people expect a slump. To make a profit they sell shares while the price is still high, hoping later on to repurchase them at the lowest possible price. The origin of this name is almost as uncertain as the result of the speculation. It might well have been suggested by a once well-known English proverb (first documented in 1580) that spoke of 'selling the bearskin before the bear has been caught'.

The Show Isn't Over Till The Fat Lady Sings

What is behind this intriguing observation?

The observation that 'the show isn't over till the fat lady sings' is of American coinage. An alternate version refers more particularly to an opera. Either way, its meaning seems obvious. Spectators unacquainted with the plot or program may depart prematurely, wrongly assuming that the performance is all over. They are told that the really important part is still to come and that the show will not be finished 'till the fat lady has sung'.

Apparently far-fetched and of concern to only a limited number of people, the words may have a much wider application: not to a single performance but to life generally. The way in which they apply has been given intriguing, though contradictory interpretations.

The saying can serve as an encouragement to those unfortunates who imagine that they are at their wit's end and without hope. For them to be told that the show is not over and something is still to come will prove a source of strength. Although at the moment things may seem dismal and almost desperate, new opportunities are still in the offing.

Completely different is an alternate but equally apt explanation. This sees in the words a warning to those rejoicing and celebrating too soon. It would be equivalent to the proverbial advice not to count your chickens till they are hatched.

As puzzling as its message is the very background of the saying and its reference to 'the fat lady' singing. Wrongly, a connection has been suggested with the fact that some operas conclude with the death of the heroine, a role taken by the most forceful singer of the cast – usually a soprano, who constitutionally was conspicuous by her stoutness. With her swan song, as it were, the performance reached a climax and, simultaneously, the finale.

Much more plausible and sensible is the actual identification of 'the fat lady' and of the relevant circumstances. Kathryn (Kate) Smith was a renowned American singer of the 1930s and 40s. Nature had endowed her with a phenomenal voice and an outstandingly corpulent figure, both so prominent and well known that whoever heard a mention of 'the fat lady' singing immediately knew who was meant.

Kate was a 'natural'. The astonishing fact was that she could neither read music nor had a single singing lesson in her life, but nevertheless from earliest childhood onward had been obsessed by a burning desire to sing.

In a remarkable career, she won numerous distinctions and was the first private citizen to be awarded the American Red Cross 'Medal of Valor'. She was the American troops' favourite in the two World Wars and became a household word in the States. No wonder that she was called upon to conclude any occasion of great national importance, from political party conventions to exciting sporting events. Her singing of 'God Bless America' was the grand finale. It has been said that, in fact, through her outstanding rendition of it, next to the 'Stars and Stripes', it became the second American anthem.

There could hardly be any doubt in anyone's mind, therefore, as to who was meant and which circumstances referred to by the observation that the show was not over till the fat lady had sung.

Although sounding very convincing, the association of the phrase with Kate is merely hypothetical. Other origins have been suggested as well, though none of them has been proven correct.

The popularity of the saying has been attributed to Dan Cook. A Texan sports writer and renowned broadcaster in San Antonio, he is said to have used it in connection with his report on the encounter between two professional basketball teams. In fact, his original words are quoted to have been 'the rodeo isn't over till the bull riders ride'. The coach of one of the teams who had heard Cook's broadcast picked up the phrase to use it to caution his team not to be over-confident in a forthcoming series. Nevertheless, Kate's case is still the more convincing and acceptable.

Fame, it is said, is short-lived. However, Kate Smith will be remembered for ever in the saying 'the show isn't over till the fat lady sings'.

The Caddie In Golf

What is the background of his name?

That the 'caddie' has travelled a long distance is not surprising. In his case there is no doubt of ancestry, though as is so typical of life, he has very much come down in the world from his aristocratic beginnings.

His home was France, where at the time he was far removed from games of golf. The word 'caddie' is derived from the French *cadet*, meaning a 'diminutive chief' or a 'little head' (itself rooted in the Latin *caput*, 'head'). The title was mostly used for the younger sons of upper class families. Mary, Queen of Scots, introduced it into Scotland, where it soon assumed a derogatory connotation. In fact, the noble word deteriorated so much that it was used to describe messengers and pages waiting around for an odd job. Eventually, 'caddie' was further reduced to refer specifically to those hanging around golf courses to carry sticks and to clean them with emery paper during and after the game.

Still carrying on the Scottish queen's French pronunciation, 'cad-day', the Scots began to spell it their own way, and that is how the 'cadet' changed into the 'caddie'.

Later his task extended far beyond transportation and cleaning of clubs. Before the introduction of tee-pegs, making tees belonged to his duties as well. He did so mostly by taking a handful of sand out of the hole or the tee-box (which also deteriorated in value and changed into a refuse receptacle) and putting it onto the turf, shaped it into a small cone on top of which he placed the ball.

The Hash Key

Who invented this symbol and for what purpose?

Multiple are the present-day uses of the hash sign, the symbol consisting of two pairs of parallel lines intersecting at an angle. It is part of the dialling system of the modern telephone (the hash button) and well known in the world of computers.

It often serves as a number sign, whether applied as a prefix to the number of an apartment or flat or to one's telephone or fax connection, taking the place of the traditional 'No.'.

In the realm of measurements, it was chosen for the pound (of weight).

In music it is known as the sharp sign. Placed before a note, it raises it in pitch by a half-stage or semitone. It has been attributed in this context to Guido d'Arezzo. Born in 995 in Paris, he became a famous Benedictine monk, leaving his perpetual mark in music. His application of the hash became common in the thirteenth century, though only temporarily so. After lapsing for almost four hundred years, it was permanently adopted in the seventeenth century.

In medicine, it is applied to specify bone fractures.

Every writer or editor is well acquainted with the sign when proofreading. It denotes where to insert space, either between words or lines.

However, this modern use of the hash in such a variety of fields is merely coincidental, just as claims to have introduced it in any of them cannot be substantiated. One of the credits has been given to an engineer of the US Bell Laboratories. He is said to have invented it in the 1960s to indicate a video phone call, though subsequently it did not catch on as such.

To complicate matters, there were those who, convinced that the hash was not a novel creation, saw in it a symbol going back to times long ago – in some cases several millennia. Their assertions produced a veritable hotchpotch of suggestions, adding to the confusion. A couple of examples must suffice.

A long way back, at least prior to the fifteenth century, early cartographers are said to have used the hash on their maps for a sign they called an 'octothorp'. With it, they indicated small settlements. Their term was an intriguing choice of description. It is a combination of the Latin *octo* (for 'eight') and the Old Norse *thorp* (for a 'village', 'hamlet' or 'farmstead'). There is also the suggestion that the *thorp* is related to the Welsh for a 'dwelling'. The octothorp might well have been chosen to designate a location in which at least eight properties, perhaps fields, surrounded a central common or square.

Tracing the hash even further back, some have linked it with the misty region of early writing systems, Creto-Mycenaean ideograms, Babylonic-Assyrian script and the early Semitic alphabet. The latter, for instance, contains as its eighth letter the guttural *chet*. Looking very much like the hash, it developed from the stylised picture of a fence.

Not surprisingly, the hash found its place in the symbolism of the occult as well. It was used by astrologers (as the Zodiacal sign of the Gemini) and alchemists and, following them, early pharmacists.

Most likely, the present-day hieroglyphic is a modern symbol. Its previous appearances the world over and the many diverse functions it has fulfilled are not interrelated. To associate them in any way has no foundation and is merely a product of people's imagination or wishful thinking.

The etymology of the term is a study in itself and, partially at least, explains its various applications. Most likely, 'hash' is a popular corruption of the word 'hatch'. Derived from the French verb *hacher* (also responsible for the 'hatchet'), for to 'cut' or to 'chop', the word assumed a variety of meanings. Speaking of 'chopping something up', and 'cutting it into pieces' as a noun, 'hash' became the name of a number of dishes such as hash browns, but particularly of diced cooked meat and vegetables, somehow akin to the Scottish haggis.

Such is the complex story and such are the manifold explanations of the apparently ubiquitous hash. Whether ancient or modern, a button on the telephone or a mark on archaic maps, a doctor's reference or a musician's direction, it presents a veritable cacophony of interpretations of both its application and its etymology, easily leading the concerned inquirer to make truly a 'hash' of it.

The Tooth Fairy

Which circumstances were responsible for the belief in her existence?

Among the many superstitions of primitive society was the belief that if the clippings of one's nails or any of one's hair fell into the wrong hands, they would be used to cast evil spells and inflict hurt on their original owner. The same applied to teeth. According to old folklore, even a child who lost a milk tooth was thus in danger. The tooth growing in its stead would not take on the qualities of the one it replaced, but those of the very creature or demonic being that had found and taken possession of the lost one.

German tradition claimed that it was the 'tooth rat' which, having acquired the lost tooth, hid it in its hole. Eventually, however, the rodent was displaced by the tooth fairy.

The part she came to play changed altogether the fearsome circumstances and possible evil effects of losing a tooth, into a situation that could prove even advantageous. The myth of the tooth fairy came to assume a significant beneficial place in the life of a child.

No one likes losing a tooth and not least so children. Whether in the natural process of growing up (as in the case of the milk teeth) or the now rare occasion of having a tooth extracted, it meant apprehension, pain and unpleasant memories.

Cleverly, parents learnt to assuage their child's anguish. Before going to sleep, they made the child place the lost or extracted tooth under the pillow with the promise that doing so would bring luck the following day. During the night a fairy would visit the home and replace the tooth with a welcome present.

Obviously, the parents arranged the exchange during the child's sleep, firmly establishing in its mind the belief in the existence of that magic figure of fairyland. All the pain was taken out of losing a tooth or having it extracted, and children, sure of the profitable exchange, no longer dreaded quite as much a visit to the dentist.

Nowadays, the tooth fairy is no longer so much a superstition, but part of modern times and present-day children's commercial instinct. Taking advantage of the myth, they demand adequate monetary compensation for their loss, not just as in former days a mere coin, but an amount much more substantial.

Children rightly wonder what the fairy eventually does with their tooth. Having, as it were, paid for it, she would not just dispense with it.

Fantasy has been given its full range, and suggestions proffered have covered a most colourful spectrum. Thus, it was claimed that the fairy used the tooth to decorate her castle with it or to transform it into one of the bricks making up its walls. She might also grind it into magical fairy dust. Or, casting it into the sky, she changed it into one of the millions of stars shining down to earth. On the other hand, not abandoning the terrestrial sphere, she would keep it for the birth of a new baby as her gift to the child.

The myth of the tooth fairy – the product of emotionally involved and concerned parents – shows the human mind's ability to change loss into gain and demonstrates how ancient superstitions once haunting people can be sublimated into an enriching and beneficial experience.

The Pocket

What is the story of the pocket?

Much has been written about people's dress, its history through the ages and the information it gives as to the needs, tastes and fashions of a race, an era, a class or a profession. Little, however, is realised about one of its smallest items, the pocket – its story, the forms it took and the varied purposes it served.

Names are given to describe the most essential features of anything or anyone so called and therefore they had much to say about their place in life. The name of the pocket (known to have been in existence in the fifteenth century) is derived from the 'poke', a small pouch or bag, etymologically rooted in the northern French *poque.* The description immediately reveals what pockets were made for. Their shape, of course, depended on the dress people wore at the time and their way of life.

Going back to the days of antiquity, it can be assumed that pockets in their present sense did not exist. In classical days their place was taken by a fold. The Romans thus used deep pleats (called the *sinus*) in the front of their toga, into which they placed small items. A mere fold therefore might be regarded as the forerunner of the pocket!

Until the middle of the sixteenth century the pocket was not part of one's dress, but a small pouch, exactly what its original name suggested. Initially, in its most primitive form, it was mainly a piece of cloth, gathered and tied up with a cord to make up a bag or, as it was then called, the 'reticule'. Totally divorced from one's garment, it was carried separately or attached to a waistband. In which way it was worn depended on the ruling fashion and, of course, differed between the sexes.

In the case of women, flat in form, reticules were affixed (often in pairs) to a belt or band tied around their waist and worn concealed under their skirt. Eventually, they were replaced by a slit in the costume and thereby became part of it.

According to the mode of dressing at the time, pockets were fitted into a man's breeches, his coat and, later still, into his waistcoat as well. The subsequent introduction of hip pockets was especially welcomed by thieves. It made it easy to steal from them, adding to vocabulary and society the 'pickpocket'.

Once having become a feature of their outfit, people were concerned to improve the pocket and in the pursuit, in the eighteenth century they added flaps, as a simple but effective protection for the contents. Decorating them with gold or silver braids made them specially conspicuous and attractive. Once merely fulfilling a practical purpose, now they also served as ornamentation and inspired extraordinary specimens.

Of all types of pockets that, through succeeding periods, were part of men's clothing, none surpassed the codpiece in conspicuousness and in its unique twofold function. Fashionable and popular between the fifteenth and seventeenth centuries, it took the place of the modern trouser fly and very noticeably enclosed a man's genitals, forming a truly outstanding section of his breeches. Indeed, it was the oddest piece of male attire and, apart from drawing attention to his virility, doubled up as an outsize (and outside) pocket to carry many items he cherished. This explains its very description as a codpiece, as *cod* was the Old English word for a 'bag'. Cynical observers would refer to it as a 'sex purse', which by its bulging volume seemed to promise lots of change!

In the nineteenth century, with the introduction of modern men's suits, pockets became mainly functional. They have remained so ever since.

It has been said that history repeats itself. This applies equally to fashion. It has rightly been observed that if women kept their discarded, out-of-date clothing items long enough, in time these would become the vogue again. Another example of modern days applies to the return of the practice of wearing purses securely tied around the waist. Women as well as men have resurrected the custom, this time not for fashion's sake but as a safety precaution in an era of bag snatchers.

Cheerio

Why, on departing, does one use this greeting?

To bid each other 'farewell' is not always easy, particularly so if there is a close communion of spirit, a sharing of joys and of thoughts. People may say goodbye in several ways. Each has its own background and explanation.

Au revoir, in German *Auf Wiedersehen,* says in French what friends really hope for: to see one another again. To some, the English 'ta-ta' may sound rather childish, while many a person who calls out 'see you later' well knows (and hopes) that the two may never meet again. 'Cheerio', however, with its happy sound, taking leave and yet looking into the future to a reunion, has attracted diverse explanations.

First of all, it recalls early days of transportation. One way to move about then was by being carried in a sedan chair. To start with, this was privately owned and reserved for the wealthy and noble. But with the passing of time, the sedan chair became a public vehicle, functioning as a taxi for all and sundry.

Without personal transport at their disposal, people have become accustomed to stand at the curb and call out to a passing cab, 'Taxi!' Earlier generations did the same. They stood in the road, outside a home or a tavern, waiting for a sedan chair to pass by. Seeing it approaching, to attract the carrier's attention, they called out, 'Chair-oh!'

A polite host always waits till his guests have departed, making sure that they have transport. And as this was mostly the case after they had called out 'chair-oh', this hailing of their cab doubled up as a farewell greeting, eventually slightly changed into 'cheerio', which thus still carries inside, though hard to see, the original sedan chair.

'Cheerio', however, may come from a completely different source. Parting is sorrow to many. The French proverb observed that 'to part is to die a little', *partir c'est mourir un peu*, and everyone knows the Shakespearean line, 'parting is such sweet sorrow'. It was to encourage both the person who went away and the one who stayed behind not to take the parting too hard that they said to each other, 'cheerio'. It was a reminder to 'cheer up' and consider their separation only temporary.

This would conform with yet another derivation of 'cheer' that sees in it the Late Latin word for the 'face', *cara*. 'Cheerio' as a parting greeting expressed concern even at a time of farewell to remain of 'good cheer', showing a happy 'face'.

Index

[Where the reference is to a particular saying, it appears in *italics*.]